SPRINGS OF HELLAS

CAMBRIDGE
UNIVERSITY PRESS
LONDON: BENTLEY HOUSE
NEW YORK, TORONTO, BOMBAY
CALCUTTA, MADRAS: MACMILLAN

TERROT REAVELEY GLOVER

Springs of Hellas

and other Essays

BY

T. R. GLOVER

With a Memoir
by
S. C. ROBERTS

CAMBRIDGE
AT THE UNIVERSITY PRESS
1945

PRINTED IN GREAT BRITAIN

PREFACE

THIS book was prepared for press by my husband during the last months of his life. None of it has been in print before except the essay on 'The Mind of St Paul', which was given as a lecture to the British Academy on 9 July 1941, and is here included by permission of the Oxford University Press.

I desire to thank Mr Roberts for his great kindness in writing the memoir and for his advice and help; and another lifelong friend of my husband, Professor A. B. Cook, for identifying some references which were found to be uncertain.

My daughter Mary and my son Robert have helped me in making the index and correcting the proofs.

ALICE E. C. GLOVER

1945

CONTENTS

MEMOIR

I

In the final paragraph of the preface to the volume of essays entitled *The Challenge of the Greek* (1942) Glover wrote:

'From time to time of late it has been suggested to me that I should write an autobiography. I have been reluctant to do this; I cannot think the subject of it very interesting; and who wants a story without episode? But I have a confession to make. As I read the proofs of this book, it came to me that the autobiography, without set design or conscious purpose, is written in these pages. Here are the things that have made the life— the great Classics, the great lake and river by which I lived, the Dominion; interwoven are memories of friends and colleagues, outlooks, fancies, impressions, and impulses of deeper birth.'

At first sight, it might seem difficult to reconcile this paragraph with the contents of a book which contains two essays in defence of a classical education, four on various aspects of economic life in ancient Greece, one on Homer and his readers, one on Athenaeus (with a short article on Iced Water as a pendant), two short pieces on Virgil and Erasmus and only two which seem to suggest a wider range—*The Fairy Tale* and *Team or Hero?* Such a book, it might be thought, represents but one side of Glover—the classical don. What can it reveal of the President of the Baptist Union, of the restless, enquiring traveller, of the passionate Liberal, of the fervent champion of the Dominion?

Yet, we have Glover's own word for it and, if no record of him, other than *The Challenge of the Greek*, had survived, it might be an interesting exercise to reconstruct the man from the book. Certainly, his love of Canada and particularly of the 'corner of empire' where he had lived and taught is evident enough. His essay on *The Greek and the Forest*, for example, is full of illustrations taken from Canada and North America. But why should he choose to write on the *Deipnosophistae* of Athenaeus? When he told me that this essay was to be included in the book,

I expressed some mild surprise and I find the conversation duly recorded in the text:

'"What do *you* know of gastronomy?" asked my friend, the publisher. Little enough, I admitted; but I modestly claimed (and he allowed my claim) to understand irrelevance; and there lies the fascination of Athenaeus.'

And there, for Glover, lay the fascination of innumerable books and innumerable people. Like Burton or Cervantes or Charles Lamb, or Pausanias ('Prince of Digressors') to whom an essay is devoted in the present volume, Athenaeus led him into a hundred byways of speculative interest:

'Athenaeus' subject is dinner, a theme lowly enough at first sight. We shall associate with cooks and learn how they look at their own art, but their dishes do not remain in the kitchen, nor shall we; and we shall meet a large variety of interesting people, poets, philosophers and kings, medical men and naturalists, taking them as we find them, in their hours of leisure and enjoyment, content not to be impressive, occupied with meat and drink, but Greeks still, open-eyed for the world and not altogether missing it, even at table. "We feed on questions", he says.'

A serious student of gastronomy would be shocked by the notion of regarding dinner as a lowly theme, even at first sight. Glover, though not indifferent to the pleasures of the table, was roused to a keener interest by the prospect of 'feeding on questions'. 'What is the good', he quoted in another essay, 'of reading a book, when you agree with all of it?'

The Fairy Tale is another example of Glover's delight in dipping into an illimitable sea of legend and literature. 'Once upon a time', he properly begins, 'there were three brothers, who lived in Russia, when hardly anybody else lived there.' And having recorded the story of the Scythians as told about themselves, he passes to Herodotus, to Plato, to Pliny, to Apollonius Rhodius, to Apuleius and then, by way of Clement of Alexandria, to *The Water Babies* and to Charles Lamb's protest against 'the Barbauld crew'. Later, he reveals his own passion for stories and story-tellers:

'Of course Lipoxais and his brothers wanted those golden things from heaven; we are all of us acquisitive, as the pedants call it to-day. We all of us love adventure; if we do not actually wish to be pirates ourselves, nor indeed to sail with John Silver, we draw to him when he is in a book'

and, finally, there is a characteristic reference to 'the finest contribution Oxford has made to literature'—*Alice.*

The essay entitled *Team or Hero?* springs from a contemplation of the Greek games. Now Glover, in his recollections of undergraduate life in *Cambridge Retrospect*, has not much to say about athletics. He recognises the importance of the College boat club, but he shows little interest in games and the verses beginning

> I am not athletic at all,
>> Nor destined by Nature for sport;
> My biceps is certainly small
> And my sight is excessively short.

are presumably autobiographical. In later years, though his house abutted on Fenner's, Glover, unlike another classical don, was never tempted to 'squander long summer afternoons on watching the game of cricket'. What interested him in the records of Greek athletics was the emphasis on personal distinction:

'In Pindar's day the young man won the victory; and, even if the glory covered his father's house and brought renown to the city whence they came, it was an individual achievement. There was no thought of a team in most of Greek athletics.'

For once he feels that Victorian England may claim superiority:

'Have not Tom Hughes and Henry Newbolt something to say of worth, which is not in the *Republic*?'

So he is led to the ideal picture of Democracy in the funeral speech of Pericles, to Plato's guardians ('the imagination of a man of genius who had no experience of a civil service or a board of education'), and to the place of the artist and the poet in the community:

'The progress of the community again and again has depended on the man who did his own seeing and his own thinking and would not submit to the community. But such a man often needs to be dead before the average people will forgive him; and they may owe him more than they will ever recognise...but it is still the same issue—the group or the great man.'

There follows a brief account of the battle for independent thinking fought by the early Christians against the sovereign state and the subsequent transformation of that battle into the struggle between orthodoxy and heresy.

The old question remains: the individual or the group, the rebel or the government, the heretic or the church? Glover does not pretend to give a clear-cut answer. Temperamentally, he was wholly on the side of the rebels and he applauded Dean Inge's remark that the genius of Christianity is to be recognised chiefly in its heretics. But from the categorical imperatives of Christian doctrine and Christian morality he could not escape; so he fell back on Luther's paradox: 'A Christian man is the most free lord of all and subject to none; a Christian man is the most dutiful servant of all, and subject to every one.'

These are but a few excerpts from *The Challenge of the Greek*; but they are sufficient, perhaps, to show what Glover meant when he declared that in its pages he recognised the *disjecta membra* of his autobiography.

II

There are some authors who, when encountered for the first time in the flesh, seem to contradict the impressions made by their writings. Of Glover this could not be said; in him the writer and the man were one.

In my undergraduate days I did not know him, except by sight and reputation. At that time, inter-collegiate classical teaching was planned, for the most part, on a geographical basis and, as Cambridge distances go, St John's is a long way from Pembroke. But, in my fourth year, I used to hear from friends who were reading ancient history in the second part of the Classical Tripos that in Glover's lectures there was an element of interest and excitement which went far beyond the requirements of examination papers.

Later, when I returned to Cambridge, it was not long before I established several points of contact with Glover—the Cam-

bridge Classical Society, the *Cambridge Review* committee, David's
stall in the market-place.

In Glover's relations with the University Press there had been
a break. At the suggestion of Leonard Whibley, he had produced a school edition of Demosthenes' *Olynthiacs* (1897) and
on his return from Queen's University, Kingston, Ontario,
where he held the Chair of Latin for five years, his first book,
Life and Letters in the Fourth Century, was published at the Press
in 1901. Two years later he submitted his work on Virgil. The
Syndics of the Press considered it not so much as a manuscript
offered to a publisher as a treatise to be appraised by the
strictest standards of academic scholarship. Eventually (by
8 votes to 5) they refused it. Glover took the manuscript to
Arnold and the work went through many editions. Indignant,
but not embittered, Glover published elsewhere for many years
and it was not until the 1920's that his name re-appeared in the
Cambridge catalogue. Of course, he frequently indulged in
retrospective jocularity about the rejection of one of his most
successful books; it was part of the under-current of his recurring
complaint against the rigidity of the Cambridge classical tradition. Nevertheless, it was with genuine satisfaction that he
returned to the University Press. 'I am pleased', he wrote in
February 1925, 'with the proposal of the Syndicate and happy
in the idea of re-linking the connexion dropped in 1903.' The
connexion was not dropped again and nearly everything that
Glover wrote in the last twenty years of his life (including *The
World of the New Testament*, *Democracy in the Ancient World*, *Greek
Byways*, and *The Ancient World*) was published at Cambridge.
The last book to come out in his life-time was *Cambridge Retrospect*. About this Glover and I had some argument, not so much
about its content as about its plan. For one thing, it seemed to
me that his recollections of undergraduate days ought to have
come in the first chapter rather than the last. He made some
modifications, but in the main he had his way and I am glad
of it; for further revision would have delayed publication and
he would not have lived to read the 'third leader' which *The
Times* devoted to the book.

In the spring of 1930 it happened that Glover and I travelled
to New York together on the *Aquitania*. Travelling second class,

we found an interesting group of fellow-passengers. Among
them were Miss Sperry, daughter of Dean Sperry of Harvard;
R. E. Balfour of King's (lately, alas, killed whilst serving with
the 60th Rifles in Holland); Walter Starkie, of Trinity College,
Dublin, who was going on a lecture tour in America; and
Beverley Robinson, of Toronto, returning from winter sports in
Switzerland. I had previously met Starkie and Robinson knew
Glover slightly, so the four of us shared a table in the dining-
saloon. Meals became not only friendly, but hilarious. In conversation Glover was equally fond of argument and anecdote
and we had plenty of both. On the face of it, it was not easy
to see much in common between Glover and Starkie, except that
they were both fellows of colleges. What appeal could Starkie's
stories of life in the gipsy encampments of Spain or Hungary
make to Glover's staunch and massive Puritanism? In fact, they
quite clearly enjoyed, and even admired, each other.

In some respects Glover seemed to me to be the least typical
of Puritans. Of course, he was intensely loyal to his early
training and to the tradition which discouraged alcohol, tobacco,
card-playing and the theatre. But the whole world of literature
was open to him and, in a quite literal sense, he revelled in it.
Some of his principal choices (Herodotus, Horace, Cervantes,
Charles Lamb) might seem odd favourites for a Puritan and
who but T. R. Glover would have found room in a book entitled
Poets and Puritans for an essay on James Boswell? Perhaps it was
Boswell's nationality that was part—though only part—of the
attraction. Glover had three Scottish grandparents and it was
always a grievance of his that he had not been born a High-
lander. Two centuries earlier he would have been a magnificent,
fighting clansman. As it was, his Scottish ancestry was undoubtedly one of the reasons why he instinctively felt himself at
home in Canada and why he regularly re-visited it—which
brings me back to the *Aquitania*.

On one of the days of the voyage, I succumbed to sea-sickness
and kept my bed. Glover came to see me at intervals. For some
reason it was not a good day for him, either. 'You know', he
said, sitting down on the end of my bed, 'there are times when
even books fail to satisfy me—and then I really wish that my
parents had taught me to play cards or something.'

It was an honest, and a revealing, confession. Glover's
Puritanism was an integral part of him, but there were times
when he was irked by its restrictiveness. The enquiring restlessness of his active mind, his interest in human beings and
human history, his sense of fun and his appreciation of the
ridiculous all removed him far from the category of the pietist.
In an earlier incarnation he might have been a pilgrim or a
Covenanter—he could never have been a recluse. His friend
D. D. Calvin has recalled how, after addressing a vast Baptist
rally in Toronto, Glover collapsed into a chair exclaiming
'I say, it's good to be back among sinful people. Can I have
some food?'

During that *Aquitania* voyage—and no doubt on many similar
voyages—Glover was perpetually making new acquaintances,
amongst the crew as well as amongst the passengers. Solitary
pacing of the deck made no appeal to him. Frequently after
breakfast he would seize my arm and offer me various books for
publication, for example, a collection of his Latin speeches.
Having refused this and other proposals *en bloc*,[1] I would be
carried off to chat with one of the stewards or to have a look at
the ship's printing press; and very soon we had both been
induced to write something for the ship's magazine.

Amongst the passengers there were some notable artistes.
There was an eminent violinist from Roumania, a magnificent
negress with a contralto voice of great depth and power, an
'eccentric' dancer from the Palladium, and the champion tight-
rope walker of the world. Most of their names have escaped me,
but there was on board another couple whose names it is less
easy to forget—Naughton and Gold. With all this talent—and
Walter Starkie, too, was an accomplished violinist—it was
inevitable that there should be a ship's concert; it was equally
inevitable that Glover should be asked to take the chair. He
made, of course, an appropriate little speech on behalf of sea-
men's charities; what was more interesting to me was his enjoyment of Naughton and Gold. Wearing ordinary evening dress
('We work in dinner-jackets', they told me) they did an unpre-

---

[1] There was, I find, an exception. In July 1930 Glover wrote to me:
'I propose to send you one copy of it [*The World of the New Testament*], if you
would like to see it, as you supposed on the *Aquitania*, when it seemed to be the
one small item among my proposed collected works that interested you.'

tentious little act as two British workmen, at which Glover
rocked with laughter. I was pleased to think that he had seen
a really good music-hall turn; I was pleased, too, with some
doggerel he scribbled on my menu-card:

> O Roberts, 'mid the Ocean's fury
> Packed with Panjandriots and Jewry
> Some fleet the time with Walter Starkie,
> Some look towards the beauteous darkie,
> And some more quietly make merry
> With Balfour and the bright Miss Sperry,
> But I for one would chiefly bless
> The Secretary of the Press.

These are trivialities, but I recall them because they mark the
beginning of my knowledge of Glover outside the purely academic circle of Cambridge. In that circle Glover tended to be
on the defensive. He was at some pains to emphasise that he did
not belong to a Public School or to the Anglican Church and
that the severer type of classical don disapproved of him because
his books were too readable. When he felt this too strongly, he
would book his passage to Canada and call in the new univer-
sities to redress the balance of the old.

III

Yet Cambridge held Glover very close and *Cambridge Retrospect*
is a record of affection as well as of anecdote. If it had not been
so, he would no doubt have accepted one of the many appoint-
ments that were offered to him on the other side of the
Atlantic.

'I have seen a good deal of American College life,' he wrote,
'East, West, and Central; and in spite of all the charm and
courtesy of American hospitality as you so often meet it, I feel
the balance of advantage is with our own youth...the standards
of education seem to me to be solider; and the Cambridge
College, in spite of imports and Ph.D.'s, research and practical
people, is still a nursery of culture and character.'

Like many Cambridge Radicals, Glover, as the years went on,
came to hate changes in University or College. Instinctively he
was on the side of Reform, but with an even surer instinct he
distrusted Efficiency.

He once commented to me on the contrast between the atmosphere of 'blasphemous anarchy' in the University Registry under J. W. Clark and the quiet competence of succeeding Registraries. He recognised the improvement, of course; but, in retrospect at least, he preferred the old régime.

Once again, we may discern something of Glover, the man, in the final pages of *The Challenge of the Greek*. In a short essay written for the Erasmus centenary he contemplates Erasmus in Cambridge, 'a scholar, a humorist, a satirist, a Grecian':

'All along Erasmus had a keen eye for abuses in the church, and a keen pen to note them; but, when the cataclysm came, he did not like it....He writes on Paul; and Luther borrows a phrase of his....But Luther understands Paul more intimately. Sin meant more to Luther than to Erasmus.'

Glover's sympathies were torn. Erasmus and humanist Cambridge presented a delectable picture. But was this humanism enough? Humanists, according to Professor Rand, were always normal. But the glory of the preachers and prophets who fired Glover's imagination was that they were very far from the normal; and if Glover was to range himself on the side of humanism, it must be a passionately Christian humanism, a humanism that took account of sin and salvation as well as of literature and art. In one of his early books (*The Conflict of Religions in the Early Roman Empire*) Glover had insisted that

'Jesus of Nazareth does stand in the centre of human history, that He has brought God and man into a new relation, that He is the present concern of every one of us.'

On this text he preached and on this text he wrote what was probably his best known work—*The Jesus of History*.

'Erasmus or Luther?...the antithesis is never resolved', he wrote, but comforted himself with the reflection that 'Wisdom is justified of all her children'. It was part of the fascination of T. R. Glover that, in some measure, he himself personified the antithesis.

S. C. R.

Chapter I

SPRINGS OF HELLAS

ἀλλὰ ὕδωρ μὲν οὐ μόνον πίνειν βούλεσθε καθαρόν, ἀλλὰ καὶ ὁρᾶν.

Dio Chrysostom xxxiii, 29 (Tarsus).

I

'Best of things is water', says Pindar at the opening of what Lucian called 'the most beautiful of all lyrics'. Aristotle quotes it in his *Rhetoric* and discusses whether the harder thing or the easier thing is a greater good; but he appears to suggest that we may decide this question by reflecting on the importance of the loss of the one or the other. Xenophon somewhere says that the value of a good water supply is best realized by those who lack it. Athenaeus breaks off 'oenologizing' talk, as he calls it (40f), and starts with Pindar 'of the mighty voice'; he quotes the famous sentence, and launches into the praise of water as Homer gives it to us. Water is most nourishing, says that most divine poet—clear, light, of high value, desirable (ἱμερτόν). Homer also knows the good qualities of hot water in the treatment of wounds; and like Hesiod (and others of whom we may hear) he prefers the water of springs. And then Athenaeus quotes Pindar again and Aristophanes, and Theophrastus; and poses us with a question, complicated by a doubtful text in our manuscripts. But it is as well to face it, as it brings us closer to the tastes and speculations of the Greeks. Thus, water near the mines of Mount Pangaeum in Thrace weighs heavier in winter than in summer; cold weather contracts it and gives it more density; hence the problem—can you be equally sure of the correctness of your water-clock in the two seasons? Let us waive that for the moment, and remind ourselves with Seneca (*Nat. Qu.* iii, 13) that Thales reckoned water the most powerful of elements, and the first of them, from whence the others are derived. And there we have to shirk another problem—the possibility of the ancient belief that the elements might somehow change into one another. It suggests to the modern some of the

later marvels of Chemistry and its elements—*not* the original four
of the ancients—and may serve to remind us of the vast difference
that even a minimum of Chemistry and Physical Geography
may make for us in solving problems which the ancients recognized and could only fumble with them, guessing uneasily.
Something, however, will be gained by looking into the more
obvious aspects of water questions; if nothing else, at least we
shall have the reminder of what Vitruvius sums up for us
in a sentence—'it is clear that nothing in the world is so
necessary for use as water', seeing that there are substitutes,
he says, for most forms of food, but none at all for water
(viii, 3, 28).

We begin, then, with the observations of travellers on the
physical structure of Greece. It is familiar that it is a small area,
and a land of mountains—a land, therefore, where we could not
expect to find rivers of any magnitude; and in fact in Greece
proper there are no navigable rivers, no streams of commercial
importance. On the other hand, there are abundant springs.
'Throughout the whole of Messenia and Western Arcadia',
writes William Mure of Caldwell,[1] 'a striking feature of the
scenery are these copious perennial springs, gushing from the
base of the mountains. They are for the most part similarly
adorned with gigantic plane-trees.[2]...The oriental plane
everywhere prefers a situation where it can bathe its roots in
fresh water.' Mr H. D. F. Kitto, in his delightful book *In the
Mountains of Greece*, tells the same sort of tale, of himself and his
wife going about on foot, camping in the open, and guided, as
the evenings came on, to one spring and another, some quite
small and hard to find, but familiar to the local guide. 'The
Greek countryman', he says,[3] 'is a connoisseur of waters....
Your guide will tell you not to drink at this spring; the water is
poor and thin; to drink at that, if drink you must; but better
wait half an hour when you will reach a spring whose water is
much lighter (ἐλαφρό is the term of praise). Such distinctions
we were quite unable to follow. Now the peculiarity of the
spring at Hephta Psomia is that it is stimulating to the appetite';

[1] W. Mure, *A Tour in Greece* (1842), vol. ii, p. 258; another 'copious fountain of
pure water from the roots of gigantic planes' on p. 273.
[2] Cf. Pausanias, iv, 34, 4.
[3] *In the Mountains of Greece*, p. 122.

but they did not eat as a recent predecessor had done; still roasting potatoes, with bread, sardines, eggs, tea, honey, cherry jam and stewed pears, they did very well, had a merry party, and slept comfortably—at intervals—by a great fire which their guide from time to time replenished. This happy episode may be a sort of prelude to our story—of springs and not of rivers, nothing about deltas, but water to drink, and Greek tastes in it, wells and waters that earth as it were volunteers and by and by herself may swallow—the things that the Greeks note and guess about; and a little perhaps (but how essential to the Greek historian!) about their efforts to bring the water where they most wanted it, a matter that in a wetter land, abounding this last century in water companies, very few of us, historians or others, think very much about; it is so easy to turn a tap or faucet or whatever you call it, and forget the sources of the 'copious stream' that it liberates.

Our two travellers wrote of the Peloponnese. Every student of Greece, however, thinks first of Athens and Attica. 'There is no part of Greece', wrote Edward Dodwell, in his *Tour* (1819), 'where the soil is so arid, and water so scarce as in Attica' (vol. i, p. 468); and conversely, 'there is no place in Greece which is better supplied with water than Thebes; its numerous fountains are celebrated in early classical history. Those which are mentioned by ancient authors are the fountains of Dirce; the Oedipodia, or fount of Oedipus, the Aretia or Aretiades, the fount of Mars; the Arethusa, Epikrene, and Psamathe. It is difficult to identify their situations; and in a country so subject to earthquakes, some of them may have changed their places, or may even have totally disappeared.' To some of these fountains we may return, and add to their number. In the meantime we must note the earthquakes. Pausanias, giving the signs of approaching earthquake, notes the disappearance of springs (vii, 24, 7). In a similar but less cataclysmic way Bristol lost her most famous Hot Wells; a project to make the river Avon more available meant shifting the road beside it and cutting away the rocks whence the hot spring came. It was found again somewhere near; but the experts said no, it was not the same spring at all; and, later on, a fresh competitor (with a temperature of 70° F.) appeared some couple of hundred feet higher, on Sion Hill.[1] But, tempting as it always is to look back

ad patrios montes et ad incunabula nostra,

let us return to Attica. 'The air of Attica was always esteemed for its purity', says Dodwell (vol. ii, p. 7), 'and it is still the best in Greece. Its extreme dryness has greatly contributed to the admirable preservation of the Athenian edifices', but the daily wind, the *Imbat*, modifies the summer heat. The climate, writes Henry Holland[2] (1815), 'affords an atmosphere for the most part clear, dry and temperate; very different from that which hangs over the low plains and marshes of Boeotia'; the peninsular position of Attica and the nature of the surface contribute to this, and the temperature is more uniform than elsewhere in Greece; that is, less rain. Less rain than of old, says Mrs R. C. Bosanquet,[3] because of deforestation; yet Plutarch and Strabo give evidence of Attic rivulets dry in summer; 'the dryness of the Attic climate', she concludes, 'is due not to a low rainfall but to an extremely rapid evaporation. It is this that gives the atmosphere its peculiar scintillating brilliance'; and she quotes Euripides on the Athenians 'walking with delicate feet through the most luminous ether':

Ἐρεχθεῖδαι…φερβόμενοι
κλεινοτάταν σοφίαν, αἰεὶ διὰ λαμπροτάτου
βαίνοντες ἁβρῶς αἰθέρος (*Medea*, 824–830).

Readers of her book will remember Thrasybulus on his hilltop visible through that air from Athens (p. 323). A modern geographer, L. W. Lyde,[4] notes that 'of course the summer drought has always been most favourable to the olive; and olive-oil is an admirable food in such a climate—with great nourishment in small bulk, easily assimilated, and so sustaining that there is no need for heavy or constant meals'. That explains some part of Athenian life, and its commerce; to the water question at Athens we return later, merely noting here the wicked scepticism of Athenaeus (43 b) about Athenian water, in

[1] See John Latimer, *Annals of Bristol*, Nineteenth Century, p. 504. Latimer on p. 280 almost echoes Dodwell on Athens; in and about 1845 officials reporting described Bristol as 'worse supplied with water than any great city in England'.
[2] Henry Holland, *Travels in the Ionian Isles, etc.* p. 411.
[3] Mrs R. C. Bosanquet, *Days in Attica*, p. 299.
[4] Lionel W. Lyde, *The Continent of Europe*, p. 156.

spite of the comic poet Antiphanes, who is almost Pindaric about it—'one would know in a minute one was drinking Attic water'. Incidentally, one may note the reference of Pausanias to 'rain-making' in Arcadia (viii, 38, 4). Elsewhere he speaks of prayer being tried to this end.

One feature of the Greek water system has already been hinted at—the habit that Greek streams have had, and still have, of disappearing underground in all their volume, running so many miles (it may be) underground, and then re-appearing, apparently undiminished. The ancients believed—or at least told the story—that the stream would sometimes go under the sea and re-appear, as the Alpheius did, which, after a long under-sea passage, united its waters with the spring Arethusa near Syracuse. Strabo cites Pindar as an authority for the legend (which makes Artemis the object of the river-god's passion, *Nemean* i, 1–4); he advances reasons against accepting the story (C 271), yet recognizes the fact of rivers flowing underground. The phenomenon is not unfamiliar in England, in Derbyshire in particular; and the causes appear to be the same, limestone and slate, full of natural caverns and fissures.[1] Katavothra is the modern Greek name—χάσματα, βάραθρα, φάραγγες in antiquity. Associated with this habit of Greek rivers, we find noted the otherwise strange phenomenon of springs of fresh water in the sea itself—hot springs, too; 'fresh water', says Pausanias,[2] 'rising in the sea may be seen here in Argolis...still more wonderful is the boiling water in the Maeander.... Off Dicaearchia, which belongs to the Etruscans, there is boiling water in the sea, and an island has been constructed artificially, that the water may be used for warm baths.'

---

[1] Cf. Dodwell, *Tour*, vol. i, p. 238; vol. ii, p. 228; H. F. Tozer, *Geography of Greece*, pp. 111, 112; J. I. Manatt, *Aegean Days*, p. 182; Herodotus, vi, 76; Strabo, C 275, 343, 389, 578, 834; Pausanias, v, 7, 5; Athenaeus, 43 d; Pliny, *Nat. Hist.* ii, 225.

[2] Cf. Pausanias, viii, 7; ánd for such springs on the seashore Pliny, *Nat. Hist.* ii, 224. For modern views on this subject see W. Coles-Finch, *Water, its Origin and Use*, p. 251, with a reference to such a fresh-water spring in Syracuse harbour.

II

Mr Kitto, in the passage already quoted, spoke of the Greek peasant as a connoisseur in waters. Other travellers confirm this. 'The Greeks', writes Mr William Miller,[1] 'will discriminate as nicely between the respective merits of neighbouring springs as a connoisseur between the vintages of different years, and the traveller soon learns to measure his journey by the distance from one well to the next....Andros produces an excellent table water, which, as the English advertisement on the label epigrammatically states, "is superior to its equals"....Greece is very rich in mineral waters.' Athenaeus offers evidence for similar delicacy of taste in ancient Greece—springs 'rather good to drink from' ($\pi o \tau \iota \mu \acute{\omega} \tau \epsilon \rho a \iota$) in Paphlagonia, with a flavour of wine; 'royal waters' near the Mysian Mount Olympus; very pleasant water near Dorylaeum (42 e–43 b). 'For the variety of taste in water', says Seneca (*Nat. Qu.* iii, 20), 'there are four causes', which for the moment we may postpone. Athenaeus would have you drink the best water obtainable ($\dot{\omega}s \chi \rho \eta \sigma \tau \acute{o} \tau a \tau o \nu$), in winter and spring as hot as you can bear it, in summer cold (45 d). Running waters ($\tau \grave{a} \ \dot{\epsilon} \pi \acute{\iota} \rho \rho \upsilon \tau a$), he says, even from an aqueduct, are as a rule better than standing water, and when aerated are softer ($\kappa o \pi \tau \acute{o} \mu \epsilon \nu \acute{a} \ \tau \epsilon \ \mu a \lambda a \kappa \acute{\omega} \tau \epsilon \rho a \ \gamma \acute{\iota} \nu \epsilon \tau a \iota$, 42 c). The modern authorities say the same. 'The best water', says Dr A. T. Schofield, quoted by Coles-Finch,[2] 'is fresh spring water. This however is a luxury that is rarer than good wine, and the bulk of the population have no idea what such a water is like.' *Punch* dealt with the matter at the time of the Great Exhibition of 1851; 'the Contractor is bound to supply *gratis* pure water...but the committee must have forgotten that whoever can produce in London a glass of water fit to drink will contribute the rarest and most universally useful article in the whole exhibition.'[3] A man in health and strength, we read in Hippocrates, may drink any water that is to hand[4]—of course excluding poisonous waters which we shall notice; and after dealing with springs he passes on to rain—'the lightest, sweetest,

---

[1] W. Miller, *Greek Life in Town and Country*, pp. 298–299.
[2] W. Coles-Finch, *Water, its Orign and Use*, p. 130.
[3] Quoted by Drummond and Wilbraham, *The Englishman's Food*, p. 370.
[4] Hippocrates, *Airs, Waters, Places*, ch. 7, 80 (p. 88 in Loeb vol. i).

finest and clearest of water', for the sun takes the best. For some
reason the ancients classed rain among the 'hard' (σκληρά)
waters, which I have not seen explained. Once again, the
want of chemistry leaves things indistinct, and the general
statement (Athenaeus, 42d) that cold waters are hard seems
inadequate. Rain water is lightest, says Celsus (ii, 18, 12); after
it, spring water (*fontana*), then river water (*ex flumine*), then well
water (*ex puteo*), after these water from snow or ice; heavier than
all of them lake water, heaviest of all marsh water (*ex palude*);
and he adds tests by which waters of equal weight may be
judged—do they heat or cool quickly? and how are they for the
cooking of vegetables? Vitruvius bears the same testimony to
rain water—its qualities are more wholesome, 'because it is
drawn from the lightest and most delicately pure parts of all
the springs, and then, after being filtered through the agitated
air, it is liquefied by storms and so returns to the earth'
(viii, 2, 1).

A paragraph of Seneca's[1] sums up the varieties of spring—
some sweet, some with pungent flavour, salt, bitter, medicinal,
in which last class he groups waters tinged with sulphur, iron
and alum. Then there are other differences—hot and cold—
light and heavy—varieties of colour, pure, muddy, dark blue
and yellowish. (There are further hints as to colour in
Pausanias, iv, 35—the bluest of water at Thermopylae, red near
Joppa in the land of the Hebrews—red as blood, and legend
associated it with Perseus washing off the blood of the sea-beast
he slew there—black water at Astyra opposite Lesbos, white
water somewhere across the Anio above Rome—*Sulphurea Nar
albus aqua.*) Seneca continues: 'there are waters wholesome,
useful, and waters deadly and putrid; thick and thin; some
nourish and others pass through the system without benefiting
it at all; some remove barrenness'—a belief found in other
authors.[2]

Athenaeus (42c) condemns 'the heavier, harder and colder'
waters as inferior; they are hard to boil; and most spring water
is too hard (46b), where, in view of all we read in modern books
of chalk and limestone and bicarbonate of lime, we find belief

---

[1] Seneca, *Nat. Qu.* iii, 2.
[2] Athenaeus, 41f, quotes Theophrastus, *Hist. of Plants*, to this effect.

easier. The earliest use of 'hard' in our modern sense as applied to water that the Oxford Dictionary quotes is in 1660. The modern medical man, as we have seen, seems to prefer spring water to rain, and the *Lancet*[1] is quoted against popular notions that a hard water is bad for health or contributes to the growth of stone; on the contrary, we are told that children in particular cannot drink too much of it; it helps to build bone and teeth, and safeguards against rickets. Loch Katrine water has been criticized as not bringing the Glasgow children all the lime they needed; hence the bandy legs, and the quip of a wild humourist that 'you should always sit down for a little after drinking Glasgow water', to safeguard your legs. Sir George Adam Smith quotes a friend of his on 'Jacob's Well' near Nablus or Samaria; the water is hard, or, as the natives call it, 'heavy'— which is not very far from Greek terminology; the well is esteemed, and it is recorded that here, as elsewhere in the East, people will send for a particular water rather than another that may be a mile nearer—again, something like Greek practice, as we have seen. We need not perhaps linger longer over light and heavy, except to record that Athenaeus tells us he weighed the water from the Corinthian spring Peirene and found it the lightest of all Greek waters (43b), and that the Greeks (as we shall see) were well aware that water picks up solid matter (τὸ γεῶδες), which causes the variety in its shades of colour (42e). Peneius, writes Mr Tozer,[2] is never clear, and disappoints travellers, who find it a white and turbid river in springtime, though summer changes it to a more pleasing pale green. Canadians may think of the junction of the Ottawa and the St Lawrence, where for a spell the streams run side by side, the Ottawa turbid from its peaty area, while the St Lawrence has left its earthy matter (τὸ γεῶδες) in the great lakes and runs clear and blue. Dodwell[3] compares the Cephissus in Boeotia with its sluggish and muddy current to the Cam at Cambridge, both as to width and colour, but he has scant patience for the belief recorded by Pliny and by Vitruvius that its waters, entering the bodies of sheep, give a whitish colour to the lambs.

[1] See W. Coles-Finch, *Water, its Origin and Use*, p. 127.
[2] H. F. Tozer, *Geography of Greece*, pp. 86–87.
[3] Dodwell, *Tour*, vol. i, p. 242; Vitruvius, viii, 3, 14; Pliny, *Nat. Hist.* ii, 230; Seneca, *Nat. Qu.* iii, 25.

There are of course salt springs, about which Hippocrates has
to correct a popular belief; their water is not laxative, he says,
but the reverse.[1] Here again differences may be explained by
chemistry; Epsom salts, magnesium sulphate, are firmly established in popular and medical regard; but Hippocrates will
have used 'salt' in a more specialized sense. The Nile, Athenaeus
says (41 e), contains 'a soda ingredient' (μῖξιν ἔχον λιτρώδη);
so it promotes conception, is pleasant to drink, and opens the
bowels. Lady Duff Gordon, in one of her letters, records how
her maid declared that other waters after you had drunk of the
Nile were like poor beer after good. Poisonous springs were
familiar—'fatal', says Seneca,[2] 'though they do not betray the
fact either by smell or taste'; and he and Pliny both instance the
Styx. Here we touch a famous story, Why did Alexander the
Great die so suddenly at Babylon on 13 June 323? Because,
suggested Sir Clements Markham, there was not yet quinine from
Peru, a stiff dose of which might have cured his fever. Because,
said sundry of the ancients, the water of Styx was craftily administered to him. No vessel of man's contrivance could hold the
water of the Styx, horn, bone or metal—nothing but the hollow
hoof of an ass, or (as some said, according to Pausanias), of a
mule or a horse would hold it; and in that it was brought over
to Asia and given to the king. 'Whether Alexander really died
of this poison', says Pausanias, 'I do not know for certain, but
I know that people say so' (viii, 18, 6). Plutarch says there
was no suspicion of poison for some five years; and then the
tale became current that the son of Antipater administered it,
to which scandal added that Aristotle himself was behind the
deed.[3] W. G. Clark, in his *Peloponnesus*, has a chapter (ch. xxi)
on the river and the problem of its identification; there was the
waterfall that Pausanias believed to be the Styx—Mavro-Nero
to-day—a thin stream of water falling over a cliff; was Pausanias
right? At all events, 'as we crossed the river I tasted the water
and found it excellent. Neither its temperature, colour nor
flavour is such as to suggest or support the notion of its having

[1] Hippocrates, *Airs, Waters, Places*, 7.
[2] Seneca, *Nat. Qu.* iii, 25. Cf. Vitruvius, viii, 3, 15; Pliny, *Nat. Hist.* ii,
231.
[3] See Plutarch, *Alexander*, 77, 2; Vitruvius, viii, 3, 16; and of course it is too
sensational a tale for Q. Curtius to omit, x, 10, 14, 31.

a preternatural origin.' Tozer[1] attributes the discovery of the river to Colonel Leake and tells us that it falls 500 feet. Whether Pausanias was right or not about the Styx, we may honour his doubt about the Alexander story, and the other story which he quotes of the wrath of the gods; 'I do not believe', he says (and in view of his critics let us welcome it), 'that one of the gods would so ruthlessly have quenched at a blow the life of Alexander and the glory of Macedon', 'leaving', as Demades said, 'Macedon helpless as the blinded Cyclops'; 'but this has been a digression', concludes Pausanias.

But there certainly were strange springs. Henry Holland came on a spring, through whose water rose a vast number of air-bubbles. He had some guess as to their nature, and collected a lot of them in a glass jar, and set a light to it, and the gas burnt with considerable vividness. His Albanian guards were immensely surprised, and then he set fire to the bubbles as they came up through the water. They did not know nor did the ancients that the gas was, as Holland guessed, sulphuretted hydrogen. This story he tells after discussing data of Strabo, Plutarch and Dio about what we may call burning wells.[2] Strabo, again, and Virgil and Lucretius[3] remind us of Avernus in the volcanic region round Naples—a lake so-called because a vapour rose from it that killed birds flying over it—"Αορνος—a mephitic vapour such as rises, Strabo says, from all *Plutonia*, natural shrines of Pluto, entrances to the world of Hades.[4] All the same there was a well of drinkable water nearby on the sea-shore, but the people would not drink of it; it must have come from the Styx, and there are hot springs not far off, which again suggested the rivers of hell. As to *mephites*, Strabo tells us that the vapour at Hierapolis will kill a bull, and that he himself threw in sparrows which died at once. At the Neapolitan one the experiment is tried with small dogs, which the guides plunge into the neighbouring lake to recover them 'because another carriage is coming down the hill'. A. H. Norway refused to

[1] Tozer, *Geography of Greece*, pp. 33, 118.
[2] Henry Holland, *Travels in the Ionian Isles*, p. 522. Cf. Strabo, C 316, the Nymphaeon in the territory of the Apolloniates, a rock that gives forth fire with a spring of warm water and asphalt; Plutarch, *Sulla*, 27, streams of perpetually flowing fire.   [3] Strabo, C 244; Virgil, *Aeneid*, vi, 239; Lucretius, vi, 740.
[4] E.g. one at Hierapolis in Asia, cf. Strabo, C 629; Virgil, *Aeneid*, vii, 84.

have the dog exposed to the gas—'Ah!' said the guide, 'you are Englees! If you had been American, you would have said "Why, certainly".'[1] The commentators and dictionary-makers are reluctant to define the gas in chemical language, but they are all agreed, on the testimony of Strabo and Virgil, that it must have been unpleasant. One supposes it to be carbon dioxide, which we shall find elsewhere, still without a chemical name.

Hot springs are mentioned by Strabo at both places, and we read of them elsewhere, in Etruria and Tunis.[2] Homer and Sir Charles Fellows speak of them in the region of Troy; Homer says that one of the two sources of the Scamander 'flows with hot water and about it smoke rises as from a blazing fire', while the other is cold as hail or snow or ice which forms from water.[3] Sir Charles had a thermometer which quickly registered 140° F.;[4] he adds that the springs were strongly chalybeate. Seneca and Vitruvius attempt explanations,[5] Vitruvius adding that in some instances the hot water is delightful to drink. Britain has only one hot spring, at Bath—900 miles, we are told, from the nearest volcano—a spring which yields about 400,000 gallons a day of a temperature about 120° F.; the water, the authorities add, is radio-active. The place and its water, as we all know, were familiar to the Romans, who associated them with a goddess Sulis, who is otherwise little known.[6] The Greeks linked such places with another divinity, as Aristophanes reminds us in the dispute between Right and Wrong Reason:[7]

W.R. You said that always from warm baths the stripling must
      abstain:
      Why must he? on what grounds do you of those warm
      baths complain?

R.R. Why, it's the worst thing possible, it quite unstrings a man.

[1] A. H. Norway, *Naples Past and Present*, pp. 26–27.
[2] Strabo, C 227, 275, 578, 834; Athenaeus, 42f, 43a; Pausanias, ii, 34, 1; viii, 7, 2–3.
[3] Homer, *Iliad*, xxii, 149; quoted by Athenaeus, 41c.
[4] Fellows, *Asia Minor* (1838), p. 58.
[5] Seneca, *Nat. Qu.* iii, 24; Vitruvius, viii, 3, 1.
[6] One may add hot springs found in the making of the Simplon tunnel.
[7] Aristophanes, *Clouds*, 1044–1051 (tr. of B. B. Rogers). See Strabo, C 428 and Herodotus, vii, 176 (not quite so definite).

W.R. Hold there: I've got you round the waist: escape me if
       you can.
       And first: of all the sons of Zeus which think you was
       the best?
       Which was the manliest? which endured more toils than
       all the rest?

R.R. Well, I suppose that Heracles was bravest and most bold.

W.R. And are the 'baths of Heracles' so wonderfully cold?

Of course, they were not cold, they were hot—120° F., says
Baedeker of the baths supposed to be meant, the hot springs
of Thermopylae—the bluest water, we remember, that Pausanias
had ever seen;[1] a grey-green colour, says Mr Tozer, and the
water salt and sulphurous,[2] who tells of other 'Baths of Hercules'
on Euboea, once used by Sulla and now turned into an extensive
bathing establishment. (One might add a similar development
by the Italian government of medicinal springs a little West of
the city of Rhodes.) Helen herself had lukewarm baths on the
Isthmus of Corinth.

But the Greeks were also interested in cold springs, very
intelligibly. Pausanias tells us of a stream at Gortys in Arcadia
with water colder than that of any other.[3] It was called the
Lousios, because Zeus on his birth was washed in it, which
recalls the treatment of Italian babies, of which Remulus
Numanus boasts so unseasonably.

> Durum a stirpe genus natos ad flumina primum
> Deferimus, saevoque gelu duramus et undis.[4]

Of course, Pausanias does not compare this Arcadian stream
with the Danube and the Rhine and the rivers of Russia, whose
waters freeze in winter, the rivers of snow-clad lands—he
explains that; but he thinks of lands with a temperate climate
and rivers refreshing in summer to bathe in or to drink, and
not disagreeable in winter; it is cold on that scale that he means.
And he picks out St Paul's native river, the Cydnus that flows
through Tarsus, as agreeably cold; and one or two more over
which we need not linger. An epigram from Mr Mackail's

---

[1] Pausanias, iv, 35, 9. [2] H. F. Tozer, *Geography of Greece*, p. 104.
[3] Pausanias, viii, 28, 2. [4] *Aeneid*, ix, 603.

selection[1] will suffice, and will perhaps recall points already noticed in the Greek habit of life:

'Drink not here, traveller, from this warm pool in the brook, full of mud stirred by the sheep at pasture; but going a very little way over the ridge where the heifers are grazing, there by yonder pastoral stonepine thou wilt find bubbling through the fountained rock a spring colder than northern snow.'

So Leonidas of Tarentum. St Matthew is with him, adding the attractive adjective *cold* to the cup of water.

Hippocrates[2] tells us that the best springs flow from high places and earthy hills (λόφων γεηρῶν). By themselves they are sweet and clear, and the wine they can stand is but little. In winter, they are warm, in summer cold—which may astonish; but he adds a reason—'they would naturally be so, coming from very deep springs'. He goes on to commend especially springs that flow toward the rising sun, particularly toward the point where he rises in summer; for they must be brighter, sweet-smelling and light. Surely a pleasanter test than some of the others suggested by Athenaeus, Celsus and Vitruvius, which involve boiling vegetables and the inspection of the cauldron.[3] Vitruvius also suggests that the physique of the people who live near the spring would be a good guide—are their frames strong, their complexions fresh, their legs sound, their eyes clear? If so, go ahead with your conduit plans. One feels somehow that this test should be better than the flow toward the sun.

III

The tests of good water suggested by Vitruvius raise the general question of the effects that various waters have upon human health. As we saw, Hippocrates suggests that a man in sound health may safely drink almost any water; but he himself supplies endless cautions. Water from swampy land with no outflow—stagnant, hot, thick and stinking—bad in winter as well as summer—what consequences it may bring—enlarged spleen, bad digestion, dropsy, in summer dysentery and diarrhoea, and difficulties of pregnancy for women and un-

---

[1] *Select Epigrams from the Greek Anthology*, p. 203; App. Plan. 230.
[2] Hippocrates, *Airs, Waters, Places*, ch. 7.
[3] Athenaeus, 46 a–c; Celsus, ii, 18, 12; Vitruvius, viii, 4, 1.

satisfactory babies; and other troubles, not to prolong the catalogue.[1]

On the other hand, there are waters named as specifics for various diseases, and water generally is prescribed as useful for digestion. Modern authorities tell us how largely the human body consists of water, which needs constant renewal. Man, wrote Frank Buckland, has been aptly defined as forty-five pounds of carbon and nitrogen diffused through five and a half pailfuls of water.[2] Man, says Charles Van Hise, is 80 per cent water and needs (if you take his average weight to be about 150 lb.) 264 gallons of water a year.[3] An English writer, W. Coles-Finch, thinks a man of that weight needs rather less; he puts it at $5\frac{1}{2}$ lb. of water, or rather more than half a gallon per day.[4] There may be differences of climate to consider. Less wheat is reckoned necessary per man per annum in the United States than in France, in the proportion of 6 to 8 bushels.

But to come to special complaints, and the waters of healing, here are a few statements of belief. Leprosy might be washed away in the Anigrus in Elis; so Pausanias (v, 5, 11) and Strabo (C 346). Gout was cured by bathing in the Cydnus at Tarsus; so Vitruvius (viii, 3, 6). The springs of Pamisus in Arcadia 'are cures for little children', says Pausanias (iv, 31, 4). Vitruvius mentions waters in Italy which, used as drinks, have the power of breaking up stone that forms in the human bladder; this is due to some natural cause, i.e. not to magic, but to some 'sharp and acid juice' that the soil gives it (viii, 3, 17–18). Pausanias is commonly counted a matter-of-fact writer, not very apt to attempt humour; but the account he gives of the water of Selemnus in Achaia half tempts one to revise this judgment. 'I have heard', he writes (vii, 23, 3), 'that the water of the Selemnus is a cure for love in man and woman, for they wash in the river and forget their love. If there is any truth in this story, great riches are less precious to mankind than the water of Selemnus.' Do we need to remind ourselves that, like Herodotus—so far, at least, like him—Pausanias feels bound to

---

[1] Hippocrates, *Airs, Waters, Places*, ch. 7 (pp. 84–86 in Loeb vol. i); referred to by Athenaeus, 46 c.
[2] *Curiosities of Natural History*, vol. i, p. 12.
[3] C. R. Van Hise, *Conservation of Natural Resources in U.S.A.*, p. 104.
[4] W. Coles-Finch, *Water, its Origin and Use*, p. 136.

set down what he is told, but avows that he does not always feel
bound to believe it (cf. vi, 3, 8; ii, 17, 4)?

At this point it may be fitting to recall a caution given by
Aristotle; it is well, he says, to be careful in keeping your
drinking water separate from all other water.[1]

These medical records, and not least the warning of Aristotle,
bring us to the consideration of the bath. Here national usages
differ. The Eskimo, for instance, has less opportunity for the
frequent bath than the Hindu, and less temptation; he has not
the same fresh-water rivers, and climatic conditions give a
different bent to his habits and his religion. But even where
the climate is the same, we find interesting differences. In the
early story of Christianity in Saxon England, we read how the
Saxon saint (memory seems to suggest it was more commonly
a woman) 'went woolward', and abstained for terribly long
periods from washing herself or her woollen garments; this by
way of spiritual discipline. The Celtic saint on the other hand
would spend the night, reciting the whole Psalter, neck-deep in
the river. It might be trivial to suggest that one of them would
be pleasanter to sit next in the daytime than the other; but
when piety headed one to the river and the other away from it,
we might properly ask which of the two had the stronger natural
instinct for cleanliness; and the answer might not be quite easy.
Roman remains in this island are generally supposed by amateur
antiquaries to have been baths, and water-pipes and hypocausts
offer some evidence. What of the Greek? We read constantly
in Homer of a guest's entertainment beginning with a bath,
where attendants wash and anoint him, and he comes out
looking like a god—looking younger perhaps as Odysseus did—

$$\text{ἔκ ῥ' ἀσαμίνθου βῆ δέμας ἀθανάτοισιν ὅμοιος}$$
(*Odyssey*, iii, 468),

and people wonder (xxiv, 370). And what was the bath like?
A priest in Phocis boards with the goddess and bathes after the
ancient manner in an *asaminth*; and the translators render it *tub*.
The modern traveller recalls the white man's bath in India—
the room apart; the little enclosure cut off by a three-inch 'wall',
the huge clay jar of water (that is very often quite opaque) and

---

[1] See Newman, on Aristotle, *The Politics of Aristotle*, essays, vol. iii, p. 402.

the 'dipper' with which he pours the water over himself, as he stands in that enclosure, and what is spilled runs away into the garden through a hole in the wall, a cool lurking place for a cobra. But the most famous bath of Greek history—or of all human history—seems to imply something more like our English 'slipper bath'. The story deserves detail, and this is how Vitruvius tells it (ix, *Intr.* 9) :[1]

'Hiero, after gaining the royal power in Syracuse, resolved to place in a certain temple a golden crown, which he had vowed to the immortal gods. He contracted for its making at a fixed price, and weighed out a precise amount of gold to the contractor. At the appointed time the latter delivered to the king's satisfaction an exquisitely finished piece of handiwork, and it appeared that in weight the crown corresponded precisely to what the gold had weighed. But afterwards a charge was brought that gold had been abstracted, and an equivalent weight of silver had been added in the manufacture of the crown. Hiero thought it an outrage, but, not knowing how to detect the theft, he asked Archimedes to consider the matter. He, with the case still in mind, chanced to go to the bath and on getting into a tub he observed that the more his body sank into it, the more water ran over the tub. Without a moment's delay, transported with joy, he leapt out of the tub and rushed home naked, shouting repeatedly in Greek εὕρηκα, εὕρηκα.'

He then took two masses of the same weight as the crown, one of gold, the other of silver. He immersed the silver in a large vessel full of water to the brim, and the water overflowed. Thus he found that the weight of silver answered to a definite quantity of water. He did the same with the gold; this was of the same weight as the silver, but of less bulk; so less water overflowed. Finally he put the crown into the water, and found that more water ran over for it than for gold of the same weight; and it was plain that there was after all silver in the crown. But Archimedes had not merely achieved a triumph in detection, a real Sherlock Holmes feat; he had given a new idea of first

---

[1] The baths of ordinary people are discussed by Mure, *A Tour in Greece*, vol. ii, p. 24, who holds the bath to have been a daily practice, citing Aristophanes and Xenophon; but not a Spartan habit. W. G. Clark, *Peloponnesus*, p. 334, cruelly says that the modern Greeks 'never take the trouble to undress'.

importance to Natural Science, which has never been lost—
Specific Gravity.

Before we pass on, I may raise again the question of water
chilled with snow, which I have discussed elsewhere. The general
ancient view was that it was unwholesome, but hardly for any
reason that modern medicine would offer. It was observed that,
when water freezes and melts again, there is less of it than
before; some has evaporated, and this would obviously be, men
said, the lightest and most volatile parts of the water, the
wholesomest; consequently what was left must be less wholesome.

Athenaeus (24 b–f) gives us a list of eminent men (some no
longer familiar to us) who were water-drinkers, teetotallers in
fact—the patriot Theodorus of Larissa, the tyrant Glaucon, the
sophists of Elis Anchimolus and Moschus, the musician Lam-
pros, other philosophers, the orator Demosthenes (at least for
a time).

IV

We have so far surveyed the variety of springs, of which ancient
observers and modern travellers speak—hot, cold, salt, bitter—
waters tinged with iron, sulphur, sulphuretted hydrogen—and
radio-active water at Bath. For the variety Seneca suggests
four causes.[1] Two of them we need not linger over; the ancients
believed in the four elements changing into one another; so
some of this variety in water may be due, he suggests, to the
earth or the air which has undergone this transformation.[2] And
there is the obvious suggestion of a taint from a foreign body.
More interesting is his first suggestion, which Vitruvius also
elaborates for us. It all depends on the soil through which the
water flows; water is water; so what gives one spring or another
its peculiar character can only be the soil, which may, says
Seneca, be full of sulphur, saltpetre or bitumen. Pausanias
gives the same explanation of the smell of the waters of Anigrus
in Elis.[3] The soil, says Vitruvius, affects the flavour of the fruit;
there are wines of countless varieties; Syria and Arabia have
their special products; the sun of course plays its part in the
production of pepper and frankincense, but the 'juices' of the
soil count; the human body has many juices, so 'we should not

[1] Seneca, *Nat. Qu.* iii, 20.   [2] Cf. Seneca, *Nat. Qu.* iii, 9.
[3] Pausanias, v, 5, 9.

be surprised to find in the great earth itself countless varieties of juices, through the veins of which the water runs and becomes saturated with them before reaching the outlets of springs'.[1]

The modern would not put it quite in the same language, but he would mean the same thing. He might speak of a deposit rather than a juice; but otherwise they would be in fair agreement. Without chemical analysis the ancient, as we saw, classified waters as to their influence on human health much in the same order as the modern does—it is the study of health that unites them. But on the general question of ultimate source, even an elementary knowledge of physical geography gives the English schoolboy an advantage over Seneca. Evaporation and condensation were not unfamiliar to the ancient. Even popular phrase to-day speaks of the sun 'drawing water'; the non-scientific ancient (with whom, I fear, we must group the Stoic or his pupils) said that the sun drew water 'to feed his flames'.[2] One can hardly imagine the serious astronomer even in those times to say this, but the early philosophers, e.g. Xenophanes and Heraclitus, believed it, and, in spite of Aristotle's contempt for a notion so ridiculous (as he says), it continued to please the poets—Lucan, for instance; and the angel in *Paradise Lost* (v, 415) repeats it, but it really suits Anacreon better.

It was recognized—or at least surmised—that there was underground an immense reserve of water—a sea of it, so Seneca says,[3] which was supplied and reinforced by seepage from the salt sea familiar above ground, the earth absorbing the salt as the water percolated. The water-table, the level of saturation, are familiar conceptions to the modern, and are explained by the rain. No, rain does not sink so far, says Seneca; witness his experiment in his vineyard—'as a diligent digger among my vines, I can affirm from observation that no rain is ever so heavy as to wet the ground to a depth of more than ten feet'. It is often said that the ancients did little in the

---

[1] Vitruvius, viii, 3, 26.

[2] Lucan, vii, 5; also i, 415; x, 258. Cf. Cicero, *de Nat. Deor.* ii, 15, 40, *cum sol igneus sit oceanique alatur humoribus*, on which see J. B. Mayor's note *ad loc.*; cf. his references.

[3] See Seneca, *Nat. Qu.* bk. iii generally; and in particular iii, 9; iii, 15; vi, 7, 5; vi, 8.

way of experiment, preferring theory; here the experiment has misled the observer.[1]

'There is no need', says Lucretius (v, 261), 'to say how sea, rivers and springs for ever well up in abundance with new waters, and their streams flow down unceasing. The great pouring down of waters from all sides makes this clear. But, bit by bit, whatever comes first of the water is taken off and the result is that there is no superabundance of liquid in the sum total; partly because strong winds sweep the surface and diminish it, and the sun on high unravelling it with his rays; partly because it is distributed abroad through all the earth underneath; for the virus (salt?) is strained off, and the substance of the water oozes back, and all meets at the sources of each river. Whence it returns over the earth in a marching column (*agmine*) of sweet water, along the path which has once been cut for it in its liquid course.'

Moderns know more of geology, of the types of soil and stone that will or will not transmit water, of faults and cracks and fissures that will swallow it in quantity; and even if brackish drinking water is found in wells near the sea, into which the salt water has seeped, whether losing salt as it comes or bringing it into wells initially fresh, the idea that the water table at large over great continents can be due to seepage from the Ocean is unthinkable. No, the rain is the great factor, gathered by the sun from the sea, and given back by the land. Three ways are recognized, by which it moves back toward the sea, at various rates of travel (for forest, if nothing else, will delay it) and after various adventures. There has been much speculation as to how much of the rainfall is at once returned to the atmosphere by evaporation, a matter vital for man and beast and tree; how much sinks into the ground, to a greater depth or a less, to reappear in well and spring—and, in modern times, Artesian wells—and under this head we may, not perhaps improperly, include water taken up by vegetation (remembering White of Selborne's aphorism that trees are perfect alembics, and take up immense quantities of water, which in turn they give out);

---

[1] See the comments of Sir Archibald Geikie in *Seneca, Physical Science*, p. 327, on Seneca's unawareness of the underground structure of the rocks; and p. xliii, Seneca an 'eclectic' in physics.

and finally how much finds its way directly into stream and river, to be water-supply and waterway for man and bird and beast. The proportions will vary with the nature of the absorbing soil or rock (and the tilt of the land), the character of the vegetation, and the dryness of the climate; and the manifold operations of man must not be forgotten, as he diverts, applies, uses or wastes water, for it is recognized that he also is a 'geological agent'.

Another, and a very different, series of ideas is connected with springs. *Felix qui potuit rerum cognoscere causas*—there is happiness in understanding Nature; the wonderful epigram of the Greek astronomer, the rapture (it is little less) that haunts Lucretius, assure us of this. But Virgil goes on with his *Fortunatus et ille*. Surely the spring is more than a larger or smaller quantity of drinkable fluid, projected by natural factors which can be almost calculated. Surely there is something in it beyond calculation; 'best of things is water', the gift of God, not least when it is so healthful, so curative. This at least is in the hymn of St Francis:[1]

> Praised be my Lord for our sister water, who is very serviceable unto us, and humble and precious and clean.

Nymphs and Nereids belong eventually to a lower order of divinity, but the swineherd of Odysseus is witness to their being taken seriously:

> Virgins of Zeus, ye fountain-nymphs divine,
> If that Odysseus thighs did ever burn
> Of lambs or kids fat-folded, at your shrine,
> Fulfil the hope wherewith in soul I yearn!
> May God yet bring him, may that man return!

The degeneration of the Nymphs perhaps began long before Greece became Christian; the fairies are a queer clan, creatures of dubious temper, in whatever land you find them. The kelpies of the brooks are ill neighbours. The point need not be laboured; but doubtless Greeks feel easier, as on the isle of Andros, when a church is built over the well. Mr Tozer speaks of the extraordinary number of sacred springs in modern Greece—ἁγιάσματα as they are called; and sometimes the same belief is attached to

[1] See Paul Sabatier, *Life of St Francis*, p. 306.

the spring now as in antiquity.[1] W. G. Clark remarked the same thing;[2] a stream or a fountain survives many successive buildings, and a local superstition attached to either has the best chance of permanence. A tradition to be lasting must be writ on water. We are told of holy wells in Asia Minor, once sacred to nymph or pagan god, by and by to a Christian saint, and still holy when a third religion holds sway. There is plenty of evidence of the healing power of nymphs, even if some of the race caught away Hylas. Hence the caution that Hesiod gives to treat a stream with respect (*Works and Days*, 737, 757). Strabo tells his readers that the Persians worship water (C 733).

V

Herodotus tells us (and it interested later Greeks who quote it from him) that 'when the Great King goes upon campaign, he goes well equipped with food and sheep from home; and water from the Choaspes which flows past Susa is carried with him whereof alone, and of none other, the king drinks. This water of the Choaspes is boiled, and many four-wheeled waggons drawn by mules carry it in silver vessels, following the king whithersoever he goes at any time.'[3] In 1863, shortly after his accession, Ismail, the Khedive of Egypt, received a visit from his suzerain, the sultan Abdul Aziz. Lady Duff Gordon was in Egypt at the time. She writes home that there was some mystery about his coming, but the fact was established that all his food and his water were brought from Constantinople.[4] Other travellers, perhaps thinking more of germs than of religion, have carried water. 'When one has lived for a month or more on bottled waters,' writes the American P. S. Marden, 'the expectation of drinking at nature's fount is not lightly to be regarded'; and if a spring Baedeker had bidden him look for in Arcadia failed to be found, at Delphi his prose becomes almost lyrical when he has the opportunity to 'drink deep' at Castalia, 'for the water is good, and the chance to drink fresh water in Greece is rare enough to be embraced wherever met'. And it would seem that the long literary traditions of the gushing spring

[1] H. F. Tozer, *Geography of Greece*, p. 332.
[2] *Peloponnesus*, p. 286.
[3] Herodotus, i, 188. Cf. Strabo, C 735, and Athenaeus, 45a.
[4] *Letters from Egypt*, dated 9 April (food) and 13 April (water).

haunted him as he drank.[1] Another traveller has spoken to me
of the bottled water, supplied to tourists in Greece; it is boiled,
he says, but not unpalatable. From a remark of William Miller,
one conjectures that it may have come from Andros.[2] In modern
Toronto, during the 'prohibition' period, the brewing house of
Gooderham turned to another industry; they chanced to own
a fine spring and they retailed its water; it was not unwelcome—
the water of the lake supplied through the domestic pipes was
so heavily chlorinated, a precaution involved by the risk of
pollution of neighbouring parts of the immense lake, not a
contribution to delight in water-drinking. One hardly needs to
be a 'connoisseur' in water to be able to recognize chlorine.

The earth, then, supplies the water, but man has to do his
share in the work, chlorinating and boiling in modern times, and
at every time lessening, if he can, the difficulty of actually getting
the water. Hence the difference between *pege*, the spring, and
krene, the fountain;[3] the well may be deep[4] or difficult, but
human ingenuity—let us add, human kindliness—will simplify
the task of water-drawing. Even the Turk built fountains
wherever he went—his only contribution to his fellow-subjects'
welfare—and travellers blame the Greek for letting the fountain
decay or sweeping it away altogether with the hated Turk's
minarets and cypresses. It is unfortunate, but only too intelligible.[5] Turn back, however, to our oldest records of Greek
life, and we find in Ithaca 'the fair-flowing spring with a basin
fashioned (τυκτήν), whence the people of the city drew water.
This well Ithacus and Neritus and Polyctor had builded. And
around it was a thicket of alders that grew by the waters, all
circlewise, and down the cold stream fell from a rock on high,
and above was reared an altar to the Nymphs whereat all
wayfarers made offering.'[6] It is interesting to note how many
of Homer's details we have met already. On Calypso's island—
a passage quoted with comment by Athenaeus (41 a)—were

[1] P. S. Marden, *Greece and the Aegean Islands*, pp. 167 and 226.
[2] W. Miller, *Greek Life in Town and Country*, p. 299.
[3] W. G. Clark, *Peloponnesus*, p. 234.
[4] Cf. Seneca, *Nat. Qu.* iii, 7, who says 200 feet.
[5] Mure, *A Tour in Greece* (1842), vol. i, p. 259 (a good account of the fountains);
Lord Carnarvon, *Athens and the Morea* (1869), p. 3; Mrs R. C. Bosanquet, *Days in
Attica*, p. 243; Sir T. Wyse, *Impressions of Greece*, p. 186.
[6] *Odyssey*, xvii, 206.

'fountains four set orderly, running with clear water (ὕδατι
λευκῷ), hard by one another, turned each to his own course'
(*Odyssey*, v, 70).

When we reach historic times, we meet Solon's very significant
law—a recognition, as always in his work, of the real needs of
actual people, and it is underlined by Plato. That supreme need
for water was to be met in another and more telling way by
Pisistratus. Plato, in drafting his second thoughts for an ideal
state—this time to be practicable—dealt with the water question, and it looks as if he had in mind, along with the waterworks
of Pisistratus and others, a simpler community and people who
were not city dwellers, but were not exempt from human
passions and hatreds. Here then is Solon's law.[1] He observed,
says Plutarch in the previous chapter, that 'the city was growing
full of people constantly streaming together into Athens from
every quarter, for greater security of living'. So 'as the country
was not supplied with water by everflowing rivers, nor lakes,
nor copious springs (ἀφθόνοις πηγαῖς), but most of the people
used wells that had been made, he enacted a law that when
there was a public well within the distance of four furlongs, that
should be used; but, where the distance was greater than this,
people must try to get water of their own; but if, after digging
to a depth of ten fathoms on their own land, they do not find
it, then they may take water from a neighbour's well, filling a
five-gallon jar twice a day. For he thought it his duty to aid
the needy.'

Plato[2] perhaps has this enactment in mind when he starts to
tell us that there are admirable laws laid down of old about
water for farmers, though there is no reason to 'tap' them in
our present discourse (παροχετεύειν λόγοις); a man shall have
the right to use the public water-supply (ἐκ τῶν κοινῶν ναμάτων),
but he must not cut into the springs that clearly belong to any
private person [or perhaps, that a private person has opened up],
nor shall he be allowed to injure house, temple, or tomb by his
channelling. If in any place there is a natural dryness of earth
which absorbs the rain from Zeus, and there is a deficiency in
the supply of water, let him dig down on his own land as far
as the brick clay (μέχρι τῆς κεραμίδος γῆς) [note how all our

---

[1] Plutarch, *Solon*, 23.   [2] Plato, *Laws*, viii, 844, 845.

modern authorities tell us that the water will not get through the clay], and then if at this depth he finds no water, let him fetch from his neighbours what water he needs for actual drinking purposes but not more (ὑδρευέσθω μέχρι τοῦ ἀναγκαίου πώματος). But if the neighbours also are short of water, he must apply for a ration of water to the proper authorities (ἀγρονόμους) for a daily allowance, and on these terms share with his neighbours. Plato then deals with regulations about flooding a neighbour's land on a lower level, and, after some suggestions about fruit crops, returns to water. A man will find it hard to poison soil or sun or air—the other elements in the nutrition of plants—but water is more amenable to attack or misuse; by poison or digging or theft, a man may injure a neighbour's supply, whether in spring or cistern; and every such ill act shall be dealt with suitably, the guilty person, thief or poisoner, fined, the spring or basin cleaned out and the cleansing shall be done as the laws of the interpreters direct for each several sufferer.

Poisoning the water supply was not done by the decorous and established processes we know so well, by discharge of sewage or factory refuse, soap, acids and so forth—the act, if you like, not of malevolence but of sheer indifference to the community—but by the more deliberate putting of malignant drugs into the water to injure health, as some Athenians believed the Peloponnesians did in the war, with the great plague at Athens as a direct consequence, intended and achieved.[1]

An anecdote that Plutarch records about Themistocles in exile illustrates another point[2]—the theft of public water, clearly an act that implies the public supply to which we shortly come, but it follows naturally on our passage from Plato. Themistocles, then, saw in a temple at Sardis a bronze statue, two cubits high, of a girl—the so-called water-carrier, which he himself when water-commissioner in Athens had had made and dedicated from the fines exacted from persons convicted of stealing public water. It had been looted when Athens was sacked in 480; and for some reason he asked if he might have it. It was refused to him, and he had some difficulty in soothing the satrap.

Our primary subject is the springs of Greece, so that it will not be supremely needful to amplify in detail the engineering or

[1] Thucydides, ii, 48.   [2] Plutarch, *Themistocles*, 31.

architectural aspects of the great constructions of the tyrants, which are discussed in their several books by the experts.[1] Let it suffice here to suggest that these great works implied real understanding of human nature and human needs—an easy water-supply enlisted the women at once; that they required the application of real intelligence of nature's laws in various spheres and a genius in using them; and (not a small point either) that they involved a great labour policy, the details of which we may lack as they bear on slave or free labour, and big expenditure (and Polybius, in dealing with the Roman Senate, emphasizes the significance of both these phases in securing the power of a government); and finally that the great projects were achieved. In all these cases—Athens, Samos, Megara—it is well to remember that, as Plutarch says, the population was growing; and modern experience ought to enlighten us. 'The water history of London, Eng.[2] and of the great new cities on the North American prairies should make it clear that to double a population may involve far more than to double the problems of transport, lighting, water, etc., while of all these the water problem is most urgent and most quickly touches the largest number of homes.' The tyrants saw this; and, as among them were some of the acutest minds of Greece (we must remember what Thucydides has to say of Pisistratus[3]), it is not surprising that with a big population, a serious problem and great resources, a big scheme was political wisdom. The futile efforts of Greek provincial towns, which Pliny describes centuries later— efforts wrecked by mismanagement, dishonesty and incompetent architects—show by contrast something of the genius of the older Greeks and their tyrants. Strabo indeed (C 235) draws a famous contrast between Greeks and Romans—the interest of Greeks, when founding a city, in site and harbour and soil, and the beauty of the city—of the Romans in roads and sewers and aqueducts. Water, he says, is brought into Rome in such quan-

---

[1] For Pisistratus and the *Enneacrounos*, see E. A. Gardner, *Ancient Athens*, pp. 16 ff.; and Neuburger, *Technical Arts and Sciences of the Ancients* (tr.), pp. 409–425 (Water supply of the Greeks), for Pisistratus and Samos; the Samian tunnel is also mentioned in Michaelis, *A Century of Archaeological Discoveries*, p. 187.

[2] A friend of mine, comparing Whitaker's *Almanack* on London's water supply and Smith's *Dictionary of Antiquities* on Rome's striking averages, reports that the Roman had eight times as much water as the Londoner.

[3] Thucydides, vi, 54.

tities that veritable rivers flow through the city and the sewers, and almost every house has cisterns and service pipes and copious fountains. The early Romans made little account of the city's beauty, but by Strabo's day that is all changed. But once more we have to remember that Athens led the way. And Herodotus (iii, 60), claiming for Samos 'the three greatest works to be seen in any Greek land', sets first the double-mouthed channel eight feet high, eight feet wide and seven furlongs long, driven through the base of a high hill, bringing water from an abundant spring to the city of Samos; and its architect or contriver was Eupalinos of Megara. The tunnel was rediscovered in 1882. It is to be noted, too, how regularly Pausanias takes the pains to mention water basins in one city after another, and tells in turn of the Emperor Hadrian who 'brought water to Corinth'.[1]

To complete our survey of this part of our subject, there remain Vitruvius and Frontinus—the one an Augustan writing on architecture generally with a special section of his work upon water, into which (to vary Plato's metaphor) we have been dipping all the way along; the other a most Roman official of something like a century later, who had charge in his day of the aqueducts that brought to Rome the abundant water of which Strabo spoke. Frontinus must have written the most business-like book of antiquity, a book that reflects its author if ever a book did. The aqueducts had been badly mismanaged; his energy and care, his resolve to know everything about them at first hand made a change—'the water-supply has been almost doubled', he wrote (de Aquis, ii, 87). He had plans made of all the aqueducts, so as to have the business always in sight and be able to plan as if on the spot (i, 17). His book tells the story; he surveys them all and sets forth their capacity, intake and delivery. There is not a hint of rhetoric in the book; but while everything is matter-of-fact and while there are pages and pages about pipes and their dimensions, which the general reader will do little more than skim, one cannot but read him with the respect that one always feels for an honest man who handles a serious subject seriously. He is honest to the core, believes in his work, serves his Emperor loyally and realizes how much he

[1] Water basins i, 40; i, 41; ii, 3; ii, 35; Corinth viii, 22.

can promote the comfort and welfare of the people—'the appearance of the City (queen and empress of the world—*regina et domina orbis*) is cleaner, the air is purer, the causes of the unwholesome atmosphere which gave the City's air a bad name in former days are removed' (ii, 88), and there are still improvements of which he thinks (ii, 89). There were 'secret pipes' all over the City, 'punctures', by which dishonest people drew off large quantities of water for private uses (ii, 115); there were repairs to be done; bad workmanship and bad neighbours, violent storms and trees were to blame (ii, 120), and the repairs must not be made in summer, which would stop the flow of water when it was most needed, and care should be taken not to repair several aqueducts at once (ii, 122). He asked for no lictors; he sought no monument—'my memory will endure if my life has deserved it' was what he said to Pliny. Statistics do not make a gay form of literature; but Frontinus somehow gets the reader's goodwill as one realizes his conscience, his efficiency, and his simplicity.

Vitruvius has a subject of much wider range, and he is a more engaging writer. One must not digress in any attempt to appraise his work on architecture, when our subject is comprised in one book, the eighth; but he lives in a real world and sticks to it; and for any one interested (let us say) in forest or water, in wind and weather (they bear a great deal on house-planning), machinery and artillery, his book is amazingly interesting. Not to stray too far, here is a practical point, which we have not yet had.[1] In the digging of wells there is danger; 'great currents of air come' and stop the breath of life in the men's nostrils by the natural strength of the exhalation. 'Let down a lighted lamp, and if it keeps on burning, a man may go down without danger'; if the light goes out, air shafts, right and left, have to be added. He had never heard of carbon dioxide; he was no chemist; but it is interesting to find such practical guidance.

[1] Vitruvius, vii, 6, 12-13.

VI

A few words may be given to some of the famous springs of Greece, though Dodwell expresses surprise at the numbers that have ceased to flow; it may be the effect of earthquakes; but at any rate many of them, he says, 'only flow and murmur in the classic page'.[1]

The swan of Dirce

says Horace—he means Pindar—

> Borne by strong winds is wafted high
> Above the clouds; the Matine bee
> Is type of me.[2]

But Dirce, says Dodwell, is not now to be identified.

There is no literature, says Macneile Dixon, in which spring waters are so often mentioned as the Greek; and he suggests at least one reason—they are so enchanting in themselves, so delightful to the eye, gushing and sparkling from the clefts and hollows of the rocks, famous some for their coolness and copiousness, others for their purity and sweetness. Dirce, Pirene, Aganippe, Hippocrene—he speaks of their legends; and in spite of Dodwell's doubts he drank of Dirce, he says, as well as Castaly and Hippocrene; no writer of verse could overlook such a chance of inspiration. (Does not Thomas Fuller tell us of Sternhold and Hopkins that they had drunk more deep of Jordan than of Helicon? He probably means Hippocrene, which Keats half suggests might have been too much for them.) Many forest springs and village fountains he tried, happy evidently as Mr Kitto, and careless of Mr Marden's bottled and boiled water. You would not want wine, says Athenaeus (43f), if you drank of Kleitor. Manatt praises the spring at Oropus, full and fresh from under the sanctuary—'after many a delicious draught, we are all ready to vouch for it as *the* water-cure of Old Greece and New.... Only at Paros in a precinct of the Healing God can one still find a source so pure and sweet.' So he goes on, through the catalogue.

But there is an exception. One British scholar tried drinking from the stream that comes down from Hierapolis; and the

---

[1] Dodwell, *Tour*, vol. ii, p. 306.   [2] *Odes*, iv, 2, 25.

effects, he told a Cambridge society, illustrated too forcibly a verse in the Apocalyptic epistle to Laodicea. He should have read Vitruvius, who tells us of the multitude of boiling springs that well up at and about Hierapolis and deposit an incrustation of stone, as certain other springs which he mentions and others in Britain coat objects left in them with stone. One thinks in connexion with Hierapolis of the yet more wonderful waters of New Zealand and of the famous pink and white terraces destroyed by earthquake or volcano or both at Rotomahana in 1886.

But do not let us end with earthquake and volcano, but turn back to Kitto, and Macneile Dixon, and Manatt, those happy travellers who tell us of the joy and beauty of the Greek springs, and set the mind wandering to another ancient author who tells us how he saw a pure river of water of life, clear as crystal, welling up—like the Greek spring from under temple or church —out of the throne of God and the Lamb. His picture seems natural and inevitable after all we have read, and his metaphor, we read, had been used more than once by another.

Chapter II

SAVAGES

I

Greek civilization was ringed about with barbarians—a word
which remains somewhat indefinite. Barbarians included highly
civilized peoples like the Egyptians, the Phoenicians, the Persians and the Lydians; peoples who might be called half
civilized like some of the outlying Greeks (if Greeks they were;
for it had to be proved) and the Macedonians; and tribes that
were frankly savage. Of these last there were more than we
sometimes realize, and colonization brought the Greeks into
close acquaintance with them. The many colonies of Miletus
and Megara, planted about the Black Sea, had endless savage
neighbours. Herodotus, in the fifth century B.C., visited Olbia
in South Russia, as we call it; and there were the Scythians,
of various degrees of barbarism and savagery—some growing
wheat to sell to the Greeks, some vastly more primitive; and
about A.D. 90 Dio Chrysostom visited the Borysthenites, and
found them still on the defensive against the same race; the
walls had to be manned while he was there. There were indeed
Scythians to be seen in Athens; but they were policemen, state
slaves literally, employed in keeping order to some extent in a
civilized city. One guesses that the first real contact of many
Greeks with savages was when Herodotus met them. But there
were others. For Cyrene and Marseilles were outposts of Greek
life on the shores of savage lands—Gaul perhaps rather less
savage than Libya, but primitive enough then and for centuries
later. The two cities were at starting almost in the position of
Montreal and Boston; but the French and the English colonists
had one great advantage which the Greeks lacked, and which
gave them very quickly an initial immunity; they had fire-arms.
It has been suggested that a Norse or Icelandic settlement in
Vinland (at whatever point on the North American coast it may
have been) would have involved the settlers in war on too equal
terms with the Skraelings (whoever they were, Eskimo or Indian)

to permit hope of much permanence. But by 1630 the settlers
at Boston and by 1640 the settlers at Montreal were less at the
mercy of savages. The savage menace to the outlying farm was
bad enough, but in each case the Indians were supported in
their raids by a European race. The Iroquois bought guns from
Dutch and English to avenge themselves on Champlain and his
Frenchmen; and the French gave their Catholic converts a
bounty on English scalps. Even so the Indian danger grew less
with years or at least with decades, and both the lands in
question are undoubted white men's country. But the Greek
never exterminated the Scythian, the Libyan or the Gaul, nor
was able, like the American Government, to shift them farther
and farther away, or confine them to Reservations. The savage
remained a problem.

A problem in several ways. A practical problem, of course;
but an intellectual problem. Herodotus says, very definitely,
that Homer flourished four hundred years before his own day;
modern scholars, many of them, have accepted that date, and
many put Homer (let us say) a good century and a half earlier.
In any case there was Homer describing a high civilization;
and whether you thought more of the Cyclopean walls of Tiryns
and Mycene or of the two great epics that bore Homer's name,
either—walls or poems—would confirm this belief. Four
hundred years—or six hundred, as you might calculate—of
civilization, of Homer's poetry, of shipbuilding, of mechanical
arts, of colonization with all it means of quickened intellect,
heightened arts, geographical interests and democratic politics;
there was bound to be a consciousness that the Greeks were not
like other men. The famous choric ode in the *Antigone* tells the
tale—πολλὰ τὰ δεινά, and nothing more wonderful than Man;
and it is clearly Greek Man that is in the mind of Sophocles,
Man the inventor of arts, and, above all, Man the thinker who
has devised the state. And when the Greek thought of the state,
his word was *polis*; he meant a city state; and whoever speaks
of politics or politicians, so far uses his vocabulary. *Polis* was
Greek. The barbarian in Egypt, Persia, Lydia, had no real *polis*;
he was the subject of a king in a vast domain where there was
no political life in the Greek sense; the barbarian north of the
Black Sea and in the environs of Cyrene and Marseilles—yes,

and perhaps even Syracuse—was a tribesman. We know something of Iroquois social organization—a good deal, in fact; we
are dealing there with a federation of tribes, and something like
statesmen, shrewd observers of at least two foreign nations. We
know much less of political life, in any sense of the word, among
the Scythians; they must have had something of the kind, they
clearly had a sort of national policy in dealing with Darius
when he invaded their country; but the general statement
stands; *polis* they knew not, and little enough of the arts and
ideas preliminary to the growth of a *polis*, as Sophocles sums
them up in the *Antigone* ode.

Hundreds of years of civilization on the one side; and on the
other whatever there was rudimentary—borrowed commodities,
like the guns that enabled Western Indians to kill off the buffalo,
their main food supply, without developing anything to save
the race of men. The obvious conclusion was one the Greeks
drew clearly enough, with more and more emphasis as the
generations passed; there was some natural difference between
Greek and barbarian. There was no thwarting Nature; and
Nature had planned two distinct types of Man—Greek and
non-Greek—and the difference was fundamental. So much was
obvious; but one of the things that marked out the Greek was
an intellectual curiosity, an insistence—you might almost call
it an itch, a mania—to have a thing explained. Then accepting
the fact of this natural cleavage between Greek and non-Greek
nature, how would you explain it? For, little as barbarians
were interested to seek it, there was always a reason about
Nature's proceedings. Perhaps we are personifying Nature too
much—attributing to her too much of the feminine mind as
Juvenal drew it—

Hoc volo, sic jubeo, sit pro ratione voluntas.

Then if Nature's *hoc volo* is not to be accepted quite as it stands,
explain how this great difference between the kinds of Man
arose—a tremendous task, not yet completely achieved.

The Greek began his explanation with geography and some
magnificent generalizations. Europe, cold and northerly, produces one kind of character; Asia, soft and enervating, produces
another. 'Those who live in a cold climate and in [northern]

Europe', says Aristotle,[1] 'are full of spirit, but wanting in intelligence and skill; and therefore they keep their freedom but have no political organization and are incapable of ruling others. Whereas the natives of Asia are intelligent and inventive, but wanting in spirit and therefore they are always in a state of subjection and slavery. But the Hellenic race, which is situated between them, is likewise intermediate in character, being high-spirited and also intelligent. Hence it continues free, and is the best governed of any nation, and if it could be formed into one state, would be able to rule the world.' But perhaps if it did, it would be a *polis* no longer. And, in fact, so we find. Almost while Aristotle was writing, the *polis* was doomed; only 'the dear city of Zeus' (as Marcus Aurelius calls it) remained, and it was rather an abstract idea than anything like the *polis* that Greeks had known and loved. But we must not digress, and Aristotle's passage does something to explain the differences that Nature designed, and quietly indicates the superiority of the Greek conception of life. Climate matters profoundly. 'These Ionians', says Herodotus (i, 142), 'had set their cities in places more favoured by skies and seasons than any country known to us. For neither to the North of them, nor to the South, nor to the East, nor to the West, do the lands do the same thing as Ionia, being afflicted here by cold and wet, there by the heat and drought.' 'Nature is no niggard in Anatolia', says D. G. Hogarth in his *Wandering Scholar* (p. 84), 'but has granted early springs, brilliant summers and sure rains —a climate like that of Central Europe' and so forth. Herodotus elsewhere (ii, 22) explains the colour of the black man by the heat.

'Η φύσις ἐβούλεθ', wrote the Greek comic poet; Nature willed it and it was; she arranged the climates of the world, and by their aid carried out her will. As Plutarch says in another connexion, to discover the *means* by which Destiny effects this or that is not to abolish the higher cause. Nature willed the Greek to be Greek, and he was; and the centuries of civilization established his title to be different from other men. Barbarians, the philosopher suggested, were φύσει δοῦλοι, slaves by nature; there could therefore be no real objection, no objection in the nature of things, to selling barbarian captives

---

[1] *Politics*, vii, 7, 2; p. 1327 b.

into slavery, while a feeling grew up that it was not right to
treat Greeks in this way. At a later stage of Greek thinking,
the Stoic, perhaps following the lead of the Cynic, who would
hold that Greek and non-Greek were alike animals, maintained
that this distinction, so long embedded in Greek consciousness,
was not in nature. That was good Stoic doctrine, linked with
the 'dear city of Zeus' which was the universe; a man *quâ* man
was naturally κόσμιος, a citizen of the universe, made of the
same atoms as another man, inspired by the same instincts,
capable of the same philosophic or spiritual development. So
it was held by the Stoic; but, as Charles Lamb said of some
philosophy of Coleridge's, it was 'only his fun'; did the world
believe it? On the whole, the Roman lawyer moved toward
believing it, and law was modified in a Stoic sense. But that
was a long way off, almost as far as St Paul with his doctrine
that in Christ is neither Greek nor Jew, barbarian nor Scythian.
And perhaps in view of all said and to be said, there is point
in this emphasis on Scythian.

II

At a fairly early stage, Greeks began to handle the question of
the origin of Man, forsaking, as it has been put, cosmology for
anthropology. Where had Man come from? Myth might speak
of his making, and Pausanias (x, 4, 4) might be shown, as he
was shown, the residual lump of clay from which Prometheus
had taken the material to mould the first man; there were
stories about Deucalion and Pyrrha; but science—or perhaps
they would have said philosophy in those days—preferred an
impersonal cause, factors instead of a Creator—the constant
preference of the scientist—neuter factors in spite .of Latin
grammar. How had Man arisen or come to be? Could he have
grown in the inside of some fish and escaped from it? Or have
grown out of the ground?[1] Could he have been the product of
a tree? Odd as these notions may appear to us, there was one
that seems stranger. Empedocles threw out the idea that Nature
might have begun by creating stray parts or limbs or members,
which coalesced somehow as chance directed, but that, if the
parts were really too incompatible, the creature did not survive

[1] Cf. Pausanias, ii, 29, 2.

or failed to propagate; and hence there were centaurs and such
things, half one creature, half another, and hence, fortunately,
they ceased to be. One wonders whether fossil remains of
extinct monsters may have suggested this explanation, or
whether it was an attempt to treat legend seriously, or lastly,
whether some allegory was intended. The notion re-appears in
Lucretius (v, 837), who proceeds to say that there never were
Centaurs—*sed neque Centauri fuerunt* (v, 878), nor any other
compound creature of double nature and incompatible parts.

When the Orphics told their story[1] of the child-god Dionysus-
Zagreus being mutilated and devoured by the Titans, and how
he was somehow rescued by Athene and swallowed by Zeus to
reappear as the new Dionysus, and how meanwhile the Titans
were reduced to ashes by a thunderbolt and how from the ashes
came Man, of twofold nature, god and Titan, an uneasy union
of good and evil, it is told, as Plato might have said, in the shape
of a myth and a man of sense would not wish to take it literally.
Plato himself had some such idea in mind, when he urged that
Man is 'a heavenly plant' ($οὐράνιον\ φυτόν$, *Timaeus*, 90 A).
But for the historian and the man of science, these dreams are
as unsubstantial as Hesiod's succession of ages named from the
metals, from gold to iron (alas!), with a special intercalation of
a rather better age to accommodate the Homeric heroes.
Lucretius, as we shall see, finds a development in human
history—in spite of all Man's delinquencies and his misuse of the
new powers he discovers. Herodotus, who must claim our
special attention as 'the father of anthropology', confines himself to actual savages, with space here or there for a legend as
to their origin, but a legend that moves (so to say) on the human
plane; he has no Titans, no Centaurs, no loose-compacted
compound creatures. No! the savage and his tribal habits are
interesting enough; Herodotus, for all the tales true or false that
he heard and reports, is what Carlyle used to call a 'son of fact'.

To the facts, therefore, of Man's early history we go; and
Lucretius shall be our guide. In a long and supremely interesting passage in his fifth book he unfolds the story of
primitive Man (v, 925–1457). In one point after another he
tells us much that the modern anthropologist confirms from the

---

[1] Cf. Dieterich, *Abraxas*, § 9, pp. 126–135. Also *Progress in Religion*, p. 87.

evidence of actual remains of primitive man's abode and even
of his food, found lying as it was stored, of the bones of animals
about his den or cave,[1] and from the widest and often the most
sympathetic study of living savages the world over. Primitive
man, then, as Lucretius pictures him, was hardier and more
robust than his modern descendant, which we can readily
believe; he was also, the poet adds, bigger, which seems
doubtful. 'Through many lustres of the sun, rolling on through
the sky'—he uses the Roman phrase for a period of five years,
and doubtless would accept the modern suggestion of centuries—
'they passed their lives after the wide-wandering fashion of wild
beasts.' There was no plough, no iron tool, no agriculture, no
woodman's craft. What sun, rain and soil volunteered, had to
suffice; there were acorns, which, as I implied, the anthropologist still finds hoarded, and arbutus berries, more perishable.
To quench thirst, rivers and springs invited them. 'They dwelt
in the known woodland precincts (*templa*) of the nymphs, from
which they knew that some running rivulet issued rippling over
the wet rocks, over the wet rocks in abundant flow, dripping on
the green moss, with plenty left over to splash and bubble across
the level plain.' So the poet sees the spring; a passage that seems
to warrant the suggestion that he is far from being the mere man
of science and nothing else; but perhaps, considering what
proved to be in the human stock, one might believe that the
mute inglorious poet was already touched by the beauty of the
spring even in the dawn of pre-history. Lucretius does not say
so, does not even imply it directly; but his picture tempts the
fancy, and whether anthropologists, ancient or modern, allow
it, there must have been at least a faculty for recognizing beauty,
latent in that primitive man, practical as Lucretius draws him,
and living a bleak and starved life. Not yet did they know how
to work things with fire, how to use skins and cover their own
bodies with spoils stripped from the beasts; they lived in woods
and caves, with little or no sense of common good; 'they knew
not to use among themselves custom or law' (*neque ullis moribus
inter se scibant nec legibus uti* (958)—the phrase suggests an almost
Virgilian outlook on human life). It was a Rob Roy rule

That they should take that have the power
And they should keep who can.

[1] The cave-dwellers, cf. Herodotus, iv, 183.

With hand and foot, with stone and club, they would hunt the woodland tribes of wild creatures, risking a return visit of boar or lion to their dens in the night. There was always danger from wild beasts, and he pictures primitive man 'seeing his living flesh buried in a living tomb' (*viva videns vivo sepeliri viscera busto*, v, 993). But, at least, in those days there was no modern battle-field, when one day gave many thousands of men in arms to destruction, no ships and men dashed on the rocks by the sea. 'The wicked art of navigation' (*improba navigii ratio*) was still unknown. But famine was a real danger then, just as plethora is to-day. Poison then was an accident in a man's diet; he had not the modern skill to administer it to others.

Then comes change; they got themselves huts and skins of beasts and fire; and marriage began, regular marriage, and home with its children, who with their winsome ways (*blanditiis*) broke the proud temper of their parents; and life grew gentler (*mollescere*), and neighbour began to stand by neighbour—not in every case, but in many, or the race would have perished. Women and children made their natural appeal; and with voice and gesture and stammering tongue men pled that it is right to pity the weak (*imbecillorum esse aecum misererier*). With voice, he says; for Nature inspired language, as she teaches young animals and birds their parts, the use of claw and wing. It is folly to suppose that some man invented and imposed speech on the rest; how could he have? No, language is natural in man (v, 1089).

At this point Lucretius introduces the origin of fire; perhaps it was lightning, perhaps the rubbing together of boughs in the winds. After that 'the sun taught them to cook food and soften it by the heat of the flame' (v, 1102).

And then he makes a big stride to city life, which the Greeks permit us to lessen, hinting at intermediate stages. There was the life of the waggon, which Herodotus reports among the Scythians, that mobile domesticity that defeated Darius (iv, 46). Strabo, centuries later, describes the tents of felt fastened to the waggon, in which the Nomads spent their lives, and, round about them, the herds which yield them milk and cheese and meat, as they follow the cattle from one grazing ground to another. It is of Russia that he speaks (Strabo, C 307). Herodotus looks at tribes that live by hunting (iv, 22), who perhaps antedate the

Nomads; and he tells us of one form of life which the nineteenth century rediscovered in ancient Switzerland and in Scotland and elsewhere—the wooden house of a sort, built on a platform raised on piles over the surface of a lake[1] (v, 16). Strabo and Plato alike touch off one phase of these early societies, by borrowing a word or a picture from Homer; they are 'Cyclopean'; the Cyclops tribe, as Homer says, have an ultra-Greek form of home-rule, every man is lawgiver for his children and wives; and the Cyclops, as we can never forget, lived in a cave, kept sheep, and, when guests were not forthcoming, lived on milk, etc.[2] Andrew Lang's ballade of primitive man tells the tale in English—how 'he lived upon oysters and foes'; but Andrew Lang adds words that the ancients would not have expected about marriage taboos, involving an 'extensive morality'. Then comes agriculture, familiar to some of the Scythians, who grew wheat to sell to the Greeks, as Herodotus tells us (iv, 17)—agriculture inspired, as Lucretius at a later point returns to tell us, by Nature herself, 'since berries and acorns falling from trees produced in due time swarms of seedlings' (v, 1361); and thence they deduced and proved that earth could tame wild fruits by kind treatment and friendly tillage (*indulgendo blandeque colendo*, v, 1369).

When Lucretius swings off to speak of kings and cities, of gold, ambition and disaster, of the slaying of kings and the interaction of magistrate and mob, he has travelled out of the region of primitive life, and is thinking of civilized man. We will not follow him, but will turn aside to half-civilized man, as another Roman poet pictures him in early Italy side by side with the early splendours of Latin royalty and architecture. That Remulus Numanus and King Latinus, with his hall of a hundred columns, should be near neighbours, was not out of the way in the ancient world, nor indeed in the modern New World. Here, at all events, is what Remulus Numanus says about himself and his people: 'The stubborn race of a stubborn stock, we take our new-born children down to the river and harden them in the pitiless chill of the water. Our boys pass sleepless nights in

---

[1] Cf. Ferdinand Keller, *The lake-dwellings of Switzerland* (tr. Lee) and Robert Munro, *Ancient Scottish Lake Dwellings*.

[2] *Odyssey*, ix, 114; Plato, *Laws*, 680B; Strabo, C 502.

hunting and outweary the forest; their sport is to rein the steed and draw the shaft upon the bow. Patient of toil, inured to want, our youth tames earth with the hoe or shakes towns in war. All our life knows the touch of iron.... On white hair we press the helmet; and ever it is our delight to gather fresh booty and live on plunder.'[1] Evander draws a similar picture, as he talks to Aeneas of the land in which he is an exile—'a generation of men, sprung from boles of trees and stout oak; they had neither rule of life nor culture (*quis neque mos nec cultus erat*); they knew not to yoke the oxen, nor to lay up stores, nor husband their gains; but the branches of the trees and hunting gave them rude sustenance' (x, 315–317). The essential savage touch lies in *nec parcere parto*, as every explorer in America has known; the supreme difficulty with the Indian, as with all uncivilized men (and with many who suppose themselves civilized), is the failure to realize the needs of to-morrow and to abstain from using up all his stores to-day. The Italian peasant, as we meet him in history, has outgrown the savage ideals of Remulus Numanus, and has learnt thrift—*et amore senescit habendi*.

But we have to return to Lucretius, who deals with the gods, and how primitive man came to people heaven with divine powers, and to cover earth with altars. Even in those days men used to see with the waking mind (*animo vigilante*), and still more in sleep, figures of beauty and strangely heightened frame; and they attributed to them sensation, enduring life, happiness with no fear of death. They could not understand the source of the regularity of the seasons, so they left it in the hands of the gods, and for an abode they gave them the sky, where there met their gaze

luna, dies, et nox, et noctis signa severa (v, 1190),

the night-wandering torches and flying flames, cloud, sun, rain and snow, winds, lightnings, hail and thunder. 'O unhappy race of men! to ascribe such deeds to the gods and add thereto bitter wrath! What groans they got for themselves, what wounds for us, what tears for our children.' Then, in the middle of this lament over the delusion that makes life miserable, comes perhaps the most famous of the passages, which a French critic

[1] *Aeneid*, ix, 603–613.

assigns to the 'anti-Lucretius' in the poet. 'For when we look up to the celestial spaces of the great world, to the aether set with glittering stars [an echo of Ennius, this], and it comes into the mind to think of the paths of sun and moon, then into hearts borne down by other woes this doubt also begins to wake and raise its head—can it perchance be that we have to do with some boundless power of gods, that wheels the bright stars each on its orbit?' (v, 1204–1210). The modern reader must involuntarily recur to Browning's *Bishop Blougram*:

> Just when we are safest, there's a sunset-touch,
> A fancy from a flower-bell, some one's death,
> A chorus-ending from Euripides,—[1]
> And that's enough for fifty hopes and fears
> As old and new at once as nature's self,
> To rap and knock and enter in our soul,
> Take hands and dance there, a fantastic ring
> Round the ancient idol, on his base again,—
> The grand Perhaps!

The grand Perhaps may come more directly from Rabelais, but here it is in Lucretius—*nequae forte deum....*

But a half-hint a little earlier in Lucretius' story, perhaps legitimate, reminds us of other ancient thinkers. 'Their refuge', he says—from questions about nature, he means—'was to leave all in the hands of gods' (v, 1186). Writing at a later day a defence of scepticism, Sextus Empiricus quotes some forty lines of iambics in which Critias, once the pupil of Socrates, gives another view of the origin of gods.[2] It is not great poetry; dogma does not often make great poetry, and anti-dogma perhaps less often. In summary, then, here is his contribution to the problem Lucretius handled: how did primitive man come to create gods? And the primitive man of Critias is much more sophisticated than the primitive man of Lucretius. Life, he says, was all in disorder, beast-like, the slave of violence; no reward for the good, no punishment for the bad; so mankind, he suggests, set up laws to punish wrong, that Justice (δίκη) might rule and keep recklessness (ὕβριν) in subjection. Laws

---

[1] Perhaps, though not strictly a *chorus* ending, *Hippolytus*, 191–197, ending μύθοις δ' ἄλλως φερόμεσθα—'and we drift on legends for ever'.

[2] See Sextus Empiricus, *adv. Mathematicos*, ix, 54; F 563.

were very well, so far as open and avowed deeds went; but
much was done in secret, and how was all that to be dealt with?
Then, says Critias, I think a shrewd and wise man brought in
the idea of the divine (τὸ θεῖον εἰσηγήσατο), to wit that there
is a divinity (δαίμων), living for ever, hearing and seeing with
his mind all that men do; silence does not mean escape from
the notice of the gods. It was a most acceptable doctrine—a lie,
no doubt, but carrying within it a truth. And he domiciled his
gods in the sky, whence come lightning and thunder, the rain
and the sun, fit home for gods; and so he quenched lawlessness
with laws. The gods were to be secret police; and if they did
not really exist, they might be supposed to exist, and be not
less efficient.

Expedit esse deos; et, ut expedit, esse putemus

is Ovid's neater and briefer version of it. Varro, too, as quoted
by Augustine, held it desirable that men should be deceived
(*falli*) in their religious beliefs. Polybius himself (vi, 56) de-
precated the modern weakening of religious sanctions; it would
be well enough for a community of philosophers to be quit of
them; but everywhere the multitude (πλῆθος) is light-minded,
full of lawless desires, unreasonable anger and violent spirit, and
can only be controlled by dim terrors and theatrical effects of
that sort (τῇ τοιαύτῃ τραγῳδίᾳ); the ancients were wise in
introducing notions about gods and hell, etc. All this represents
the reflexion of a highly civilized age, no longer believing in the
gods of its ancestors; and, as is clear to anybody who takes the
trouble to inform himself as to the mental habits of savages
ancient or modern, an age quite unintelligent of primitive man.
Lucretius hardly gives us the picture of primitive man that
results from actual study; there is conjecture and there are
omissions in his picture, but it is less frankly impossible and
unhistorical than that of Critias and Ovid and the rest.

It is worth while to set beside these more critical views the
more conservative position of Plutarch. There was a pre-
sumption for the existence of gods in the teaching of mankind's
best guides and teachers, viz. the poets, lawyers and philosophers;[1] for what they say is likely to be true.[2] And he falls

---

[1] Plutarch, *Amatorius*, 18, 763 c.   [2] Plutarch, *Consol. ad Apoll.* 34, 120 B.

back on the Stoic doctrine of the consensus of mankind; a belief
that is universally held is more than likely to be true. 'You
might find', he says, 'communities without walls, without
letters, without kings, without houses, without money, with no
need of coinage, without acquaintance with theatres or gym-
nasia; but a community without holy rite, without a god, that
uses not prayer nor oath, nor divination, nor sacrifice to win
good or to avert evil, no man ever saw, nor will see.'[1] Modern
research and intercourse with primitive tribes confirms this
affirmation in the main; the real savage does not lack beliefs in
divine or quasi-divine beings; and his invisible policeman might
be that strange and widely prevalent thing we call (from a
South Sea word, as it chances) *taboo*. But that the origin of *taboo*
is the happy thought of some Critian sophist is as unlikely as
the invention of language by some ingenious person, which
Lucretius taught us to reject.

III

Our design was to get the facts of man's long progress upward
from savagery, and Lucretius, possibly himself following Greek
guides, led us in the main aright, if we allow a poet to desert
now and then the strict chronological order of events and to see
things as a poet, with some forgetfulness or unawareness of what
does not stir the imagination. Witness how Homer cut out—
shall we say one half of Greek religion? and gave new value
and new life to the other half. But now let us leave the poets
(and the poetasters), and try to see actual savages as shrewd
observers saw them—Herodotus first and foremost. For in the
last century the credit of Herodotus has steadily risen. Juvenal
took him to be a typical Greek liar; but modern travellers have
found the traces of that Athos canal which provoked that rather
journalistic poet. Herodotus was indeed no great linguist; it is
difficult to name any Greek who was; there were interpreters,
and no doubt there were Greeks among them—they are always
interesting to note when one meets them; but so significant a
Greek man of letters as Plutarch can suggest to his countrymen
that *sine patris* is Latin. Herodotus travelled widely, and

---

[1] Plutarch, *adv. Coloten* (the Epicurean), 31, 1125D, E. Compare Seneca, *Ep.*
117, 6, on this *consensus* as an argument for gods.

evidently listened well. It is likely enough that, like other men, he mis-heard and mistook at times, but he makes it plain that he inquired, and that again and again he gives us the result of his inquiries as faithfully as he can, even if he avows now and then that to report is not necessarily to believe. And there is another thing to be remembered. Travellers' tales are a proverb; the traveller is apt to be so credulous. Of course he is; and the range of his real experience is the cause of it. Once outside your native land and its streets, there is no telling what you may meet; you acquire a habit of believing, as the street-bred and street-limited man acquires the habit of disbelieving. The result is that the traveller may accept statements that need revision, and that the home-keeping youth with his homely wit is too clever to realize the limitations of his experience.[1]

The critical capacity, then, of Herodotus is emphasized by the modern student of anthropology. He is interested in Man and his ways wherever he goes, and he is apt to relate Man to his environment. Geography is a living thing for him. There are slips, people say, in his Geography; Carpis and Alpis become rivers in his pages, and there are those who think they should be mountains. The ranges, whose names seem borrowed here, have certainly not reached his pages, and he brings the Danube across Europe, cutting, it would seem, at right angles (or nearly) through the Rhone. The town of Pyrene too looks as if it should be a range. But all this is far from proving that there were *not* rivers Carpis and Alpis and that there was *not* a town Pyrene. How many names has the Tiber had, or the Cam, or Lake Ontario? But the great rivers of the East, the great plains of Russia, interest Herodotus; and as we have seen, climate is a factor in his reflexions. Trade, and especially river trade (unfamiliar in European Greece), diet, manner of life, all catch his eye and his mind. We have noted already, in a gap in Lucretius' story of human progress, types of human life, unfamiliar to the ancient Greek, which find a place in the pages of Herodotus. He will risk an improbable story, if there is a chance of some geographical truth about it; witness the tale of the explorers among the pygmies on a river, nowadays supposed to be the

---

[1] Something like this is quoted from Cleon of Magnesia by Pausanias, x, 4, 6; Cleon's story was not very plausible. Cf. also Pausanias, ix, 21, 6.

Niger, but which he guessed might be upper waters of the Nile;
and the other tale of the circumnavigators of Africa. Russian
frost and polar night are not incredible to him; but loose talk
about the Ocean, the river Eridanus, the Cassiterides islands,
takes him too far into the unknown—into the unverifiable, he
believes, and he would not endure it. Mr H. G. Rawlinson
emphasizes the carefulness and the accuracy of much that
Herodotus writes about India.[1] Did he.draw upon the lost
narrative of Scylax, or the reports of Persian officials who had
served in India? It is not very profitable to spend time in
computing the debt of an author so vivid and so human—and
so endeared to mankind—to other authors whom mankind has
been content to lose. The practice is popular enough, but it is
amenable to the criticism Herodotus made on people who
talked of the Ocean; they carried their tale into the unseen—
and perhaps unseeable—ἐς ἀφανὲς τὸν μῦθον ἀνενείκας (iv, 23).
He did it himself once, when, from a belief in a flat earth, he
deduced that dawn is hotter than noon in India. That was a
deduction. What he says about the tribes known to us as
Dravidian, as opposed to the whiter races of the North, on the
aborigines in the marshes of the Indus in clothes made of rushes
and living on raw fish, on the tribe that killed and ate its sick
members, on the houseless hermits who lived on a grain like
millet—all this is not matter of deduction, but the fruit of
intelligent questioning.

Not to spread over into detail, nor to digress too far—since
either course would mean some challenge of the charm of
Herodotus—let us group some part at least of what he gives us
under a few main headings, which may serve to show how he
handles anthropological themes at large. For instance, think of
the racial varieties which he discusses—Scythian and Sarmatian,
Egyptian and Ethiopian, Amazon, Libyan, Pygmy and
Brahmin—and then all the pageant of strange races with their
varieties of dress and armour that marched in Xerxes' army
against Greece. A pageant indeed. Or think of the survey of
the satrapies, with their races and tributes of ingots. And with
race after race we have glimpses of their customs—how they
dress their hair (iv, 175, 180, 191), not for the anthropologist a

---

[1] H. G. Rawlinson, *Intercourse between India and the Western World*, p. 24.

trivial matter—how they tattoo themselves or their children—
ornament and amulet, tools and boats, and Scythian baths, the
enemy's skull as a cup—'here is God's plenty', as was said of
Chaucer. One point is worth remarking, perhaps; however
well one knows Herodotus, however often one has read him,
there always seems to be more to note the next time one takes
up the text. γραφικὸς ἀνήρ, as Plutarch said of him,[1] καὶ ἡδὺς ὁ
λόγος; and he is moreover 'a lover of barbarians', the same
critic notes—φιλοβάρβαρος.

To be a little more particular, we may remark how constantly
he notes the diet of a tribe or a race—not, we are assured by
students of Greek life, a matter of idle curiosity. It has taken
two long and intense wars to make the reading public of Britain
realize what a problem food may be; and in the Greek world
the margin between just enough and starvation could be
menacingly narrow. Think of the diet he records in one place
or another—fish sun-dried or preserved in brine; quails, ducks,
small birds, salted and raw; lotus root and castor oil (κίκι);
roots, dried fruits; the cherry concoction of the Bald Argippaioi
far into Russia; the monkeys and locusts of Libya; and the aged
relatives of the Massagetai. And the last item reminds one of
the Persian king's experiment with national prejudice; what
sum would induce the Greek who was with him to *eat* a dead
parent, or the Indian to burn the dead parent's body? and each
made outcry at the profanity of the suggestion made to him.

Or, again, take marriage, and note the comment of Professor
J. L. Myres that Herodotus 'is not simply emptying an ill-filled
note book on to the margins of his history'.[2] Marriage usages
have been many, and every strange marriage custom that
Herodotus notices is representative of a widespread type.
Polygamy, mother-right, purchase of wives, promiscuous and
open relations, the right of the chief, the marriage market of
Babylon, and the strange usage of the Sauromatai that a girl,
before she can marry, must kill a man of some hostile tribe, and
the limitation upon the Persian king to marry only within the
range of certain families—a limitation tempered by some
polygamy—there is variety enough about the world's ways as

---

[1] Plutarch, *de malignitate Herodoti*, § 43; and § 12.
[2] In *Anthropology and the Classics*, pp. 153–156.

Herodotus sees them. He quotes with approval Pindar's dictum that custom is king (iii, 38); every race will stand by its own ways and refuse to change.

In the same way and in the same spirit Herodotus goes about his world, looking into the religions of the races he meets. He offers no explanation of religion the least resembling those of Lucretius or Critias. No, it seems natural that every race should have its own religion, though he recognizes that races adopt new gods now and then from their neighbours or others and rather readily adopt or learn new rites. Did the Greeks borrow Herakles from the Egyptians (ii, 43)? Certainly they seem to have learnt howling at a sacrifice from the Libyans (iv, 89). Persian religion deeply interests him; and he quotes the hostile comment of Scythians on the rites of Dionysus. He sees Providence taking care of animals (iii, 108), and of the Athenians at the time of the Persian invasion—'it was all being done by God' (viii, 13)—the storm was to level the opposing forces. Those are divine judgments; if Cambyses had not been quite mad, he would not have tried to mock at the sacred usages and customs of other men, the Egyptians (iii, 38); and the injury that killed him is significant. Dreams, and mysteries, and oracles, constantly engage his attention; as he says in another connexion, he 'wishes to know'; and while he has heard of sham oracles (χρησμὸς κίβδηλος, i, 66, 75; cf. v, 91; vii, 6), he will be no party to the rejection of all oracles (viii, 77). It is not fair to say he is 'ultramontane' where oracles are concerned; their truth is a thing to examine, and he examines it. But perhaps enough has been said to show the acute interest this Greek takes in all sorts and conditions of men—'he is such a lover of barbarians', and of the most primitive savages along with the rest. Scythian or Libyan, his interest in them is kindly; he is as open-minded to mankind as Odysseus before him or Alexander the Great after him—πολλῶν ἀνθρώπων ἴδεν ἄστεα καὶ νόον ἔγνω, at least as well as he could through interpreters and permanent residents in the lands he saw. Like others among the ancients he recognized his own gods under strange names in foreign pantheons—not a practice to commend itself to precisians, but it made for goodwill. Polytheism, said a French scholar, knows no *false* gods.

The next great traveller whose work survives in Greek is
Xenophon, who clearly shares the admiration of Herodotus and
Alexander for the Persians in general—in spite of Tissaphernes.
He saw much of savages on his great retreat from the Tigris to
the Black Sea. He had to fight the Kurds, but that was natural
enough, and he does not try to balance his account in the
English way by abusing the enemy. But the savages were not
all enemies. He describes life in Armenian villages, in the
underground houses, shared by beasts and human families,
where they drank 'barley wine' through straws, a stiff drink
unless diluted with water, but 'pleasant enough when you had
acquired the taste', and he and his colleagues in turn entertained
their hosts; and then onward again (*Anabasis*, iv, 5, 25–27).
A Persian interpreter was a help in that region. More fighting
followed, as they advanced; and then on the hill top the wonderful episode of 'The sea! the sea!' (iv, 7, 21–27); and then more
savages, and the raiding of hostile villages; by and by the
Mossynoikoi, so-called from the wooden towers they lived in, a
fresh alliance and further fighting. He tells his story in pictures—
the canoes each made of a single log and each to carry three men—
the warriors in short tunics (like linen bags for carrying bedding),
with leather helmets, each tufted—battle axes, rhythmic march
and song—and in the hour of victory, dance and song and display
of the heads of the fallen enemies—and then plunder, slices of
dolphin meat in jars, dolphin blubber (which the Mossynoikoi
used as the Greeks use oil), and upstairs endless nuts, which
were somehow cooked into loaves, the bread the natives used
most—wine, too, rather sharp when taken neat, but delicious
(εὐώδης τε καὶ ἡδύς) when mixed in the Greek way with water.
The personal habits of these people, told very explicitly, and
recognized as their 'custom' (νόμος), led the Greek soldiers
to believe them the most barbarous and least Greek people
they had met, tattooed people (v, 4, 32) doing in public what
Greeks did in private, talking and laughing to themselves, and
dancing wherever they might be (v, 4, 1–34). Once clear of
the Asian coast and the Black Sea Xenophon and his forces had
some experience of Thrace with King Seuthes, among people
who might be called partially civilized; and as usual Xenophon's
story of it makes good reading. English readers have lost a great

deal through forgetting what an incomparable teller of stories he was.

Strabo, in his Geography—an admirable work—describes savage life in regions rather to the east of those that Xenophon had to traverse. 'The Albanians are more inclined to the shepherd's life than the Iberians; and closer akin to the nomad people—except that they are not ferocious (ἄγριοι), which renders them only moderately warlike.' Their country is between the Iberians and the Caspian Sea—not that they need a sea, for they even neglect to develop the resources of their land, which is very fertile. They live on what the land yields without sowing or plowing—Cyclops-fashion. Big, handsome people, they do not in general use coined money; barter is their way, without accurate weights or measures; and they are only able to count up to a hundred. They love hunting, but without being very clever at it. On occasion they have a human sacrifice, but otherwise they are 'surpassingly respectful' to old age (Strabo, C 501, 502). People still tell the old tales about the Amazons in that region—tales marvellous and beyond belief (τερατώδη τε ὄντα καὶ πίστεως πόρρω, C 504), e.g. about Alexander and their queen; but there has been a lot of falsification of history to glorify Alexander.

'Custom is King'—yet, as we saw in Lucretius' account of the progress of mankind, customs change, men gain new conceptions of life, of law and order, of pity for the weak, of honesty, of comfort and home, and on the other side of the account, of gold and its uses, of war and the means of mutual destruction. Greek legend and Italian had their tales of great civilizers; Virgil's great epic tells us of exiles who make great contributions to human life; and he suggests that Rome's real task is *pacis imponere morem* (*Aeneid*, vi, 852). All this raises in a new form an old question of the Greeks—custom or Nature? The Cynic philosopher pretended to believe that man is a beast like other beasts—himself nicknamed a 'dog', and rather proud of the nickname and apt to do disgusting things in public to emphasize that he is a dog and nobody else any better. But the story of civilization points up and not down. The great poets—Homer, Euripides, Virgil—all have their eyes upon human greatness— a greatness which lies in character; and those who read them

found it belonged to human nature to respond to the great
thoughts of poets and philosophers—especially perhaps the poets;
the madness of the Muses tended somehow to a clearer vision
of Man and his destiny. 'Custom is King'; but Nature is
stronger, and she, some said, is all for 'the dear city of Zeus'.
Meantime the *polis* of the Greek surely represented an ideal
stage of development. Who can read the *Epitaphios* speech of
Pericles and not respond to it?

IV

When we turn westward, we meet representatives of three great
races, or great names, in case doubts arise as to ethnology. For
it is not yet quite clear what the earliest population of France
and Britain may have been, or how far in either case it has been
absorbed or exterminated by later comers. Certainly the Franks
were not the people that Caesar found in Gaul. The common
feature in all Northern Europe, reckoning so all that lies to the
North of the Alps, the Danube and the Black Sea, was movement. Thus, when Strabo (C 291) writes of Germany, as we
now call it, he says: 'it is a common characteristic of all the
peoples in this part of the world that they migrate with ease,
because of the meagreness of their livelihood ($\tau\grave{\eta}\nu$ $\lambda\iota\tau\acute{o}\tau\eta\tau\alpha$ $\tauο\hat{υ}$
$\beta\acute{\iota}ο\upsilon$), and because they do not till the soil nor even store their
food ($\theta\eta\sigma\alpha\upsilon\rho\acute{\iota}\zeta\epsilon\iota\nu$; cf. Evander's *nec parcere parto*), but live in
cabins and provide for the day. They chiefly live on their
flocks, like the Nomads, and as the Nomads do they load their
belongings on waggons, and then turn wherever they think fit,
beasts and all. And there are other German tribes more
indigent.'

Mass-migration was not a new thing. When Greek history—
as distinguished from pre-history and the Homeric period—is
just beginning, there are raids from across the Black Sea into
Asia Minor and regions beyond. The tale is not altogether clear,
nor the order of events, but Scythians, Cimmerians and Trêres
are recorded to have invaded Asia.

One group of them captured Sardis (the Cimmerians, Strabo,
C 62). The Scythians, Herodotus tells us (i, 104 ff.), beat the
Medes in battle, advanced into Syria, ruled Asia for twenty-
eight years, wasting the land in their $\ddot{υ}\beta\rho\iota\varsigma$, exacting tribute and

plundering, till Cyaxares the Mede slew most of them after a drunken debauch, and Asia was rid of them. The view is sometimes advanced that the Homeric warriors came of an immigrant stock from the North; but this is perhaps problematic, and when we meet them, they are wonderfully civilized. So we return to the North and the West and the savages.

Gallia est omnis divisa in partes tres, runs the most famous of Latin sentences; but Rome and Greece met the Gauls long before Caesar penned it. Everybody knows how they captured Rome itself in 387 B.C. (Polybius' dating) after the *dies Alliensis*, how Manlius and the geese saved the Capitol, and how Brennus uttered the famous words *vae victis*—the maxim of all conquerors, and perhaps inevitable. Their invasion of Greece itself and Asia Minor was a century later. 'To the men of the Mediterranean', says Mr Edwyn Bevan,[1] 'they seemed the embodiment of brute and brainless force.' 'Titans of a later date', said Callimachus (ὀψίγονοι Τιτῆνες, 4, 174); and Titan was a name fetched out of legend to signify an enemy of gods and men, of law and order of every kind, an outrage on Nature. Polybius in the second century B.C., and Pausanias in the second century A.D., describe them, and the beautiful monument of the dying Gaul confirms the description. They were the tallest and most beautiful of men,[2] even their enemies admit, brave beyond reproach, and mad for war and fighters by nature (adds Strabo, C 196). They had a way of fighting naked, but for sword and shield, and the gold chain about the neck, as the statue reminds us; and they howled appallingly as they charged—'the hosts of the happy howling men', to borrow Chesterton's line. We are told how they ate, how their bards chanted, how furiously they fought through the ages. The Gallic sword was not as good a weapon as the Spanish, which the Romans adopted,[3] but the Gaul used it effectively. In the long run troops, drilled and armoured, who would not mind their noise, were too much for them, as similar troops in this island were for the Celts in the Battle of the Standard, at Pinkie, and elsewhere. It makes a difference, as

[1] *House of Seleucus*, vol. i, p. 138.
[2] Polybius, ii, 15, 7; Pausanias, x, 20 ff. Their primitive way of life, Polybius, ii, 17; Strabo, C 195.
[3] The swords, Polybius, ii, 30, 8; 33, 5; vi, 23; xv, 15. See Jullian, *Histoire de la Gaule*, vol. i, p. 329, for the causes of their success.

Herodotus said about the battle of Plataea, whether you wear a shirt like the Persian or a breastplate like the Spartan; and the Gaul had no shirt, and in Britain he might fling off his kilt before he charged. At Cannae Polybius (iii, 104, 4) remarks upon the contrast between the Spaniard in his native dress and the naked Gaul, both in Hannibal's service. Nearly six hundred years later we meet the same Gauls in their descendants, fighting as Roman troops against the Persians and the Sassanian king Shapur.[1] They figure in the siege of Amid, and were a difficulty to the Roman commander, till he let them make a sortie, in the course of which they all but captured Shapur himself. And perhaps a reference to Alan Breck may be forgiven; he is of the same race and the same genus, a 'bonny fighter', as every honest Greek admitted they were. Of course there are stories of their cruelty. That instinct of pity, which Lucretius recognized in primitive man, limits itself to clan and family; but the later Brennus and his Gauls, if they were to argue the case, might plead that Philip V of Macedon could do things in cold blood which they did in hot. And it appears that one Macedonian dynast after another was always ready to hire the savage against his rival, as French and English used Micmacs and Iroquois in North America in the eighteenth century A.D.—tribes more savage a great deal than the Celt. Of their settlement in central Asia Minor we need not speak—unless to say that the 'Galatians' to whom St Paul's letter is addressed were not necessarily Celtic, probably not at all; for the boundaries of the Roman province called 'Galatia' included at that time Antioch and Iconium and the neighbouring cities which St Paul visited and which were not Gallic. We must not forget their 'bards'; the Greeks preserve the very word βάρδοι;[2] nor should we omit to notice their response to the Greek appeal of Marseilles.

Across the English Channel from France lies the island which Julius Caesar twice invaded—*territa quaesitis ostendit terga Britannis*, as the Roman poet absurdly says.[3] The story is familiar to us all from childhood, and the authorities for it are all set out in Latin and Greek and English by Mr T. D. Kendrick in his book *The Druids*. The mistletoe and the oak forest come from Pliny; the wicker-work holocaust, 'a colossus of straw and

---

[1] Ammianus Marcellinus, xix, 5, 1.   [2] Strabo, C 197.   [3] Lucan, ii, 572.

wood', filled with cattle, wild animals, and human beings, from
Strabo (C 198) and Caesar; the Druids from everybody. But
Mr Kendrick supplies us with a caution; while Caesar, Cicero,
Diodorus Siculus, and others tell us of the Druids, and Lucan in
a characteristic quip touches off their theology (or philosophy)—
'to you alone among men is it given to know the gods and the
powers of heaven, or to you alone *not* to know them'—

> *solis nosse deos et caeli numina vobis*
> *aut solis nescire datum* (i, 452)

—with the rule of the Romans and with their withdrawal all
knowledge of the Druids was lost; the Saxon was not interested
in them, cared for none of these things; for centuries they were
forgotten. And then with the renaissance and the revival of
Classical learning in this island, men were reminded of the
Druids, who, as long as learning was a little uncritical, and we
depended on popular histories, flourished exceedingly (they
were so picturesque and patriotic) and became the builders of
Stonehenge. But knowledge more exact has stripped them of
much of their impressiveness, and leaves it highly doubtful who
were the builders of Stonehenge instead of the Druids deposed.
One or two things, of little importance perhaps, may be noted:
taboos among the Britons forbade the eating of hare or poultry,
Caesar says; and to this day the East Anglian labourer will
refuse hare—'would as lief eat dog'. Tacitus, who, as we shall
see, draws a moving picture of German virtues, seems un-
sympathetic where Britons and Druids are concerned. They
figure in his *Annals* (xiv, 30) lifting hands to heaven and hurling
imprecations on the Roman enemy; but in his life of Agricola,
his father-in-law, for seven years an administrator in this island,
the Druids are not mentioned—a fact from which little or much
may be deduced. It was not worth the Roman's while to
conquer Britain, Strabo says in the reign of Augustus; a savage
people, says Horace,

> *Visam Britannos hospitibus feros,*

but, as Cicero learnt, possessed of nothing to tempt conqueror or
plunderer—pearls, perhaps, it was said, might have been Julius
Caesar's inducement, but probably they were not. A generation
after Strabo, about a century after Caesar, the conquest began
in the reign of Claudius.

Allusion has been made already to the glorification of the Germans by Tacitus, those unspoiled children of Nature, a contrast in every honest particular to a degenerate and wicked Rome—a land where marriage is sacred, divorces unknown, children many and sturdy, *nec corrumpere et corrumpi saeculum vocatur*; and so forth. Horace already had begun to glorify the child of Nature, selecting another tribe for eulogy, *campestres melius Scythae*. It was just as in the eighteenth century, a reaction and a sentimentalism. The experts among archaeologists do not accept Tacitus' picture of the Germans as it stands; and without being an archaeologist, a mere reader of his *Histories* (iv, 73) may find a less golden view of the race, a view perhaps a little too congenial to the rest of Europe and to this century. It is put in the mouth of a Gaul, not inappropriately, one feels. 'There have ever been the same causes at work to make the Germans cross over into Gaul—lust, avarice, and the longing for a new home, prompting them to leave their own marshes and deserts, and to possess themselves of this most fertile soil and of you, its inhabitants. Liberty, indeed, and the like specious names are their pretexts; but never did any man seek to enslave his fellows and secure dominion for himself without using the very same words.'

All round the civilized minorities of the ancient world lay savagery—Sarmatian and Celt, Libyan and Albanian, cave-dweller, nomad, cannibal. Stranger people still were talked of now and then; but we may leave the dog-headed, the headless, the one-footed to Ctesias and Sir John Mandeville. Language, Lucretius said, was a gift of Nature; and the future was not to lie with a race (even if it existed) which, tens of thousands strong (I quote Ctesias), could only bark. Nature or custom? which should in the long run be 'king'? Nature must be King, the Greek said; and he held that the city state was Nature's last and highest development; and yet while the last great philosophic exponent of the city state was busy defining its possibilities and its ideals, his pupil had swept far into Asia and made one empire for the time being of the civilized world. Alexander's successors believed, like himself, in the value of Greek urban civilization; but that was hardly a synonym for the city state. The city state indeed survived; there were reasons to induce the dynasts to let it survive; but it was as a curiosity—it was not the last word of Nature. But Nature stood with the city state for an ideal—not the ideal of Cleon, not quite the ideal of Pericles though very like it. Cynic philosopher, acting the dog, and primitive man, dubious of neighbour, dubious of thought, ignorant of books—sooner or later they made it clear that they did not represent Nature—no, mere theory, or custom at best. If you thought life out, if you began to realize what Nature could do for Man, you thought with Marcus of 'the dear city of Zeus', or, if that were too large and vague, there was Homer, there was Euripides, men who realized life and interpreted it. And their interpretation of life, fortified and reinforced by ideals that came from Galilee, proved to be the voice of Nature; and gradually—*pedetemptim progredientes*, as Lucretius put it—the races have accepted it.

Chapter III

THE EXILES

I

In the year 324 B.C. Alexander the Great issued a rescript, addressed in fact to all the cities of Greece. By the terms of the League, framed or renewed at Corinth in 336, he had been elected general for the invasion of Asia, but among the provisions of the League was a clause securing freedom and self-government to the allies, in the promise that there would be no interference with their internal constitutions.[1] But Alexander had conquered the Persians and the Indians and endless other tribes; he was monarch of the world and his godhead was announced, and more or less accepted by the Greek states—inevitably but without faith or enthusiasm. It has been supposed that his godhead would absolve him from his oath to respect the constitutions of his allies; but it is not quite clear whether this was his own actual view or was intended to be the view of his allies; and it may be no more than an apology invented by historians. At all events his rescript was for the return to their cities of all Greek exiles with their families—Thebes naturally being excepted, the city which he had destroyed.[2] The decree was to be read at the Olympian games, and it was read there in the presence (so we are told) of twenty thousand exiles. This figure appears to go unchallenged; and, if it is right, it involves a much larger figure, as we cannot suppose every Greek exile to have been present at the festival. But if twenty thousand is the maximum, it is not a small number.

The King did it, we read in Diodorus, whatever be the authority he is quoting, 'at once for glory and from the wish to have in each city many private persons well-disposed to him, in view of changes and revolts that the Greeks might make'.[3]

Our modern historians are divided in their judgments about the King's action. Mr Tarn is favourable;[4] the object was

---

[1] See W. W. Tarn in *Cambridge Ancient History*, vol. vi, p. 355.

[2] W. W. Tarn, *ib.* pp. 418–419.   [3] Diodorus Siculus, xviii, 8.

[4] W. W. Tarn, *Cambridge Ancient History*, vol. vi, p. 418.

twofold. He was making his satraps discharge their mercenaries, and this rescript for the restoration of the exiles was the logical accompaniment of that order to disband; there should be no longer so great a floating mass of homeless men, available to be hired by any governor or other person who would pay them. We are warned not to suppose that every mercenary soldier was an exile; far from it, but we have evidence enough that exiles were apt to become mercenaries. It was also a piece of the King's idealism, Mr Tarn suggests—a dream of ending faction and its fights in Greek cities, compulsory reconciliation. A generous act, says the Frenchman Jouguet, and likely to cure one of the greatest evils of Greece; statesmanlike, says the German Wilcken, to heal one of the worst cancers of the Greek *polis*; but a violation of the covenant, they both admit.[1] Sir John Mahaffy is less admiring; there was no room in most Greek states for exiles without new banishments and new confiscations; how was this returning crowd of impoverished men to be provided for? or their claims on their former property to be settled? It was a warning that the King would condone no more disloyalty, that the treaty of Corinth was not necessarily his last word. Mahaffy echoes the authority of Diodorus; the King let loose on the cities twenty thousand men, most of them trained soldiers, who would form a nucleus of adherents in every city and give the Greeks something to think about at home.[2] It is difficult to accept any other view of the probable consequences, whatever the King's motive. There was, we understand, great delight among the exiles at Olympia; we hardly need this assurance; but we are told that, while most Greek communities put up with it and took it as for the best, the Aetolians and the Athenians resented it, for intelligible reasons. But in 323 Alexander died at Babylon, and the story of the world began anew; every factor in every situation was changed. Τῷ κρατίστῳ, said the dying King; his empire was to go—was that his meaning—'to the strongest', and who would that be?

Alexander's rescript did not finish the exile question; it was ever present in Greece, till Fortune's kindest turn, as Polybius

[1] Jouguet, *Macedonian Imperialism* (tr.), p. 115; Wilcken, *Alexander* (tr.), p. 214.
[2] Mahaffy, *Greek Life and Thought*, pp. 13, 14.

put it,[1] brought all Greece under Roman control, imposing an end on factions and revolution and exile—and an end, one is tempted to say, on any real Greek life. It is arguable that for long—from Philip's day, perhaps—the glory and the inspiration had passed from Greek life; it does not need to be argued that after Mummius and the fall of Corinth in 146, there was nothing left for Greece but decay—decay and patchwork, reminiscence in place of life.

II

At the very dawn of Greek history, we meet the exile. Patroclus was an exile—from childhood, from the time when he 'slew the son of Amphidamas, a child himself, not willing it, in wrath over dice', and his father had to find another home for him, a blood-guilty child.[2] A strange story, but it illustrates a phase of ancient life. It was Draco, of all people, who established for the Athenians for ever the distinction between a murder by intention and an accidental killing, which primeval religion had not so far recognized.

But we may turn at once to historical Greece, the Greece of which Herodotus and the historians tell us, and of which Aristotle analyses the political instincts—instincts not yet dead. Mr W. Miller writes of the disinclination to obey a leader and the consequent tendency to split up into cliques and groups; and he quotes a Venetian saying about them: 'Every five Greeks, six generals.'[3]

Aristotle, apart from our three historians, is the incomparable authority on Greek city life. He is deeply interested in it, as the normal, the ideal life of man—oddly enough, when we reflect that under his eyes the world was changing to a new regime, under which the city state decayed, growing more and more obsolete. He shows the forces that worked to disintegrate society in the small state, political factors and personal, and always poverty not very far away. The fundamental difference, he says, between democracy and oligarchy is poverty and wealth (*Politics*, iii, 8, 7; p. 1280a). Faction throve in these small towns; everybody knew everybody else, and jealousy

---

[1] Polybius, i, 4, 4: τὸ κάλλιστον ἅμα κὠφελιμώτατον ἐπιτήδευμα τῆς τύχης.
[2] *Iliad*, xxiii, 85–88.
[3] Miller, *Greek Life in Town and Country*, p. 7.

flourished—or, to give it a nobler but hardly a truer name, a passion for equality. People got the notion that those who are equal in any respect are equal in all respects; when men are equally free, they claim to be absolutely equal (1301a). Mr Delisle Burns makes the point that there is a difference between the modern demand for liberty and the ancient; we want to be free, or as free as possible, from state regulation—by now a hopeless dream; the Greek was not worried by that, it was people of superior status and greater wealth of whom he wanted to be independent. And every Greek, as Aristotle says, wishes to live as he pleases (ζῆν ἐν ταῖς τοιαύταις δημοκρατίαις ἕκαστος ὡς βούλεται, 1310a)—in the words of Euripides according to his fancy; and everybody claims to have political ability, and to be fit to fill most offices (1291b). Nor does anybody like to see the laws over-ridden by sudden votes of the assembly, unless of course he is the demagogue who starts the ball rolling (1292a). Consequently we may expect jealousies; and other writers tell us how they abound. Read the speech of Lysias against Agoratus and note what he says of private hatreds (§ 44), or Isocrates 'on the Peace' and mark his complaints that there is no freedom of speech in a democracy (§ 14). Your neighbours are always interfering; really the fewer you have, the better. Hence the Greek passion, recognized to the full by moderns, for the smallest possible group, the utmost subdivision of government, no league, no suzerain, no overlord, man or community. Plato's famous democratic man, who is a law to himself, everything by turns and nothing long, may have been sketched from Alcibiades—not indeed as a portrait but as a fancy picture with many borrowed features—notably the central element, the guidance of life by the inclination of the moment, which in the long run is the distinctive mark of all hedonism. Alcibiades may have been the model, or at least a model; but there was no lack of models, and it is suggested that a fruitful source of such characters was to be found in the sophistic movement. Plato's *Gorgias* suggests as much. But generations before that telling dialogue was written, there were factors enough—the smallness of the community, the restlessness that Greek conditions always produced, the sea and its opportunities, poverty, human nature, and, above all, Greek nature. There is something unexplained

in every national character. Poverty must be emphasized—
arable land was scarce in that country of mountains; water, in
many places and notably in Attica, was scarce; and starvation
was no pleasanter then than now, and apt to be a good deal
nearer. The margin that separated a community, or large classes
in it, from starvation was a painfully narrow one; and scenes of
the kind that we associate with the French revolution were apt
to be enacted. In Megara Theagenes rises to power by
slaughtering the cattle of the rich when he caught them being
grazed in the river meadows.[1] At Argos, says Isocrates, the
citizens themselves destroy the men of most fame and wealth,
and do it with zest.[2] At Cios, on the shores of Propontis, not at
all a famous town, there was, says Polybius,[3] 'one Molpagoras,
a capable speaker and politician, but in character a demagogue
and greedy of power. He by flattering the mob and throwing
those who were well off to the multitude, finally by killing some
of them and driving some into exile (φυγαδεύων), confiscating
their property and distributing it among the many [hoi polloi—
the Greek phrase is familiar enough English], quickly rose by
such means to a monarchic power.' These three instances come
from periods centuries apart, and are typical. No wonder that
private hatreds are part of the story.

Every Greek state had near neighbours, generally jealous,
eager often to annex acres of good land—as in the early war of
Chalcis and Eretria for the Lelantine plain—eager as often to
supply a refuge or a starting-point for an exiled faction.
Pisistratus, when expelled, goes to Eretria;[4] when the Thirty
ruled Athens, Megara and Thebes offered safety and a base to
the democrats in exile. The Spartans, says Isocrates,[5] set the
Greeks quarrelling—set stasis on foot among them—'it is a sort
of art with them'; you might compare them to pirates who go
about pillaging and sinking ships. Distances were not great,
and, if the Athenian oligarch does say that the Greeks at large
prefer each their own dialect, there was little difficulty about
language; they all knew Homer; and one thinks how French
authors and pressmen in the reign of the third Napoleon found

[1] Aristotle, Politics, v, 5, 9; p. 1305a.
[2] Isocrates, Philip, 52.
[3] Polybius, xv, 21, 1–2.
[4] Herodotus, i, 61.
[5] Isocrates, Panath. 226.

a French-speaking refuge across the frontier in Belgium—as indeed Louis Napoleon himself had earlier, on escaping from the fortress of Ham. And the Greek neighbour was always ready to lend a helping hand; 'in the old times of the Athenian and Spartan supremacies,' says Aristotle,[1] 'the Athenians everywhere put down the oligarchies and the Spartans the democracies'. The exiles from Mitylene and the rest of Lesbos, in 424, were able to hire mercenaries from the Peloponnese and elsewhere, nearer home, and, through treachery of its citizens, to capture Antandros, a place with every facility for shipbuilding and an ideal base for attacks on Lesbos.[2] Athenians and Megarian exiles ravaged the Megarid in the same year.[3] A plea for help, urged by Sicilian exiles, was a prelude to the Syracusan expedition of the Athenians.[4] It was useless for Nicias to warn the Athenians against exiles begging for armed assistance as men whose interest it is to lie cleverly and at their neighbour's cost, who themselves supply nothing but words, and in case of success have no gratitude or in the event of failure involve their friends in ruin with themselves.[5] He was not speaking without book. A little labour with the historians will put the reader in possession of endless material about exiles, and there is, as I said, always Aristotle with a dozen illustrations of how revolutions come about; private scandals, party politics, the sense of inequality, poverty—we need not recapitulate.

It will be remarked, however, that there are no 'Big-endian exiles' in Greek history, nor Jesuits plotting to murder a Queen Elizabeth. Polytheism, as Gaston Boissier said, knows no false gods; the intolerant religions are monotheistic; polytheists are only intolerant where such matters as caste are concerned, or where there is some threat from a monotheistic faith.

III

With so much faction, so many grounds for jealousy and antipathy in the Greek state, there is little wonder that exile was a common experience, and the exile, with his heart full of hate, a figure to be thought of, to be guarded against. Thus when

[1] Aristotle, *Politics*, v, 7, 14; p. 1307 b.
[2] Thucydides, iv, 52.   [3] Thucydides, iv, 66.
[4] Thucydides, iv, 19.   [5] Thucydides, vi, 12.

nce the house of Pisistratus was gone (as we shall see), there
vas *stasis* at Athens; what should be the next government?
Cleisthenes is a familiar name; it was he who ordered the new
democracy and gave citizenship to the aliens who had gathered
n Athens as a result of the legislation of Solon and during the
eigns of Pisistratus and his sons.[1] But this did not suit the other
party, and Isagoras its leader invoked the aid of Sparta and
King Cleomenes, who had already had a hand in expelling
Hippias; let the king come back; there was more work for him
o do. And Cleomenes came readily enough; an oligarchic
government at Athens installed by the Spartans would be as
good as a garrison. Isagoras named seven hundred households
which might be suitably banished, and banished they were.
But the king and Isagoras could not get everything their own
way, and there was fresh fighting; they seized and held the
Acropolis for two days and then surrendered, and the Spartans
vere allowed to go. Not all the adherents of Isagoras were so
ucky; a number were put to death, not undeservedly one feels;
and Cleisthenes and the seven hundred households were recalled.[2] So Athenian democracy began, and lasted a hundred
years.

Sometimes there was more care taken, or at least suggested.
When the Thirty in 404 were busy sending opponents and
others into exile, Theramenes urged caution—there was no
sense in killing *metics*, the resident alien class, and making
enemies of them, nor in banishing such men as Thrasybulus,
Anytus or Alcibiades, and giving leaders, and capable ones, to
the democratic faction.[3]

There was another way, however, of getting doubtful people
away. Thus in the reign of Pisistratus, there was a notable
Athenian of family and substance, 'of a house that kept four-
horse chariots (οἰκίης τεθριπποτρόφου)', who chafed at the
present regime. As he sat one day in his porch, he saw some
people passing, evidently from their dress and their spears
foreigners. They had come some distance, it was clear; and he
hailed them, called them in, and offered lodging and hospitality.
The guests, we can believe, looked at one another. They came

[1] Aristotle, *Politics*, iii, 2, 3; p. 1276a. Cf. Herodotus, v, 69.
[2] Herodotus, v, 69; 70; 72; 73.   [3] Xenophon, *Hellenica*, ii, 3, 41; 42.

from the Thracian Chersonese and had consulted the god at
Delphi as to their people's need; and the oracle bade make him
king who first entertained them. So they told their story and
begged their host to 'obey the god'. So Miltiades went off to
Delphi to consult the god for himself, and was bidden to consent.[1]
And Pisistratus supported the plan; it would get Miltiades
away from Athens where he did not want him, and would make
him dependent, and Pisistratus would thus have a foothold on
the Dardanelles. In our own day we have seen a similar thing.
The French government made it very clear that they did not
wish the Jesuits and other orders in France, but they could be
very useful in Madagascar and perhaps other places overseas.

But there was a stronger power in the world than any Greek
neighbour state. In the sixth century Greece had become
abruptly aware of a new empire in Asia; the invincible Lydian
was swept away; Miletus was the only Greek state that even
surmised this could happen, but on the Halys river and again
at the gates of Sardis Cyrus defeated Croesus. The camels of
the Persians disorganized the Lydian cavalry; horses hate
camels, and they fled; and though the riders dismounted and
fought valiantly, it was the end of Lydian rule; and the Persian
gradually annexed the littoral and the Greek towns upon it.
The Persian king was the new factor in Greek history. Cleisthenes
and his democrats made overtures to him when they were once
quit of Hippias and Cleomenes; but Hippias anticipated them,
and the rest of his long life 'left no stone unturned' ($\pi\hat{a}\nu$ $\chi\rho\hat{\eta}\mu a$
$\dot{\epsilon}\kappa\acute{\iota}\nu\epsilon\epsilon$), we read, maligning the Athenians to Artaphrenes and
doing everything to bring Athens into subjection to himself
and Darius. The Athenians sent envoys to Sardis to bid the
Persians not to believe the Athenian exiles. But Artaphrenes
bade them receive Hippias back, if they wished to be safe. To
refuse meant war, and, as we all know, they did refuse and war
came, and for a brief day Hippias saw Attica again, but
Marathon was the first assurance the Greeks had that Persians
were not invincible on land.

About the same time (it is dated in the year of Marathon
490 B.C.) a Spartan king was deposed on the rumour of his
illegitimacy, supported by the Delphic oracle, not without the

[1] Herodotus, vi, 34–36.

secret machinations of Cleomenes. An insult led to his leaving Sparta, and by the round-about route of Elis and Zacynthus he got away to Asia, whose King Darius received him royally (μεγαλωστί) and gave him land and cities. It must have interested moralists to note that both his royal enemies in Sparta, Cleomenes (who went mad, or people said so) and his successor Leutychides, came to bad ends. But Demaratus remained among the Persians and was a figure of significance at Xerxes' side in the great invasion of 480. Herodotus, it is pretty clear, must have known intimately some member of his family; for it is hard to suppose that an outsider would have known so much of Demaratus' relations with Xerxes—of his suggestions to the Persian king, his shrewd advice (of course, not taken by Xerxes) as to means of breaking up the Greek fleet, his account (a noble one) of the Spartan character, and so forth—or would have supposed that the exile counted so much. The story is full of interest, and it does not end there. For when the younger Cyrus was killed at Cunaxa, the news of his death was brought to the Greeks by a descendant of Demaratus, named after his remote ancestor Procles—a prince who with his brother appears elsewhere in the *Anabasis* and in the *Hellenica*, domiciled where Demaratus had been settled; and numismatists tell us of the coinage of this Procles.[1]

Xerxes had other Athenian exiles in his train; and when he had taken Athens, he made them go and offer sacrifice in the Acropolis in the Greek manner; and Herodotus wonders whether this was so required of him in some dream or whether he repented burning the temple.[2]

Greeks of more importance had recourse to the Persians after the Great War—the Spartan regent Pausanias who, it would seem, had completely lost his head and over-estimated himself after his victory at Plataea,[3] and the much greater and more interesting Themistocles. Pausanias, for all his intrigues with Xerxes and his agents, did not get away. Plutarch tells us that, when he himself was a student at Athens 'in the school of

[1] For the story, see Herodotus, vi, 61–70 (the exile); vii, 3; 101; 209; 235; 237 (conversations with Xerxes); Xenophon, *Anabasis*, ii, 1, 3; vii, 8, 17; *Hellenica*, iii, 1, 6. Also Babelon, *Les Perses*, p. lxixf., the coins of Procles; G. B. Grundy, *Great Persian War*, p. 207.

[2] Herodotus, iii, 54; 55. [3] Thucydides, ii, 71; i, 94, 95, 128–130.

Ammonius the philosopher', among his friends was 'another
Themistocles still enjoying the revenues assigned by the Persian
king to the great exile'.[1] He tells us that a splendid tomb of
Themistocles was shown by the Magnesians in their market-
place; but Thucydides has an interesting story told by his
relatives that at his own request his remains had been carried
back to Greece and buried in Attica, but secretly; for in view
of his being exiled on a charge of treason, this was not lawful.[2]
Yet another notable Athenian took refuge among the Persians
when Sparta had become too hot to hold him; and he gave
Tissaphernes the suggestion, so Thucydides tells us, which
became the policy of Persia in the fourth century, to be in no
hurry to put an end to the Peloponnesian war, and to take care
that the same power did not rule on sea and on land; let the
dominion be divided, and the Persian king could always use the
less troublesome of the two rivals.[3] As is familiar, some sixteen
years later Pharnabazus acted on this plan, supported the
Athenian admiral Conon, and, after his great victory, backed
him up in rebuilding the Long Walls of Athens, which linked
the city with the sea and made her far more independent of
Sparta[4] (394 B.C.).

Persia was not the only resort of Spartan kings in exile. Tegea
in Arcadia received King Pausanias,[5] the victim of Lysander,[6]
and there he spent the rest of his life, writing, it would seem—an
unexpected form of activity in a Spartan king—a work about
oracles and perhaps Lycurgus.[7] Leutychides had gone there
before him.[8]

IV

We have looked, if only cursorily, at the general condition of
political life in Greek states, and at different phases of exile,
voluntary or involuntary or something between. Our next task
is to look at revolution as it raged, when it fairly broke out.
There will be few students of the Classics to whom memory will

---

[1] Plutarch, *Themistocles*, 31 (last paragraph); on these revenues, see Thucydides, i, 138.
[2] Thucydides, i, 138.   [3] Thucydides, viii, 46.
[4] Xenophon, *Hellenica*, iv, 3, 11; Isocrates, *Philip*, 64.
[5] *Hellenica*, iii, 5, 25.   [6] Aristotle, *Politics*, 1301 b.
[7] Strabo, C 366; the text has had to be restored; the oracles are more secure
than Lycurgus.
[8] Herodotus, vi, 72.

not at once suggest in this connexion the troubles of Corcyra.
There were before the war of 1939 German scholars who opined
that the chapters which describe them are a supreme example
of Thucydides' art, of his gift for bringing the tragic into history.
Is there exaggeration in it? The conduct of government by
Hitler and his group makes that seem unlikely. 'As false as a
bulletin', was a proverb of Napoleon's time; 'gouverner c'est
mentir', said Henri Rochefort at some point during the Dreyfus
agitation. Thucydides is notorious for his passion for the exact—
τὸ ἀκριβές; if he says that fifty people were killed as an overture
to the Corcyraean *stasis*, we may be sure that the figure was not
ten. In one place, where he knows a figure, he refuses to give
it, because, he says, no one would believe it. So revolution took
its course in Corcyra, and this is what Thucydides says.[1]

They continued killing those of their fellow-citizens whom
they counted enemies; they professed to punish them for their
designs against the democracy, but in fact some were killed from
motives of personal enmity; others because money was owing
to them were slain by the borrowers. Death in every form was
to be seen, and everything that commonly occurs at such a
moment happened then, and more besides. Father slew son;
men were dragged from the temples and slain near them; and
some were walled up in the temple of Dionysus, and perished
in the shrine. To such extremes of savagery did revolution go;
and this seemed the worst of revolutions because it was the first.
For afterwards the whole Hellenic world, you might say, was
convulsed, since in each state the leaders of the democratic
factions were at variance with the oligarchs, the democrats
wishing to bring in the Athenians, the oligarchs the Spartans.
In time of peace they would have had no pretext nor been
ready to call them in; but they were at war, and both sides if
they wished revolution could easily obtain allies to injure their
opponents and to strengthen their own cause. Revolution, he
continues, always brings calamity and always will, while human
nature is the same, but circumstances may heighten it. In peace
and prosperity cities and men have better dispositions; but war
takes away the comfortable provision of daily life and is a
violent teacher (βίαιος διδάσκαλος) and creates in most people

[1] Thucydides, iii, 81–83, but I do not give all of it.

a temper that matches their condition. Fresh devices for outrage
were thought out, and revenge grew more monstrous (ἀτοπίᾳ).
Words changed their meanings; reckless daring became loyal
courage; prudence was the excuse of a coward, moderation a
cloak for unmanly weakness; frantic energy was the mark of
a man. The hot-headed was trusted, and a man who detected
a plot was shrewder than the man who devised one. The tie
of party was stronger than the tie of blood; the seal of good faith
was fellowship in crime; revenge was dearer than self-preserva-
tion. Political catchwords were fair-sounding enough; but
justice and the public good were sacrificed to the caprice of the
moment, and the neutral was the prey of both parties. But
enough.

Can it be true? Unless we have been grossly deceived, the
atrocities of our own time make the story of Corcyra quite
probable; and there is plenty to be read in the Greek historians
and elsewhere in the same vein. For instance, the proceedings of
the Thirty in Athens in 404 are made known to us by Xenophon,
who appears to have been in Athens at the time; Isocrates has
the same sort of tale to tell as he looks back after fifty years; and
the speeches of Lysias against Eratosthenes and Agoratus were
delivered in the year after the events to an audience that had
witnessed them. Whatever may be said of the tone and spirit of
the speeches (and Lysias had had a brother killed by the
oligarchs), a man cannot falsify the major events of last year.
Or compare the massacre at Corinth in 392 B.C., planned to
take place at a religious festival 'because they reckoned they
would catch more people in the market-place, so as to kill them'
—murder in a circle of friends, with the judge on the bench, the
spectator in the theatre. The better-class people fled to the
statues of the gods in the market-place, to the altars; and then,
without a thought of common usage, those of the other party,
whether giving orders for it all or obeying them, kept up the
slaughter in the shrines. Men turned to thoughts of exile, but
their womenfolk were against it. So the attempt to make one
state of Corinth and Argos failed.[1] Or compare the sack of
Thermus by Philip V of Macedon in 218 B.C., with its tale of
sacrilege and the destruction of art and architecture.[2] Or the

---

[1] Xenophon, *Hellenica*, iv, 4.   [2] Polybius, v, 9.

factions of Cynaetha, the Arcadian town that abandoned the
national devotion to music,[1] and the lengths to which they went
in massacre, pillage, confiscation and the exiling of opponents,
till they had outdone all Greeks of that day in savagery and
lawlessness.[2] Polybius elsewhere tells us of the wholesale de-
portations carried out by Philip V,[3] and how Antipater devised
a squad of 'exile-hunters' (φυγαδοθήρας).[4] Revolution was not
a pleasant thing in Greece. I recall an old English soldier's
comment of about the year 1920–21, when he heard working-
men airily talking of a revolution to come in England; 'have
you ever seen a revolution?' he asked; for he had seen one in
Russia. And friends of Greece recall with shame how history
repeated itself and how in November 1922, as in ancient Athens,
generals and statesmen were shot when the Asia Minor campaign
went wrong. It looks as if the gloomy words of Thucydides are
true, that, as long as human nature continues the same, we may
expect revolution to be bloodstained; but, as a French observer
said, it kills its own children.

Perhaps enough has been said here, but the reader will do
well to turn to the eighth book of Thucydides and read the
tremendous story of the Athenian revolution of 411. It is hard
to understand the view of a modern English scholar that in that
book Thucydides writes as one who has lost his way.

V

We have now to turn to the exiles themselves and study for a
little what they felt—about their own condition and about the
authors of their banishment.

Cicero was a great reader of Homer, and it is of interest to
remark passages that haunt his memory and clearly touch his
heart. More than once he recurs to Ulysses, wisest of men, and
how he preferred to immortality itself that Ithaca of his, stuck
like a little nest among the rough crags (*Ithacam illam in asperrimis
saxulis tanquam nidulum adfixam*).[5] The passage perhaps in his

---

[1] Arcadian music, Polybius, iv, 20. [2] Polybius, iv, 17–20.
[3] Polybius, xxiii, 10.
[4] Polybius, ix, 29. I have omitted reference to Phlius, not a town of first interest
to the modern reader; but the story of its factions and exiles can be followed very
easily in the *Hellenica* and it repays the trouble.
[5] Cicero, *de Oratore*, i, 44, 196; the diminutives are interesting and not accidental.
Little is accidental in Cicero's writings. Cf. also *de Legibus*, ii, 1, 3; *Odyssey*, i, 56–59.

mind—certainly in the English reader's mind—is in the first book of the *Odyssey*, where Athena tells her father how Calypso would beguile Odysseus to forget Ithaca, but he longs to see were it but the smoke rising from his own land, and craves to die. So it was, and so it is with the Greeks. Before the war there was much exodus of Greeks to the United States, where they would live for a while, keeping fruit-stalls and remitting among them something like a million sterling per annum to the home-land. It was the Greek fruit-stall that gave rise to the terribly popular song of 1923 and those years—'Yes, we have no bananas'; and it is from those fruit-stalls that the man in every village of the Peloponnese who speaks English caught his American accent. The Greek village must be a great contrast to the American city, but there is the old instinct that took Odysseus away from Calypso and made a thousand upheavals in Greek history.

So Homer at the dawn of history—himself a wanderer, as later Greeks noted. And in Plato's *Crito* we see yet another phase of the matter. Crito would have Socrates break prison; it could be managed. But Socrates pictures the laws of Athens talking to him, pleading that he should not break his old standing covenant with them; above all other Athenians he had seemed to love Athens—never stirred out of her—the halt and the blind were not more stationary. And now, suppose he did break prison, what good would it do himself or his friends? They would be driven into exile, and lose their citizenship and their property; that was only too likely; and suppose Socrates himself got away, say to Thebes or to Megara, both well-governed cities, he would come as an enemy; and law-abiding citizens would look askance on him as a subverter of the laws and say that the court which had condemned him was justified. Or Thessaly perhaps? but what would be the good of living in Thessaly? Oh! they would enjoy the story of Socrates getting out of prison, wrapped up in a goat-skin or some such disguise, rigged up like any other runaway; very likely! But would there be no one there at all to hint to him that in his old age he was not ashamed to break the most sacred laws—and just for a little spell of life? If they lost their tempers, they would be sure to say it. And what would he be doing? flattering people for his

dinner! And where would all his fine sentiments be, about
justice and virtue? Would he take his children to Thessaly?
How would they get on there, deprived of their Athenian
citizenship?[1]

Of course, in theory there was Zeus Xenios, the god who
protected strangers—'Zeus, the avenger of suppliants and so-
journers, Zeus the god of the stranger, who fareth in company
with revered strangers.' So we read in the *Odyssey* (ix, 270):
they are the words of Odysseus; but the rejoinder of the Cyclops
is also of moment. He says that the Cyclops tribe pay no heed
to Zeus, nor to the blessed gods, 'for of a truth we are better
men than they'. If the Cyclops was a fable, we have seen in the
accounts of massacre at Corcyra and at Corinth that plenty of
actual human beings shared the Cyclops view of the gods. It
deeply shocks Xenophon, who, as we read in the *Memorabilia*
and in the *Anabasis*, believed that Socrates taught piety and
who certainly practised it himself.

Theognis shows us how men felt about the political upsets too
familiar in his age. He foresaw trouble in Megara—the inevitable outcome of *hybris*. 'Think not that that city shall long
go unshaken—no, not though even yet it lieth in great quietness
—when to evil men these things grow dear, to wit gains that come
to them with evil to the state. For of this arise revolutions
($\sigma\tau\acute{a}\sigma\iota\epsilon\varsigma$, plural) and murderings of men by their own kin, and
tyrants ($\mu o\acute{v}v\alpha\rho\chi o\iota$).' So he predicted and it came to pass; and
he records: 'Kyrnos, this city is still a city, but the folk are other
folk, who in time past knew not laws nor customs, but with pelts
of goats about their loins they lived, and fed like stags outside
this city. And now they are the noble ($\dot{a}\gamma\alpha\theta o\acute{\iota}$), and they that
aforetime were good are base. Who could endure to see it?
And one another they deceive, laughing one on another, with
no knowledge of evil or good.' '*Hybris*', he adds at a later point,
'destroyed the Magnesians and Colophon and Smyrna; yes,
Kyrnos, and you also ($\check{v}\mu\mu$') shall it destroy.'[2] It is the aristo-
crat's—or the oligarch's—picture of the new nobility—people
from outside with no traditions, peasants in goat-skins; and
there we leave them, for Theognis has nothing to tell us of a
happy restoration.

[1] Plato, *Crito*, 53–54.   [2] Theognis, 39–60; 1103–1104.

Pindar's 'greatest poem', as Basil Gildersleeve very justly calls
it—the poem in which he tells the story of the Argo and the
Argonauts and links it with the foundation of Cyrene—is
addressed to Arcesilas, King of Cyrene 'city of fair steeds', a
long poem brilliant and fascinating from whatever angle one
comes at it.[1] And then at the very end another note is struck.
An exile from Cyrene has been at Thebes and has become the
guest-friend of the poet. Dimly we make out something of old
troubles; but men learn wisdom; and there is forgiveness, Zeus
at last released the Titans. The god of healing honours Arcesilas,
who may well set a gentle hand to a sore wound. There is a right
moment (καιρός) in the affairs of men, but its span is short-lived.
And Damophilos hath hope yet again to see his home and the
fountain of Apollo, to handle the carven lute among the
citizens, men of wisdom, hurting and hurt of none. 'Then shall
he tell'—and Pindar looks back on his great ode, as conscious
(he ever was) of its greatness as any critic—'then shall he tell
how fair a fountain of deathless verse he made to flow for
Arcesilas, a guest of late at Thebes.' It is a magnificent peace-
offering; and perhaps the most poignant of an exile's griefs,
though a modern exile might not think so, is touched here—

> The bitterest fate of all, men say,
> Is his, who clearly hath descried
> The right thing, and no part may play,
> But stands, perforce, aside.

But now let us turn to Athens and the reign of Pisistratus, an
interrupted reign, but a great one. Herodotus (i, 61), on whom
all our authorities depend, tells us that Pisistratus was twice
driven out and twice restored. Perhaps the historians generally
accept the story, and it is attractive, when we see the great man
driving back into Athens with the goddess at his side, whom
wicked opponents in the end identified with the beautiful and tall
Phye who kept a garden in such and such a deme or parish. And
an even greater improbability is generally accepted. But I incline,
and I find that Julius Beloch also inclines, to surmise—perhaps
I owe the idea to him, but I am not sure—to surmise that there
was only one break, one exile, made by narrators into two to

---

[1] Pindar, *Pythian*, iv, 270–299; a few sentences only are taken from the passage.

accommodate two accounts of his restoration; but that need not be argued here. On his expulsion we read that the tyrant betook himself to Eretria, and there took counsel with his sons; and the advice of Hippias prevailed that they should recover the tyranny. So they began to gather gifts from the cities that owed them some requital. Many men gave great gifts, but the Thebans overshot all in the bestowal of money. Afterwards, not to make a long story (μέτα δέ, οὐ πολλῷ λόγῳ εἰπεῖν), time passed and all was ready for their return—Argive mercenaries, and a man of Naxos, Lygdamis by name, a volunteer most zealous in their cause, who brought both money and men. So— and now comes the amazing statement (i, 62)—after ten years (διὰ ἑνδεκάτου ἔτεος)[1] they came back to Athens. *Can* this be right? It seems odd indeed that, with his son egging him on and his friends supplying such generous aid, a real leader of men should wait ten years—or perhaps the Greek means eleven. Cleisthenes, or whoever invented ostracism, thought that any Athenian would be politically dead and done with after *ten* years of exile. Then is there a mistake? Can it be that Herodotus wrote διὰ ἔτεος (after a year), that ἑνδεκάτου is due to some copyist who found the last letters of διά duplicated—διαια—and wrote out the ια in full—with a correction to match it in the arithmetic of v, 65. (Herodotus seems often to get astray in simple arithmetic; the *abacus* was not so useful as the Arabic numerals, reinforced by the most valuable symbol 0.) As things are, the chronology of the reign is further entangled by the *Athenaion Politeia*, which is 'hopelessly confused'; and scholars guess, and guess again, the dates and periods of the exiles and the restorations. But a ten years' absence surely seems improbable in the highest degree.

That is not the only memorable story of exile that belongs to the reign. Quite apart from anything Herodotus tells us of Megacles and his deal with Pisistratus and the break off of their relations, there was other opposition, and armed attempts by the exiles to return. Memory of these survived in song—'a cup too for Kêdon!' and the four-line *skolion* long familiar among

---

[1] Διά with the genitive, meaning 'after an interval'; cf. Herodotus, ii, 37, διὰ τρίτης ἡμέρας; iii, 97, διὰ τρίτου ἔτεος; and iv, i, διὰ χρόνου τοσούτου (28 years); and add St Paul, *Galatians*, iv, i, διὰ δεκατεσσάρων ἐτέων, 'fourteen years later'.

many *skolia* ('catches') in Athenaeus[1]—'Alas! alas! for
Leipsydrion [a place on the Southern flank of Mount Parnes],
betrayer of comrades, what heroes hast thou slain! Brave men
in battle, and sons of nobles, who showed on that day what
fathers they had.'

There have been memorials less simple and less appealing.

One more story of exile, a great one, and we can pass on to
certain illustrations of the temper of banished men. In 371 at
Leuctra Epameinondas inflicted on the Spartans the greatest
defeat in their history. It was the end of their dominance, and
Greece could breathe again—particularly the Greeks of the
Peloponnese. Epameinondas made several invasions of the
Peloponnese, and set up Arcadians and Messenians as independent powers. Xenophon says drily that 'the helots revolted'.
Centuries later Pausanias tells it better. He gives great space
to Messenia and its history; and then 'for nearly three hundred
years the Messenians had to wander, outside the Peloponnese,
and in all that time they are known to have dropped none of
their native (οἴκοθεν) customs, nor did they unlearn their Doric,
but even to this day [about A.D. 180] they kept their dialect with
greater purity than any other Peloponnesians.'[2]

We have seen a number of instances of appeal being made by
exiles to the foreigner, Greek or Persian, to restore them. Of all
such episodes the restoration of Syloson to Samos is perhaps
most striking. It is given us very fully by Herodotus (v, 139–
145). Syloson was a brother of Polycrates of Samos, but was in
exile in Egypt at the time of its invasion by Cambyses. He was
in the market at Memphis, wearing a red cloak, when a Persian
officer of Cambyses' bodyguard, 'a *doryphoros* of no great account',
came up to him and offered to buy the red cloak. 'Some divine
chance' (θείη τύχη) stirred Syloson to say he would not sell it,
but would give it him, and he did; and the Persian took the
cloak and went away. But within not many years that '*doryphoros*
of no great account' succeeded Cambyses on the Persian throne;
he was Darius. So Syloson went to Susa and reminded the
Great King of the cloak. No, he didn't want gold or silver; he

---

[1] Athenaeus, *Gastronomus*, xv, p. 695e; and Ἀθηναίων Πολιτεία, c. 19, both give
the *skolion*. Herodotus, v, 62, tells of Leipsydrion. Cedon in Ἀθηναίων Πολιτεία,
c. 19.

[2] Xenophon, *Hellenica*, vii, 2, 2; Pausanias, iv, 27, 11.

wanted Samos. Darius sent orders and an army to effect the
restoration. But the vice-gerent of Polycrates held Samos, and
a crazy brother of his denounced him for submitting too easily.
Treacherous murder of Persian nobles followed, and then war;
and the Persians 'swept Samos clear' and handed it over to
Syloson 'uninhabited'. Centuries later the proverb survives in
Strabo's *Geography* (xiv, C 638),

$$\H{\epsilon}κητι \: Συλοσῶντος \: εὐρυχωρίη—$$

'plenty of room for Syloson'. The story deserves reflexion on a
good many grounds—the red cloak, Persian rule, the exile's
temper.

Again, when Alcibiades is exiled from Athens, he goes to
Sparta and harangues the Spartans on how to fight the
Athenians. Thucydides gives us the speech. There have been
many discussions about the speeches in his History, and they
have been variously grouped according to their supposed
authenticity by modern critics; and the caution that Thucydides
gives us is not forgotten—in the speeches he sets down not the
exact words, but 'the sentiments proper to the occasion', but
also as far as he could achieve it 'the general purport of what
was actually said'.[1] For one reason and another it is felt that
Thucydides in exile was in touch with Alcibiades in exile; he is
always closely informed—somehow—of what Alcibiades is doing
and saying. And here is part of what Alcibiades said to the
Spartans.[2]

'You ought not in fairness to think the worse of me, because,
having been once distinguished as a lover of my country, I now
cast in my lot with her worst foes and attack her with all my
might; or suspect that I speak only with the forwardness of an
exile. An exile I am indeed; I have lost an ungrateful country,
but I have not lost the power of doing you service if you will
listen to me. The true enemies of my country are not those
who, like you, have injured her in open war, but those who have
compelled her friends to become her enemies. I love Athens,
not in so far as I am wronged by her, but in so far as I once
enjoyed the privileges of a citizen. The country which I am
attacking is no longer mine, but a lost country which I am

---

[1] Thucydides, i, 22.
[2] Thucydides, vi, 92 (Jowett's translation here).

seeking to regain. He is the true patriot, not who, when unjustly exiled, abstains from attacking his country, but who in the warmth of his affection seeks to recover her without regard to the means.'

Nothing could be more explicit; and whether Thucydides is putting into his mouth the sentiments proper to the occasion, or whether Alcibiades really said something of this kind (which is indeed highly likely), it is equally illuminative. It was thus, Thucydides believes, that an exile would speak. It is not the language that will in general win him the admiration of modern patriots who read him at home. A defence of Alcibiades, which makes him almost a bonnie Prince Charlie, may be read in Mr Bernard Henderson's book *The Great War between Athens and Sparta.*

It was not, one judges, Thucydides' own temper. 'It befel me to be in exile from my country for twenty years, after my command at Amphipolis' (v, 26)—a quiet enough statement, introduced to explain how it was that he could at his leisure gain a better acquaintance with the course of events, as in exile he could (and did) see more of the Peloponnesus than he otherwise could have. He makes no protest, unless the comment on the condemnation of Sophocles and Eurymedon, about the same time, be one; the Athenians had been so uniformly successful that they expected to achieve equally what was possible and what was more difficult whether their force was a big one or inadequate (iv, 65). There was a chance that he might be recalled in 411, but the Athenians would not recall the exiles 'because of Alcibiades' (viii, 70); but in 404 he did come back with the other exiles, and we have a glimpse of him investigating the foundations laid bare by the destruction of the walls—a small bit of historical research upon the actual ground (i, 93). And before we pass on, a note may be made as to the destruction of those walls. 'After this', writes Xenophon,[1] 'Lysander sailed into the Peiraeus, and the exiles came back and dug down the walls with great enthusiasm, to the music of flute-girls, and reckoned that day the first of Greek freedom.'

---

[1] Xenophon, *Hellenica*, ii, 2, 23. The Loeb translator, Mr C. L. Brownson, introduces a new subject (not visible to Mr Dakyns in the Greek) and makes the Spartans do the digging down of the walls.

One of the returning exiles of 404, conspicuous among them, was Critias—'headlong in his eagerness to put many men to death, because he too had been sent into exile by the democracy'.[1] A pupil of Socrates, a kinsman of Plato, a rather minor poet (one set of whose verses on the origin of gods survives in the pages of Sextus Empiricus), something of an orator (for some of his speeches survived to be read by Cicero)[2]—his name is for ever associated with the worst outrages of the Thirty, and his association with Socrates told against his teacher. It was a happy thing for Athens when he fell fighting at Munychia against Thrasybulus and the returning democrats.[3]

The return of Thrasybulus is one of the happiest episodes in Xenophon's pages. The democratic exiles had taken refuge in Thebes and Megara—as well they might, for we read that the Thirty and their adherents slew more Athenians in eight months than the Spartans had killed in a war of ten years. And then came quarrels among the Thirty themselves, and the dramatic death of Theramenes, dragged from the altar and shouting to the people as they hauled him away; and then men told how, when he was made to drink the hemlock, he jerked out the dregs like a man playing at *kottabos*, with the words, 'let this be for the noble Critias'. 'I know quite well', says Xenophon,[4] 'that these are not sayings worthy of record, but I count it admirable in a man so near death that neither self-possession nor playfulness failed in his soul' (μήτε τὸ φρόνιμον μήτε τὸ παιγνιῶδες ἀπολιπεῖν ἐκ τῆς ψυχῆς).

And the next thing (ἐκ δὲ τούτου) was Thrasybulus. It is a Garibaldi-like story. He set out from Thebes with seventy men, and seized the strong position of Phyle. 'As a post of observation', says Mrs R. C. Bosanquet, 'its position is unequalled'; Athens and the sea are well in view. He had to be driven out, and the Thirty marched against him with their troops—in fine weather; but they failed, and then determined to wall Thrasybulus off and cut off his supplies, when a heavy snow-storm surprised them in the night, continuing next day. They fell back to the city through the driving snow, but lost a lot of men on the way; the men of Phyle seized their chance.

[1] *Hellenica*, ii, 3, 15.   [2] Cicero, *de Oratore*, ii, 22, 93.
[3] Xenophon, *Hellenica*, ii, 4, 19.   [4] Xenophon, *Hellenica*, ii, 3, 56.

Fresh recruits came in; we read of Thrasybulus having seven hundred men, and by and by a thousand. And in spite of the Spartan garrison the Thirty lose ground as steadily, and fall back on Eleusis, while Thrasybulus troops down to the Peiraieus. Then the Spartan king comes with an army, jealous of the too powerful Lysander. A battle follows, in which the Liberators had the good luck to be beaten, which cleared the way for the Spartan king to make peace; and the hateful episode of the Thirty was over. Thrasybulus was able to offer sacrifice on the Acropolis; magistrates were appointed; the remnants of the Tyrant party at Eleusis were defeated and a number of them put to death. And then in noble words Xenophon tells the end of the story—reconciliation; 'and they swore oaths that there should be no recollection of evil deeds, and to this day [he was writing perhaps as late as 355 B.C.] they share one state, and *Dêmos* abides by his oaths'.[1]

VI

So far we have had to do with banishments and battles, with alien allies and violent restorations, with rage and murder. But there were exiles who stayed away and sought no return, content like the Huguenots in England and Prussia, and men of how many races in Britain to-day, to live at a distance from their enemies. One thinks of Xenophon at Scillus near Olympia, hunting, writing books that lived, and bringing up his boys—the noble Gryllos one of them. One thinks of the swarms of *metics* brought to Athens by the wise laws of Solon, continued by Pisistratus—welcome in Athens if they had a trade, if they brought their families or were definitely exiles. One thinks of later centuries when in Alexandria and Antioch and innumerable other new Greek cities of the Eastern Mediterranean, of Mesopotamia and still farther East to Kandahar and Buce-phala, Greeks were content with a new kind of life—less politics, no foreign policy, a monarch, but a real Greek city with theatre and palaestra, and in more than one of these cities philosophic schools and men of letters.

Finally, there is Virgil. His first eclogue is a story of an exile

---

[1] The story is in *Hellenica*, ii, 4; and these are the telling words with which the book ends.

with a fate much like his own. In the *Georgic* we find the old man of Corycus—a town of Cilicia near St Paul's Tarsus, whose past is conjectured to have been one of piracy, whose present is the garden, beautifully told. And the *Aeneid* is all exiles together. Dido has left Tyre and founded Carthage. Evander, an exquisite figure of simple greatness, tells a similar tale—

> *Me pulsum patria pelagique extrema petentem*
> *Fortuna omnipotens et ineluctabile fatum*
> *His posuere locis, matrisque egere tremenda*
> *Carmentis nymphae monita et deus auctor Apollo.*[1]

But the whole theme of the book is exile—*campos ubi Troja fuit*—and the promise of a new world won by a man whose life was shattered and his home destroyed—an exile, but a life of victory.

[1] *Aeneid*, x, 333–336.

Chapter IV

THE WELDING OF MANKIND

I

I spent some days lately upon H. J. R. Murray's *History of Chess*, a most learned and fascinating book. Of course, it is full of chess 'problems'; and I can never do anything with 'problems', chess or arithmetic or cross-words. But the archaeology of the book was a delight. Chess is an Indian game, a war-game—with a king, a vizier, and four types of troops, cavalry, elephants, chariots, and foot soldiers—a great invention; and Persians and Arabs adopted it. It went East, and it came West. The game has been modified here and there; the vizier has become a European queen (a sort of Cleopatra or Queen Elizabeth); the elephant is disguised as a bishop; the chariot is now a 'rook' (nobody quite knows what that is) or a castle. But it is still chess; it still has the Oriental name; and, when you win, you talk Persian to your opponent and say 'Shah mat', the King is dead.

The problems reminded me of something else. One of the happiest things in my college life has been the friendship of the late Sir Joseph Larmor, the physicist. One day he suggested to me that among mankind's most ingenious achievements not the least is the invention of the symbol 0—the cypher or zero, as we call it, both words being awkward attempts at the same Arabic word, though in truth our 'Arabic' numerals come from India. On the 0, Sir Joseph said, all modern arithmetic and mathematics rest.[1] Of course twelve times twelve was always one hundred and forty-four, whether you wrote CXLIV or 144. But, if you wanted to multiply it—say, by thirty-seven—try to multiply CXLIV by XXXVII; you will need an *abacus*, and long experience in using it; but any school-boy can multiply 144 by 37—anybody can do it (except me).

[1] The reader may consult on this zero question Bertram Thomas, *The Arabs*, p. 190; and C. H. Haskins, *Twelfth Century*, p. 312; Skeat's *Etymological Dictionary*.

Thence I passed in mind to a third Indian invention, familiar to everybody. Whether you say with the Germans *zucker*, or with the French *sucre*, or with the Lancashire people *shugger*, you are trying to say an Indian word that means sugar-cane. Once again, Persians and Arabs brought the thing West; the Spaniards got it in North Africa, and took it to the Canaries and to the West Indies.

Now put the three Indian inventions together, and what do you deduce? Surely this: that, when mankind sees a good thing, it will have it and keep it. Europe has played chess for a thousand years, eaten sugar and used the cypher 0 for hundreds of years. Amusement, food, the mind—a pretty fair summary of human life; and in each sphere a foreign invention borrowed, adopted, incorporated, and made our own so that we forget it ever was foreign. And when one begins to study History in earnest the thought suggested by the story of chess, by the numerals and the nought, and by the plant that has done so much to shape the destiny of nations and of races, grows more significant. Acute as national and racial hatreds have been, there is something more fundamental—a deep unity in the human race. The ancient Stoics were right; we are one race; there are no foreigners; we are all essentially citizens of one community; and Nature has enacted one code for all mankind. There are local usages, various enough; climate differentiates clothing, for instance, for Hindu and Eskimo—clothing and foods; sari and sealskin are different, blubber and rice make different appeals and have diverse origins. But as the Stoic will tell us, clothing and food are common ideas; East or West, North or South, there is the same interest in both. *Homo sum; humani nihil a me alienum puto.*

It is worth while to look into the testimony of History; it will, if we treat it quietly, suggest things that may, in Carlyle's phrase, operate changes in our way of thought. What we learn will not all be pleasant perhaps—not all chess and mathematics and sugar. These last years have made one re-think the achievement of the American Commodore Perry. How proud some Americans were in the past of his triumph in forcing the Japanese to open their ports and their minds to the West and its ideas; how regrettable, since the day of Pearl Harbour—yes, and long

before it—that triumph of ninety years ago has come to look!
Mankind, we might be tempted to say, may borrow too much.
But chess in Europe and aeroplanes in Japan are incidents, so
to say, in a long history—trifles, if you look before and after,
if you survey mankind from China to Peru, if you look at things
sub specie aeternitatis or even (in J. B. Bury's lowered phrase)
sub specie perennitatis. Our verdict on the story will not quite
ignore chess and aeroplanes, but it will not be given on the sole
consideration of either. We shall find a more or less steady
movement toward unity among peoples, not necessarily political
union, but a trend toward a similar view of the world, toward
the absorption of one another's ideas and inventions; and we
may recall Stoic teaching about a common sense among men,
a law of Nature, the 'dear city of Zeus', and perhaps find a new
hope in old experience re-thought.

II

When we look into the history of our Western world, the first
great ecumenical fact (so to put it) is Homer. True, there were
all sorts of people in one area of Europe and another millen-
niums before Homer; they chipped flints, fought wild beasts and
killed their neighbours time out of mind; and that is not all, for
Homer implies a long and a high civilization—great arts, high
skill in metallurgy, architecture and navigation, wide interest
in the world and its geography, its seas and climates and peoples.
Odysseus 'saw the cities of many men and learnt their mind'.
Yet Homer marks an era. Say what we may of his literary and
spiritual antecedents—we do not know much about them, when
all is said; we have to divine them. But here, as so often in the
history of literature and of religion, whatever fascination there
may be in the attempt to be sure of the antecedents, they are not
of supreme importance. They never are—in spite of archaeologists and antiquaries. There has been much study, for instance,
of Shakespeare's library—and for that matter, of Chaucer's; and
it cannot be denied that either study contributes something to
our knowledge of the great man, but it is arguable that the one
and the other great man has himself made his library irrelevant
to mankind. *Antony and Cleopatra* does not depend on Plutarch's
Life of Antony for its value, even if Shakespeare used North's

translation of that book, and (as we are told and can believe) used it far more faithfully than the run of his 'sources' as they are called. That is a very relevant fact, if we are studying Plutarch, but not after all very important in the study of Shakespeare; it will help us to a real judgment of Plutarch, but Shakespeare's estimate of Plutarch is a minor fact in his own story. We read Plutarch's *Life* of Antony because of Shakespeare's play; of course historians read everything, but one surmises that Plutarch's Life of Antony might have been more read, if Shakespeare had not made his play out of it; Plutarch's book would have been the supreme work on Antony and the queen of Egypt; but for the mass of mankind Shakespeare has superseded Plutarch's book. Let us look at Homer.

> Seven Grecian cities fought for Homer dead,
> Through which the living Homer begged for bread.

So the Greeks said. They were not quite sure which the seven cities were; and their 'fighting' was done in this case (like so much of our own) by brave assertion and braver guess. But they were pretty sure that Homer was a blind man, who tramped about, and 'sang', and begged his bread. (We may be equally sure that at some stage of his life he could see, and did see— better than most of us.) Whether he wrote out his poems, or others did it for him, is of little importance; they were written out, and all Greece adopted them, read them, and learned them by heart, century after century; and Rome adopted them. So did the Christian Church. (Clement of Alexandria is one of the most charming of Christian writers, and he is always quoting Homer.) So did all Europe. Even America uses a translation of the *Odyssey* in her schools.

When we try to estimate the factors that contributed to the unity of the Greek race—a unity which their incessant jealousies and their savage wars never really obscured—we are told that 'the Greek race is of one blood and one speech; it has the temples of the gods in common, common sacrifices, and ways of like kind'. So the Greeks avowed, and so their historian tells us;[1] and no doubt it is true; and how much of it all was to be traced to Homer? Is this to exaggerate the effect of great

[1] Herodotus, viii, 144.

literature—the bookish man's constant temptation? To-day we are less certain about blood than the Greeks were. Sancho Panza's proverb 'Not of whom you are bred, But with whom you have fed' has a great deal of truth about it. Britain and America have received ceaseless streams of immigrants, and in three generations their children (apart from the Jews, who make a special case) are indistinguishable from their neighbours. The Pilgrims went to New England in James the First's reign, the northern Irish followed in the eighteenth century, Germans in great numbers after the Revolutionary Year 1848. Surnames may hint at this diversity of origin, and Greece in general had no surnames; and little enough the surnames imply to-day. Americans have not in fact assimilated the Eastern European and Italian hordes as quickly as they expected to do it; yet American is a type, and Greek was a type. One speech prevails throughout the United States, a speech moulded by the Authorized Version of the Bible, and by Tyndale's great version behind it; and this book has affected all their religious ideas, even more than we or themselves might suppose. 'Common temples of the gods, common sacrifices, ways of like kind'—so we read; and we do not have to go far to learn what influences produced this unity. All Greeks knew Homer, he is the common background; and we know very well how men and women standardize their ideas, we know the pressure they bring on one another to get those ideas adjusted to common belief and common ideal. Three wars in our lifetime have shown us how we insist on conformity among our people. Partly, no doubt, it is due to loyalty to a common government, which Greece conspicuously had not; but, apart from stress of war, there are what we might call national ideals. It would be interesting to trace out the origins of these, but for the moment it is enough to emphasize this clear fact that the man must be strong-minded indeed—or an oddity, if you prefer to say so—who will venture to criticize the standards of the nation. Matthew Arnold might suggest that 'they do these things better in France'; that was his 'little way', his 'fun' (in Lamb's phrase about Coleridge), a pose; the things which they did better in France were things of no consequence; Matthew Arnold was as English as anybody. You have only to read him on Burns to realize it. *Echt britische*

Beschränktheit is not exactly a sympathetic phrase, but who deserved it more than Matthew Arnold, where anything fundamental was concerned?

Homer was written and read and recited. Rhapsodes haunted Greek centres and recited him. Nicomachus in Xenophon says he listens to the rhapsodes every day; and this statement follows his story of his education. His father had wished him to be a good man, a man of high character; so the boy learned *Iliad* and *Odyssey* by heart, and tells us he could recite them himself— and yet day by day he will listen to the rhapsodes. A modern scholar says that the Middle Ages liked monotony. Could we say that of the Greeks? Homer is not monotonous; he does not grow stale. On the contrary Greeks invented somehow other long epics on his model, epics long familiar, but in the end lost, while Homer survived. At the very end (if one may use the expression) of the long story of Greek literature (that could be called literature) comes a last imitation of Homer:

> Which, cast in later Grecian mould,
> Quintus Calaber
> Somewhat lazily handled of old.

And how many epics of legend or learning come between? epics of gods and heroes, of frogs and mice, even of snake-bite? And other races followed Greek tradition—Romans and our own people; every epic speaks somehow of Homer.

What is more, people who did not write epics—and they were the great majority (fortunately)—

> Well, I could never write a verse—could you?

—quoted Homer interminably. They knew him as Nicomachus did, could recite him as they said ἀπὸ στόματος—had him 'by heart', as we more pleasantly put it—had him in their hearts; and, as the old Puritans knew their Bible and used it, so did the Greeks know and use Homer. I have elsewhere suggested what a great volume might be made of the quotations of Homer, bearing on every phase of life. It would be difficult to over-estimate his influence on Greece. History and geography began with him, and were never quite detached from him, as we can see in Polybius and Strabo. And as Herodotus says in so many

words, he with Hesiod made the theology of the Greeks. This
statement is challenged by modern literalists of the schools that
believe in corn-spirits and year-daemons and so on; but
challenge does not mean refutation. We have to remember
Dr Johnson's contempt for the sort of person that would rebut
the statement that there is no fruit in the orchard by noting that
in fact there are five apples and half a dozen pears. There was
no doubt much in Greek religion that had no place in Homer;
every town, every village, one might say, had its local god or
goddess, its local heroes at all events, half divine if not quite
divine; its local traditions and superstitions, its peculiar usages,
its own preference in images and idols, rites and sacrifices,
'black Demeters', and so on; Pausanias is full of such curiosities;
Homer is not, and Homer was everybody's book. Quote Homer
and the world knew what you were talking about; everybody
knew Homer's gods, and knew his stories about them; what was
more—and much worse, if you trust Plato—everybody assumed
that the gods were truthfully depicted in Homer, everybody was
apt to think about the gods on Homeric lines. But Homer did
more. Boswell boasts that his *Hebrides* and the great *Life* have
'Johnsonized' the land. *Iliad* and *Odyssey* 'Homerized' Greece.
Character was shaped and trained by the poems. It is not an
idle story that Homer was Alexander the Great's 'reading all
across Asia'. It is not enough to say that Homer tells the best
stories in the world; what is it that makes us say so, that has
made a hundred generations say so? He shows us what human
character can be, what men and women have to do and to bear,
how great they can be; life means more, is better worth living,
when one has got Homer written in one's heart. Goethe's
Autobiography, so Crabb Robinson notes (21 January 1815),
'is a book to make a man wish to live'. That is the Greek
experience of Homer.

So the Greeks felt about Homer; so have felt countless other
men; but Homer was not the only Greek whose word pulled
Greece together, welded the thoughts of men. Plutarch tells us
of the appeal of Euripides to the Sicilians—proved by what
they would do for the straggling Athenians after the failure of
the Syracusan expedition; and Browning has given it us again
in *Balaustion's Adventure*:

                    Any who could speak
A chorus to the end, or prologize,
Roll out a rhesis, wield some golden length
Stiffened by wisdom out into a line,
Or thrust and parry in bright monostich,
Teaching Euripides to Syracuse—
Any such happy man had prompt reward:
If he lay bleeding on the battle-field
They staunched his wounds and gave him drink and food;
If he were slave i' the house, for reverence
They rose up, bowed to who proved master now,
And bade him go free, thank Euripides!
Ay, and such did so; many such, he said,
Returning home to Athens, sought him out
The old bard in the solitary house,
And thanked him ere they went to sacrifice.

And the appeal of Euripides did not die. Greece kept more
of his plays than of any other poet; and Ennius and other Latins
read him, translated him, assimilated him.

                A chorus-ending from Euripides

says Bishop Blougram, in another of Browning's poems, and
comparing it with
                            , a sunset touch,
            A fancy from a flower-bell, some one's death,

he finds it has the same effect on his mind as the starry sky on
Lucretius, scattering and shattering the whole structure of
rationalism—much as Cicero used Ennius' copies of Euripides
to demolish Epicurus.[1]

But there were other poets, and they did the same thing; and
so did some of the writers in prose. It is strange to think of
Isocrates as one of the master-minds who influenced Greece, but
none the less it is true that a 'speech' of Isocrates—a pamphlet
or a tract we might say, that he had slowly written out—was
a factor in Greek life, as a century before an ode of Pindar had
been. Men read both writers for their matter, and learned far
more than they might at first guess from the touch of the artist;
it was thus that sentences had to be built; it was thus that the
poet saw the life of man. The change in outlook that Athens

[1] See p. 155.

made for all Greece is significant; the Athenian statesman had called the city 'the education of Greece'; and it was true. All that Greeks did had in the long run to be checked and judged by Athenian standards; and, what was more—and it reinforces what was said above—they came to feel that the real link that bound men together was not so much Greek blood in their veins as their response to the great ideas of Greek thinkers—a suggestion of our thesis. Let us take a rather wider range of survey.

III

Outstanding among Greek statesmen and economists was the 'sage' Solon. He created a new kind of city. Not so new, some will say; was not Miletus long before Athens a commercial city? It was indeed, and a great one, with a story that illustrates our thesis. But again and again in human story new significance is given to familiar facts by giving them a new name. The fresh phrase is interpretation, it illuminates and so it changes the bearing and value of what everybody knows and makes it new. Solon, in the happy phrase of a modern historian, associated the idea of the State with the conception of kindness. His first great measure he called by the poetic name of 'the shaking off of the burden'; in plain prose he enacted that a man's wife and children should not be sold to pay his debts, but that, instead, debts on land should be cancelled; and so he set the farm people, tenants or indebted free-holders, free in mind from the greatest of all dreads. They would stand by the State, now that it was a State to stand by; and they did. And during the 'tyranny' of Pisistratus and his sons the same feeling prevailed; the Alcmaeonids might hate the tyrant and go into exile; common people in later days called his reign the Golden Age. Further, just as England and Prussia, after the Revocation of the Edict of Nantes, opened their doors to French Huguenots, Athens became a city of refuge for honest men with families, who were sick of civil strife and interference in other towns. They came in numbers, like the Huguenots, and, like them, brought trades to their new home. Solon, as the late Greek historian pedantically and rather vaguely phrased it, 'put honour on trades'. A new city, like the old, no doubt—'like, but oh! how different!'—this city, of new outlook and new ideas and new

names, became the nidus of all that was to live in Greece or in
the world:

> Whate'er we hold of beauty, half is hers.

A century or so after Solon comes Herodotus, the first writer
of prose that Greece cared much to keep, not unaptly called by
a great Greek critic 'the most Homeric of men'.[1] He too could
tell a story that every man wanted to read—γραφικὸς γὰρ ἀνήρ[2]—
a story of national moment, of heroism, of great deeds, the
greatest of naval victories and of land victories, but not less the
story of other and subtler victories of the human spirit. For if
he avails mightily to make Greece conscious of its unity,
centuries later a captious Greek dubbed Herodotus 'a lover of
barbarians'—φιλοβάρβαρος. Why not? What was there of
shame in Carian blood? It ran in the veins of Herodotus, but
who was more Greek? He had praise for the national enemy;
the Persian was as brave and spirited a fighter as the Spartan,
but, armed with a bow and clad in a shirt, he was at a dis-
advantage against the man in armour. But it was a true
Homeric touch to admire the enemy. Pindar has it explicitly—
'if any of the citizens be friend—yea, even if he be foe—let him
not hide good work done for the common weal, and thus do
wrong to the word of the old man of the sea [Nereus]; for he
bade us praise with full justice and the whole heart even an
enemy, when he doeth high deeds of worth.'[3] It is not precisely
the same thing, but it shows the same spirit.

Herodotus goes further. In one place and another, he traces
Greek ideas to foreign sources—religious practices for instance,
derived, he holds, from Egypt and Libya, gods borrowed and
adopted (a point of which we shall have constantly to think)
and—in another range of ideas—the alphabet itself. Yes, and
he thinks more still might be borrowed—the straight simplicity
of Persian religious belief, the truer astronomy of the Egyptian
calendar, and perhaps when he emphasized that every Persian
taught his son three things, he meant further borrowing; for
might it not occur to his reader that it would be a good thing
for every Greek boy to learn to ride, to shoot with the bow and
to tell the truth? It is not unlike our modern ideals—so far as

---

[1] Longinus, 13, 3; and was he the only Greek who deserved the superlative?
he asks.   [2] Plutarch's phrase.   [3] Pindar, *Pythian*, ix, 93–96.

they are ideals in the true sense—and it was the 'national enemy' that suggested it. Lover of barbarians—it is really praise; and the same praise belongs to Xenophon and Alexander; these three men were the Greeks who knew the Persian best, and it was they who thought most highly of him. Trojan, Persian or Egyptian—real men, with real characters, and sound ideas—and in a later day Polybius adds the Roman to the list. It took time and thought to bring the Greek world to the feeling that it was wrong for a Greek conqueror to destroy a Greek city, to kill the men and sell the women and children into slavery. Alexander did it to Thebes—under provocation; a later king restored Thebes as far as possible; an *hetaira* was reported to have suggested that she would like to do it. Ought Greeks to sell Greeks into slavery? On the whole, they ought not to do this; barbarians, the philosopher suggested, stood on a different footing; they were by nature slaves; Nature intended them for slaves, built them on that principle; then why not sell them for slaves? It was long before the Stoics could get the world to see that this was a mis-reading of Nature; she had meant no such thing. And here such spirits as Homer and Euripides—yes, and Alexander himself, when he came to know Persian and Indian— told the Greek the same thing before the Stoic—not always in his language. But when Hector talks to Andromache about the fortunes of war and what it may mean for woman and child, are we to say his words, Homer's words, convey less than Epictetus or Seneca might put in a discourse or a 'moral epistle'?

Yet for all the splendour of Homer—in spite of the reverence and love he waked in the Greek boy—Plato, grown a man, found Homer defective. Homer could not be right in his pictures of the gods; somehow or other, those pictures revolted the moral sense; and it is worth while to ask how that came about. It did not come from the temples and the cults; the priests of Greece are not associated with the moral development of Greece. For one thing, they were not highly organized; and religion limited itself too closely to ritual and *taboo*. Certain things might be forbidden in the cult which the moralist also condemned; but the prohibition rested on very different grounds. The priest forbade a physical act; it was natural

enough perhaps, but after all *taboo*; the thinker looked at it in
another way; it injured the soul. Slowly enough, the moral
sense of Greece grew; and at last Plato claims it as the real
nature of man, the revelation of the real nature of God. Homer
has taught men what they should be; he has given ideals for
human character; may we not deduce something further from
this, somewhat on the lines of the modern Scottish poet—

> By all that He requires of me
> I know what God Himself must be?

Or, if that is too modern, there is a striking passage of Juvenal,
for once grave and clear of rhetoric—

> *ducimus autem*
> *Hos quoque felices, qui ferre incommoda vitae*
> *Nec jactare jugum vita didicere magistra.*

Vita magistra sums the thing up; Greece learnt her morality
taught by life; and that morality Plato applied as a test to the
Homeric gods, and they fell short of it. It was not the end of
them, if we are to be literal and stick to a blank chronology;
but spiritually it was the end of them, and throughout the
Greek world, and the Roman world, wherever men thought in
earnest, there was the problem of the gods to settle. In Virgil
we see the gods making their last great effort to conform at once
to Homeric standards and to Platonic, an endeavour at compromise, which failed. Euripides—for instance, and very
notably, in the *Trojan Women*—had drawn the traditional gods
against the background of human suffering; and Virgil had read
and assimilated Euripides; and his gods, divided in their
allegiance between Plato, Homer and the Stoics, were yet more
embarrassed by the claims of human life. Sainte-Beuve says
well that the coming of Christ itself has nothing to astonish us
when we have read Virgil. That a very great poet should have
such difficulties with the gods gives the measure of Plato's
influence.

That influence is still potent among moderns as among
ancients. Coleridge, for instance, declares: 'But I love Plato,
his dear *gorgeous* nonsense'[1]—a sentence not to be taken perhaps
too literally. Less humorously Gilbert Murray says something

[1] Letter to Thelwall, December 1796; see L. Hanson, *Early Life of Coleridge*, p. 301.

very similar: 'It is just this inconclusiveness of Plato's thought that has made it immortal. We get in him not a system but a spirit.'[1] James Adam, in a letter, wrote to me: 'There is none like him, none. It is tremendous how he searches the depths of one's whole being.' In short, the feeling of mankind is expressed by Cicero in a famous sentence:[2] *errare mehercule malo cum Platone...quam cum istis vera sentire*; and *isti*, if they were in the first instance the Epicureans, may serve for a good many schools.

Plato's criticism of Athens is notorious, but it is worth while to put it alongside of Greek comment on the two other great Greek cities of mixed origin. Syracuse, the Greeks said, owed its political ups and downs, its democratic interludes and occasional tyrannies (very successful tyrannies, by the way) to the central fact that its people were not knit together by blood and tradition. Alexandria was worse, a city, according to Polybius (no addict of superlatives), of brutal and beastly ways; he had seen them at work. The aberrations of the Athenian, as Plato describes them, were intellectual; the 'democratic man', whom he describes, has too much movement of mind, to one thing constant never. But in Athens young girls did not, as at Alexandria, take a hand in mob-murders. The Athenians had indeed put Socrates to death—'worse than a crime, a blunder', for which posterity has never ceased to condemn them. It is worth while however to recall certain other democratic outbursts; the savage hatred felt for 'pro-Boers' in England may be remembered, and the doing to death of Sacco and Vanzetti in the United States, where from revolutionary days (as 80,000 United Empire Loyalists who escaped to the Maritime Provinces and Canada might testify) the bottom fact in law has been very like *sit pro ratione voluntas*. Pro-Boers, Italian agitators and Socrates seem to belong to different categories; we forget what the Athenian contemporaries could not forget that Socrates had been a steady critic of Athens, an admirer (men thought) of the triumphant enemy Sparta, and, quite apart from conjecture, the known friend and teacher of the unprincipled Alcibiades and the hateful Critias. My point is that a democracy may be as unjust and outrageous as any other form of government—no

---

[1] Gilbert Murray, *Greek Literature*, p. 312.
[2] Cicero, *Tusc. disp.* i, 17, 39.

new discovery; but against this has to be set the other fact that Plato lived for years unmenaced in Athens, that his school survived him and his name was honoured. Mankind adopted Plato as they had adopted Homer; they went to Homer for heroes, to Plato for God—two prime needs of the human spirit. Once more, as we decided when talking of chess, the cypher, and sugar, we note that mankind is apt to be clear sooner or later about its needs, and to recognize what is 'good', to take it and keep it; and if we are to give a philosophical account of what is 'good', it is once more to Plato that we have to go.

It might even be urged that mankind at times goes too far in its passion for what is 'good'. Sugar, we all concede, has been a blessing to mankind; but the African may be forgiven for thinking it not an unmixed blessing. So with things of the mind. Plato's fierce resolve to keep Homer out of his ideal republic gives us a measure of Homer's influence in Greek religion. That has long ceased to trouble us; it did not much trouble Clement of Alexandria—Homer was Homer, chief of poets, to him, and the old gods were nothing, or so nearly nothing as not to interfere with his enjoyment of the poet. Similarly we find a protest against the influence of Plato himself. *Viderint*, says Tertullian—his great word of indignation—*viderint*, 'let them look to it, who have produced a Stoic, a Platonic, a dialectic Christianity'.[1] Plato and Christ, as early Christians had now and then to point out, did not quite see eye to eye. St Augustine was greatly influenced, for a period, by Neo-Platonic books, but in the seventh book of his *Confessions* he makes it clear that Platonism and the Christian religion involved different outlooks, a different range of ideas. None the less, the power of Neo-Platonism endured; Plato and his later more modern followers gave the Church many of its fundamental ideas. The poet Spenser is full of them. So little danger is there, if we may trust human experience, that the influence of a great teacher will be lost.

IV

Ten years after the death of Plato, a new era began with the accession of Alexander the Great to the throne of Macedon; and in this era the welding of mankind, as we call it, took on a new

[1] Tertullian, *de Praescriptione Haereticorum*, 7.

significance. It became, one might say, the dominant motive, or at all events the dominant characteristic of the age. 'If a man', wrote Pindar,[1] 'succeed in what he doth, he throweth into the stream of the Muses a sweet cause of song.' Few men of action have ever done so much to inspire their fellow-men— the fact being that men of action too often have been exclusively men of action, while Alexander was an idealist, a prince among idealists. And his ideals were ——? 'He was a lucky brigand— *felix praedo*', wrote the Roman Lucan, a thought that at least suggests some failure of insight. As much might have been said of Captain Kidd; it would have been an inadequate account of Robin Hood; and Alexander filled the minds of men for generations. His empire, if you must be matter-of-fact, collapsed; his last words, as recorded, about it, τῷ κρατίστῳ, might have forecast so much. Who was to prove 'the strongest'? There was no successor, there were too many; and the empire broke up. Three outstanding kingdoms—or, if you count Pergamum, four—survived, fragments of the great empire. But if the real history of mankind matters—a thing quite different from the lists of kings and civil servants and tax collectors—then it is clear that the real work of Alexander was never undone. It was, as we suggest, the welding of mankind.

He started as a Macedonian prince, but of Greek origin, the descendant, he believed, of Achilles—no idle dream, but an inspiration; and he read Homer interminably, the story of his great ancestor. And fresh inspiration, not very clear to us, but vivid for himself, came to him at the oracle of Ammon, at Siwah. And again fresh inspiration, when he overthrew Darius and found himself Great King, with new and interesting subjects in the Persian nobles—men who were not Greek, but not, he surmised, notably the worse for that; there was something great about the Persian, which was lacking in the Greek. Not everyone realized this; but Herodotus and Xenophon had had more than an inkling of it. And in India again there was fresh inspiration—and on the Indus river—and farther still out on the Indian Ocean. It was a life of revelation and inspiration, full of mistakes, if you like, and some crimes, if you are a precisian; but a life of new ideas. He gave the world new ideals, a new

[1] Pindar, *Nemean* vii, 11.

conception of a common humanity, of 'the marriage of Europe and Asia' (whoever invented the actual phrase), and of the new outlooks that such a 'marriage' might bring, of a new kind of empire, and new cities, and new trade routes, and a new mutual intelligence of all peoples. No human element in the world was to be irrelevant. The demagogues receded in importance; they had had their day, and those who survived were, if anything, more mischievous than their predecessors. It was to prove an age of kings and scientists and philosophers, of new schemes of rule, of new realizations of the world and its peoples—botany, natural history, astronomy, geography, humanity.

The 'sweet cause of song' may be our starting-point. We need not linger over the Choerilus tribe, the poor poetasters of antiquity; a glance at the Middle Ages tells us more. Five great bodies of song occupied the minds of medieval Europe; there were the epic of Troy, the epics of Charlemagne, of Arthur and of the Nibelungs, and not least among them was the story of Alexander—μελίφρον' αἰτίαν ῥοαῖσι Μοισᾶν ἐνέβαλε.[1] The five great themes represent the whole history of man as then known to Europe. The Ramayana and the poetry of Persia and China were so far unknown, though fragments of knowledge were filtering through. The fathers of the Church knew the name Βοῦττα, which, as spelled in Greek, suggests the doubled letter more strongly than popular pronunciation gives it to-day. The story of Buddha is incorporated, with other borrowed elements, in the great book of *Barlaam and Josaphat*.

Geography was a new thing after Alexander, an old passion of the Greeks indeed, dear to Aeschylus and the breath of life to Herodotus, but now a thing of new provinces. Alexander sailed down both branches of the Indus and sent Nearchus back by sea to Babylon; and about the same time Pytheas of Marseilles made his historic voyage to Pentland Frith. The days were past when the Danube cut across the stream of the Rhone; the Cassiterides had come on to the map, if you could be quite sure of their location—they were somewhere on the map; and the sleeping place of the sun in the far North was talked of. Botany, too, we learn, had made great strides under the protection of the great empires. Man was getting to know his world in

[1] Pindar, *Nemean* vii, 11.

earnest. Science was busy with it. Eratosthenes, quoted by Strabo, gives a fair estimate of the circumference of the globe— no flat earth, but a sphere; and, more significant perhaps, he said definitely that a man sailing out of Spain and sticking to the same latitude would reach the Indies—but that the immense width of the Atlantic might prevent it. It is worth recalling that Strabo's *Geography*, with this quotation from Eratosthenes, was printed in a Latin translation, in several editions, in the decades immediately before the voyage of Columbus in 1492, and it is hardly an idle guess that one or other of these editions had been in his hands. He was, we must add, helped in measure by a later calculation of the earth's circumference, which made it too small but effectually reduced the expected distance that would have to be covered on the sea. Such are the links between ancient Egypt and modern Spain—vital links, not mere antiquary work. But there were other men of science in Greek Egypt. Aristarchus of Samos scandalized the pious of those times as Galileo did the less pious of his day, by turning the earth out of the centre of the universe; Plutarch was greatly shocked by this revolutionary doctrine. Caesar, on becoming master of the Roman world, put an end to confusion in the calendar (which was three months wrong) by 'correcting the year to the course of the sun'; and he got his astronomy from Egypt; and, as we all know, it was good enough for Europe for fifteen centuries and for Britain for two more. A little time ago an outstanding mathematician told Cambridge that Archimedes would outlast Aeschylus; this seems optimistic—mankind does remember the names of some men of science, keeps them in manuals, in fact, but the poets, when they survive at all, are read in earnest. Mankind does not act as if it wanted to discard either the poet or the physicist.

But in many ways the most interesting effect of the campaigns of Alexander is to be seen in the world's new conceptions of deity—once again not wholly new in themselves, but full of a new significance. The Homeric Zeus told the gods in plain language that he was their master: let him throw out a golden cord and all the gods pull against him, and he would fetch them up, earth and sea and all—a naïve enough picture of omnipotence. Then we recall the tyrant of Sicyon who took a spite against the local hero, and resolved to clear him out—by establishing his rival of the days of his flesh in a competing shrine.[1] And one wonders what Adrastus looked like to men who went with Xenophon through the Kurd country, to men who reached India with Alexander—a small and distant attempt at divinity, one feels; so dim and far-away, that he could hardly count very much in these strange lands. The Orientals had their own gods, and some of them no inconspicuous figures, whatever the pantheon. So one surmises; and evidence accumulates of the greater gods of the Orient forcing their way into Western worship—Isis and Serapis from Egypt, Cybele from Phrygia, and, rather later, Mithras from Persia.

But what was more significant was the new trend to monotheism—not quite the monotheism of the Church and Islam, but a great central Original of all, with a hierarchy of deputy gods around him, rulers of provinces, men said. Alexander had for the moment made one world of the nations, and, even if his new world broke up, the conception remained. The successor kings were not without the dream that the heritage might again be united. It was not to be. But, as so often in human affairs, the same group of ideas is apt to be operative in more spheres than one. If Alexander united Greek republics and Asian monarchies in one great and amazing whole, it seemed at least germane that in things divine (the vague phrase is best) a similar concentration, a similar co-ordination, should be thinkable. Accordingly, we find the 'dear city of Zeus'—the coinage is that of Marcus Aurelius adapting an ejaculation of Aristophanes— 'says he "Dear city of Cecrops"; and thou—wilt not thou say "Dear city of Zeus"?'[2] In one way and another the universe is presented to men as a unity; and, eventually, in the fourth century, we find in the pages of Macrobius a long series of propositions, the drift of which is that all the gods are one god, manifested as the New Testament writer put it.

Meanwhile, monotheism looks rather like an abstract noun; and in the great solitude which the huge despotisms seemed to involve, as opposed to the snug and homely city states in which everybody, at least in theory, knew everybody else, and the gods, demi-gods or heroes were old and familiar local figures,

---

[1] Herodotus, v, 67.   [2] Marcus Aurelius, iv, 23.

men wanted more than an abstract noun to be the centre of their lives. The Homeric gods did not lend themselves to this affectionate devotion, which comes to be the essence of religion; and men and women turned to the more emotional divinities of Egypt and Asia, personal goddesses with personal interests. The individual asks more in a universe, which cuts him off from his old interests and leaves him nothing to do. The foreign rituals offered plenty of occupation for the mind; the great writers, one and another, take note of the new range of superstition. If Marcus Aurelius on the whole is content with an abstract noun—'Nature' can be very abstract—another note is struck by his contemporary Apuleius of Madaura, a note of exaggerative pietism. What is perhaps stranger—for Apuleius' deity is Isis, long entitled to such devotion—Julian the Apostate has a similar feeling for Athene.

Thus heaven as well as earth is remodelled; ideas are borrowed and new conceptions of religion spread, which have never been lost. Isis is no longer worshipped, no, nor Mithras; but what men and women sought in them, they have long sought elsewhere. The outcome of Alexander's campaigns and his concentration of empire is this new double movement in religion, anticipated (though the ancient world in the main ignored it) in Judaism—a double movement to belief in the unity of God and in His personality, an intellectual and an emotional conception linked. In other words, Homeric religion passes away for ever; the little local cults of an Adrastus or a black Demeter are transformed; Greece knows to-day a Saint Artemidos, a Saint Demetrius, a great Elias (once Helios, we are told). It took, however, a long time for Homeric religion to die out; almost to the end the Christian apologists afford evidence that it seemed worth attack. They say little enough about the mystery religions which have been so interesting to modern scholars. Probably both types of religion were to be met, if you knew where to look. There was still great variety; coin types preserved old figures and reminded men of old legends; but, in one way and another, it is plain that men thought of religion in new ways, asked more of it, and, with new demands and heightened instincts, looked one way and another for a valid faith. Forward movements and backward are to be seen; as always, new ideas provoke criticism and reaction, valuable habits of mind in the long run, clearing issues, raising questions and suggesting answers. 'A question is a sort of education, too', says someone in a book of Xenophon's. Alexander's conquest meant a gradual change in the religious outlook of mankind, which no backward swing availed to undo. The *Confessions* of St Augustine is an illuminative book; the old paganism has no appeal to him, but Platonism in its more modern form and the Oriental philosophy of Mani are in strong competition with the Christian religion. Intellectual interests are involved, for Manichaeanism broke down as a result of its bad astronomy, and Platonism was after all too abstract. A personal nexus was essential for a moral and religious life, and he found it in his mother's religion. But the whole story is unthinkable in the days of Aristophanes or Demosthenes; even Euripides, one feels, would have been perplexed by it and very doubtful of Augustine's conclusions, perhaps of his premises; but those premises came in after Alexander, and they remain. The modern man who thinks at all about religion thinks along lines suggested by Stoic and pietist of the Hellenistic period. 'Nothing worth keeping is ever lost in this world', says the student Schramm, in Browning's *Pippa Passes*, and as he develops his thesis, 'put Schramm's pipe into his mouth again', says one of his friends. Yes, shut his mouth, but has he not said something of moment, something conceivably true, relevant to our thesis of the welding of mankind, and suggestive after all of hope?

V

In a book recently published, a brilliant book, entitled *The Roman Commonwealth*, the new Headmaster of Harrow, Mr R. W. Moore, calls attention in his preface to the amount of space he has allowed to consideration of things Greek in a book about Rome. 'It may be observed', he says, 'that it is an essential part of our debt to Rome that she preserved for us so much of the Greek culture. The world of Greece in time runs into the world of Rome, so much so that it is hard to separate them, nor would such a separation be of great value. It is then no disproportion or distraction to subsume at certain points the Greek culture under the Roman. For we are taking the section

of a world.' Accordingly, in his ninth chapter, he deals at some
length (I take his list from his table of contents) with Mathematics, Physics, Astronomy, Geography, Medicine; and then
with Literature, Architecture, Sculpture and Painting. A previous historian of Rome of some note had, centuries before him,
suggested that a real history must be σωματοειδής, an 'organic
whole'. All the world must be included in the history of
Polybius. In earlier days the doings of the world (τὰς τῆς
οἰκουμένης πράξεις) had been, you might say, sporadically
treated, as they were held together by no unity of initiative,
results or locality;[1] but that was now impossible, or, at least,
it would not be consonant with truth; the real history must 'see
life steadily and see it whole'. Perhaps, in quoting this line,
I move from Polybius to Mr Moore; but that is my intention.
Our theme is the welding of mankind; and, in treating Roman
life as he does, Mr Moore is helping our thesis forward. To
reinforce the student Schramm, quoted from Browning a page
or two earlier, let us recall Emerson's couplet—optimistic as
Browning's student; but our thesis makes for optimism, whatever
deductions the matter-of-fact insist on making. Here then are
Emerson's lines, bold and sweeping in his own way, but so far
as Mr Moore's summary of Rome's incorporation of Greek ideas
goes, substantially true:

> One accent of the Holy Ghost
> A heedless world has never lost.

Take Mr Moore's list of subjects—one after another is handled
by Roman writers, not one of whom loses his nationality or
forgets that he is a Roman; but one and another, be the subject
Nature, Literature or Painting, naturally assumes himself to
be, as Tennyson puts it, 'heir of all the ages'. A passage in the
sixth *Aeneid* might be taken to imply that the Roman would
leave all these arts to the various Greeks, to concentrate on the
rule of the world—*hae tibi erunt artes*; but one has read Virgil to
little purpose, if he takes that passage at the foot of the letter.
All the wisdom of Greece is Virgil's heritage, and he entered
upon it, and gave it a higher meaning than it had gained even
from Cicero's handling of it. The two men did in their way

---

[1] Polybius, i, 3.

what Alexander had done three centuries before; he had linked Greece and the East, they linked Greece and the West—the Greece already linked with the East. Nothing that touched the human heart or the human mind was henceforth to be alien to Rome. And what they did for the intellectual and spiritual life of mankind, Caesar supported by his treatment of the political problems of the world. His work is in truth of the same order as Alexander's; he conquers the world to make sure for it a better and a higher life—a life, it is true, in which the demagogue and his adherents would have much less to say, but in which peace and personal freedom, literature and reflective living, would have more scope. The world under Augustus has very evidently lost something—has lost much we might say— that was of value in the Athens of Pericles—much! But much is saved and was never to be lost. It has been the fashion to talk of dark ages, and Dean Inge insists that they were really dark; but there is this to be said. The essence of culture is not to know all that was ever in the encyclopaedias, but 'to bring with you a heart that watches and receives'; and that heart was never quite lost even in the darkest days of decline and fall. New men of strange races surged into the Roman Empire, some of them savages, but some 'noble savages'. The German invader's mind was not to destroy but to absorb, and he kept enough to re-make the Western World.

The Christian poet Prudentius saw truly that there was meaning in the movement of History, that 'nothing moves with aimless feet'. If the modern reader does not quite put it as he does, is he not after all an advocate for our thesis? We began with chess and sugar and the cypher—things that man recognized as 'good' in their various ways; and we have seen how in matters of more moment mankind has done the same thing again and again, struck, and decisively, for the ideal—for Homer, for Plato, for Virgil—for God. The whole history of literature confirms our belief. Literature does not perish; men still read Homer and *Don Quixote*, Plato and St Paul; and it is growingly clear that the great things are not lost. In one passage and another the ancient critic, Longinus—it would be difficult to find a modern more alive—tells us the same story. What is the real thing in literature? he asks. What every age and every generation will read and enjoy; and why? Because the soul naturally—by nature—takes wings at the breath of the real thing and soars on high with proud uplift as glad and happy as if it had itself created what it finds so good. And he, we remember, cites 'the legislator of the Hebrews' as one who achieves 'the sublime'. And what he says is still true; the real things live and men will not 'do without them'. If the young man in *Locksley Hall* calls himself 'heir of all the ages', it is worth noting that the words come in an older book. Another is there described as 'heir of all things', and the writer implies, surely, that in God's universe real things are real and belong to the eternal order. Mankind is built with an instinct for the real; it may at times be slow in recognizing it; but it does recognize it and sticks to it and will not let it go. We have to reckon of course, as theologians and pessimists will tell us, with the devil and human stupidity, the government and the foreign enemy, all sorts of forces of evil, bent on disintegrating all that is good. And yet—mankind draws together in the quest of the best things; the welding, as a young critic friend of mine tells me, is 'not complete'; no, it is not complete, but we see it moving towards a greater fulness. Let us end with a famous suggestion of St Augustine's, very relevant to at least some of the ideas that we have been trying to handle:

fecisti nos ad te, et inquietum est cor nostrum donec requiescat in te.

Chapter V

A QUIP OF QUINTILIAN'S

Si vacet. The simple phrase haunted me. I had naturally taken
no exact note of the section and page where it belonged; but
the lexicon gave me a clue, and I found it—but in the wrong
place. *Si vacet*, then, will have been a qualification that Quintilian was apt to apply. Later on, reading Quintilian himself,
I found my passage. Two poets are mentioned as 'not unworthy
to be read'—which is not high praise in any case, and is heavily
reduced at once by the words *si vacet*—'if you have nothing
better to do'. One of these two poets was Rabirius, a name not
very familiar to students of literature. The historian Velleius
Paterculus, a satellite (they tell us) of Sejanus, couples Rabirius
with Virgil, as the two outstanding names of the reign of
Augustus. A military man's judgment—or an echo, perhaps,
of vague memories of the talk of men of letters; he is

> Moving about in worlds not realized;

but he thinks, no doubt, that he is saying the right thing.

In a long list of contemporary poets, Ovid spares half a line
and two words to Rabirius—*magnique Rabirius oris*. It has been
suggested that his phrase is not unlike Tennyson's account of
Milton—'O mighty-mouth'd inventor of harmonies'—a suggestion hardly to be taken very seriously. For look at the
passage; Milton is described as 'inventor of harmonies', and
one thinks not only of *Paradise Lost* but of *L'Allegro* and the
sonnets—a wide range in harmonies, assuredly; and the next
line speaks of the tremendous compass over which the harmonist
ranges in thought—'O skill'd to sing of Time or Eternity'; and
a third line, developing the idea of richness and variety of music,
adds the deeply English character of the man and the poet—

> God-gifted organ-voice of England.

Magni oris is a mere fraction of what Tennyson says; no real
equivalent. And, besides, it would be at least as well justified a
rendering of something else. Here let an old memory introduce

a variant suggestion—an old memory of a ship, and a pleasant
Southern voice on a sofa behind me explaining something
American to a British fellow passenger; a pleasant voice,
speaking of 'one of our great thinkers'. I listened; but I doubt
if the most savage critic of contemporary America would have
accepted the young man's estimate of his country and its
thinkers. He spoke of William Jennings Bryan—'the boy orator
of the Platte', that river of Nebraska, so like the orator himself
(men said), 'hundreds of miles long, eighteen inches deep, and
a mile wide at the mouth'. If you wanted a real native Latin
rendering of the apostolic phrase 'great swelling words of
vanity', would not Ovid's two words come pat for your purpose?

But, probably enough, Ovid neither thought of gifts like
Milton's, nor meant a fierce criticism of the late Rabirius.
Probably he meant very little; people who make lists of poets
with appropriate two-word labels must not be cross-examined
very closely. Perhaps Rabirius was what the Americans call
'orotund'; perhaps Ovid merely meant that Rabirius could roll
out a great resounding line, as a good many Roman and other
poets have been able to do—a resounding line, that might do
very well, like many in Lucan, taken by itself, less well in
connexion with the lines before and after it, and of no consequence at all if you read the page or the poem. This, of course,
is all conjecture; for we have not the works of Rabirius. *Si vacet*,
says Quintilian; and antiquity had not the leisure needed to
preserve his works; for it involves far more labour for a poet to
survive in manuscript than in print. Rabirius is lost—apart
from these three references in Quintilian and Velleius and Ovid,
and perhaps a few odd lines found somewhere—in a charred
manuscript of Herculaneum, it would seem. And the poet
coupled with him by Quintilian is also lost; people had 'something better to do' than to transcribe Pedo.

Quintilian is not really an unkind critic. He is quite explicit
in admitting that all sorts of writers have their merits—some
merits. George Dyer, if you read the Letters of Charles Lamb,
cannot believe that a whole epic could have been written
without some good lines here or there. A man must, by accident,
if nohow else, hit off a good line now and then. But it does not
necessarily mean that he will repay your reading him—unless,

indeed, you have the awful leisure of Robinson Crusoe's island and no other book. Gold miners, said Heraclitus, turn over a great deal of soil for a very little gold.[1] So said Heraclitus. In my Canadian days the Klondyke gold-field was opened up; and you will read about it in T. A. Rickard's *Through the Yukon and Alaska* and will probably remember the amazing picture of the huge crowd of gold-seekers climbing in single file over the Chilkoot Pass; and perhaps you will reflect on the millions of dollars worth of gold that they—some of them—took out of the icy river-bottoms and then on the still more millions they spent in getting that gold. It will be a sort of parable to illustrate George Dyer's hopes and their prospect of fulfilment. But that is not all. In his poem, *The Spell of the Yukon*, R. W. Service gives a very real view of the appeal of that life of the gold-seeker, the magic of the strange frozen land—

The freshness, the freedom, the farness—O God! how I'm
    stuck on it all—

and then something perhaps subtler,

> There's gold, and it's haunting and haunting;
>   It's luring me on as of old:
> Yet it isn't the gold that I'm wanting,
>   So much as just finding the gold.

That at least is a thrill worth some of the labour and the cost; but in George Dyer's quest, it must be *si vacet*—nothing else to do—for the gold he finds will be trifling (if he finds any), and it is hard to imagine the least exhilaration in the search. The stray good line of a sub-mediocre poet is scarcely worth such labour; that is Quintilian's point in his *si vacet*. You may stumble on the line in a book of quotations, or in someone's essay; or if you miss it, *facilis jactura*.

But, while ready to admit merits in many a book, Quintilian does not recommend reading them all. He urges the student to concentrate on the best authors (x, i, 20) and to read them repeatedly (x, i, 19), until his taste is formed (x, i, 58). Here he is moving on the same lines as Longinus, whose words are always worth remembering: 'Judgment in letters is the final fruit

---

[1] Quoted by Clement of Alexandria, *Strom.* iv, 2, 54, p. 565: χρυσὸν γὰρ οἱ διζήμενοι γῆν πολλὴν ὀρύσσουσι καὶ εὑρίσκουσιν ὀλίγον.

of long experience.' The soul, he says, is stirred by the true sublime and surges upward in joy and triumph, as happy as if it had itself created what it is enjoying. That is the immediate reaction, nobly conceived and nobly phrased. But time is part of the story. Time, says the French proverb, does not care to preserve what it has had no hand in making. Longinus recognizes how long time confirms the great achievement; has it been read and enjoyed over and over, in one generation after another, by men of different stocks and variant traditions? Oddly enough Aristotle adds a material point; it is the common man, it is *hoi polloi* with whom the great choices in literature rest.[1]

Do Englishmen of the twentieth century A.D. find in Homer what he gave to Greeks thirty centuries ago, in Cervantes what Spain found in him three centuries ago?—then the case is settled; Homer and Cervantes are no longer on trial; they are become (so to say) the judges. It is not how *you* estimate *them*; it is the question now, Are you fit for them? Can you respond to them? For it is with books as with certain musical instruments. Draw the bow across the violin, and the other violin will respond without being touched; the gong will sound in response to the clarion note across the hall. The great poet strikes a note, do you answer to it?

An instance. About the year 1910 Dr Rendel Harris was weather-bound in his house near Woodbrooke, the college in Selly Oak. He took from his shelves one thing or another to pass the time, and then a Syriac manuscript which he had had for some years—a manuscript, he fancied, of the Syriac version of the Old Testament psalter. But it was something else, a novelty, a new discovery; for it was a unique manuscript of the Odes of Solomon, identified beyond a doubt as the collection so called. But its date and its origin? And all the living theological schools of Christendom fell to discussing it. I chanced to be with Dr Harris in the Cambridge University Press when the great Jewish scholar Solomon Schechter came in and spoke. No, it was not a Jewish work, this collection of Odes; he 'could not place it in Judaism'. It was Christian then; but was it of the first or the second century? If it was of the first century,

---

[1] Aristotle, *Politics*, iii; p. 1281 b.

said a great German scholar, then all our current criticism of the fourth gospel was *kaput*. It was a great moment—that in which Rendel Harris identified his find. And then after two other years Dr Burkitt was reading William Wright's catalogue of British Museum manuscripts; and among them he came on a significant entry—a manuscript of the Odes of Solomon. William Wright had catalogued it without response. Some things, as St Paul said, are 'spiritually discerned' or not discerned at all; and that has to be remembered. Judgment in literature is indeed, as Longinus said, the last fine fruit of long experience. 'All the charm of all the Muses often flowering in a lonely word', wrote Tennyson of Virgil; and there are scholars, young and old, who miss that word. Ἀνέγνως ἀλλ' οὐκ ἔγνως—'you read it but you did not take it in', said the Greek of long ago. And what is the use of reading even the *Aeneid*, if you miss Virgil?

So much turns on what you are really looking for when you go to the poets. The Romans fancied *sententiae*—the aphorism, the great phrase, the quotable. But here Longinus comes to our aid once more; in real literature there is something more, something greater, than 'what is said'; it is what is divined, πλεῖον τοῦ λεγομένου τὸ ἀναθεωρούμενον[1] (7, 3). Or there is the story—'the fable' as some call it and once again the treatment is more than the tale. It may fall away into detached episode. In any case behind the treatment is the experience of the poet, his interpretation of life, as Matthew Arnold called it. Yes, there is the story; but is it relevant to man's life? Let us take an instance; at the beginning of the third *Aeneid*, after the fall of Troy, we read how Aeneas with his men sails away for the West. The story had been long growing; and there was a whole map of places which he visited, where he settled, where he founded shrines of Venus, his mother, where he was buried, and so on; there was no end of alleged facts—most of them of no human interest whatever, unless to the stray antiquary a-dreaming. The places are of little more interest than the intermediate stations which one's train may stop at, or shoot through, on a long journey, stations at which you do not alight.

---

[1] On this see the remarkable section in Augustine, *Confessions*, xii, 18, 27; and xii, 32, 43.

Yes, the Great Western goes through Reading, Didcot, Swindon, Chippenham, and the train may or may not stop; and then one recalls the bright enthusiasm of Quiller-Couch for Paddington station—it is in some sort 'the gateway of the West', lovable, though a railway station, in consequence. Aeneas leaves the Troad *et campos ubi Troja fuit*. It is the last word that counts. Troy is no more. The 'lonely word' reminds us of all we have read with 'beating hearts' (Sainte-Beuve's word) in the miraculous second book; and one recalls how from first to last Virgil is the poet of the exile—in *Eclogue, Georgic, Aeneid*, the Corycian, Evander, and how many more.

> *Me pulsum patria pelagique extrema petentem*
> *Fortuna omnipotens et ineluctabile fatum*
> *His posuere locis.*

And in all their stories is some echo of Virgil's own, some tone that shows us his heart and the things written in it. And the question rises of itself, Is the poet or is the poem of more significance? The question has been answered both ways by serious thinkers; the poem is more than the poet; the poet is more than his poem; the supreme expression of a great soul, or the great soul expressing itself or trying to express itself? which? Even if the endeavour be not wholly successful—*in magnis voluisse sat est*; and again the word of Longinus helps us—not what Virgil has said, but what we divine in his heart. And once again, it is a case of harmonies, of response between the one instrument and the other, in this instance both of them human hearts.

> *Allein sie haben schrecklich viel gelesen*

so Seeley quotes Goethe;[1] and whoever may have been the people who had read so terribly much, Goethe puts the same idea forward as a sort of general confession to Eckermann. 'We read far too many poor things, thus losing time and gaining nothing: we should only read what we admire' (vol. ii, p. 341, tr.; 9 March 1831). In another place, he repeats his last thought from another angle with even more emphasis. 'Everywhere we learn only from those whom we love' (Eckermann, p. 264). But there is a temptation for some scholars in the idea of reading

---

[1] J. R. Seeley, *Goethe*, p. 104.

everything of a period. The late Professor Saintsbury would appear to have done something of the sort in the preparation of some immensely learned chapters in the *Cambridge History of English Literature.*

> Let not ambition mock their useful toil—

no, nor let ambition pretend it to be useful in any very high degree. The Greeks knew that type of scholar, and called him χαλκέντερος. Bentley said of Warburton that he had a voracious appetite for knowledge, but he doubted whether Warburton had a good digestion.[1] In the *Comments of Bagshot* scholars of this type are characterized as men of science astray. Their ideal is wrong; they forget the caustic Heraclitus who is still right— 'polymathy', he said, 'does not develop the mind' (νοῦν οὐ διδάσκει); and to develop the mind, that critical faculty of which Longinus speaks, is the real purpose in the study of literature. 'I wish', wrote Crabb Robinson in his diary (31 March 1816), 'I could keep my hands off worthless books.'

It is the masterpiece that educates, and to the masterpiece everything must be referred. The ancient moralist, particularly if a Stoic, bade the disciple always have before his eyes the example of some great man; very generally it was Socrates, sometimes Zeno, in either case one of the greatest of human characters so far known; how would that great man have acted, how would he have reacted to the stimulus whatever it was? That was the test in conduct. In the same spirit Longinus offers three suggestions to the man ambitious of writing well. Whatever the theme, ask yourself how the man of genius who treated that theme and cognate themes in the past would handle it; imagine Homer, Thucydides, Demosthenes, busy with your task. Or, secondly, and better, imagine them listening to you as you read what you wrote—which in ancient days was sometimes a synonym for reading it themselves; how would Homer enjoy, or tolerate, *your* handling of epic? And his third rule is, Ask yourself what a future generation will make of your attempt at literature. This is a development of Quintilian's bidding to concentrate on the best. Adam Smith says much the same: 'You will learn more as to poetry by reading one good poem than

---

[1] Monk's *Bentley*, vol. ii, p. 410.

by a thousand volumes of criticism.'[1] By *reading* one good poem
he obviously means a more intensive study, a closer assimilation,
than we commonly give to text-books and newspapers; and by
'a good poem' we may be pretty sure he meant the best poetry,
the supreme poem rather than the merely admirable. Once
again a deep knowledge of Virgil carries a man beyond the
literary critics, and *a fortiori* far beyond the tribe of Lucan and
Silius. You must be quite sure that you have nothing better
to do—no fresh insight to gain into Virgil—before you spend
time on Rabirius. We read that Aristarchus said that the best
commentator on Homer was—Homer.[2]

Nor is this only true in the sphere of poetry. Quintilian has
the same conception as to prose, which he phrases rather
differently. 'Let a man understand that he has made real
progress when he finds intense enjoyment in Cicero' (*Ille se
profecisse sciat cui Cicero valde placebit*).[3]

Si vacet. It is a great principle that Quintilian gives us,
positively and negatively. The second best will not do. Homer
nods, as we all remember being told by one of his great ad-
mirers; yes, and Apollonius does not nod, says Longinus: which
would you prefer to be? Supreme genius blundering—or great
gifts, ingeniously applied? Why was there so much talent and
so little genius in Hellenistic literature? The question is asked
and there is no very clear answer.[4] With a quip of Horace let
us end. An interesting character in an American novel declares
that 'a middling doctor is a poor thing, and so is a middling
lawyer; but save *me* from a middling man of God'.[5] Horace
adds the poet to this list—a middling poet? No! Gods and
men won't endure it, nor the booksellers either.

[1] John Rae, *Life of Adam Smith*, p. 370.
[2] Cf. J. W. H. Atkins, *Literary Criticism in Antiquity*, vol. i, p. 188.
[3] Quintilian, x, i, 112.
[4] M. Cary, *Greek World*, 323–146 B.C., p. 342.
[5] Owen Wister, *The Virginian*.

Chapter VI

POLYBIUS AT ROME

I

It was the year 168 B.C., and Antiochus Epiphanes, chiefly famous with posterity for his futile persecution of his Jewish subjects, had realized that he might without much difficulty conquer Egypt. There was dissension among the Ptolemies which meant opportunity, while, since the death of Alexander in 323 B.C., there had never failed pretext. Alexander had been monarch of all mankind—apart from barbarians in the West; and Philip V of Macedon put the thing in a nutshell—'the big fish eat the little fish'. Polybius notes that this Macedonian dynasty always seemed to cherish the idea of reuniting the empire of Alexander. So Epiphanes, the King of Syria, would begin by adding Egypt to his family heritage. He raised his troops, organized his campaign, marched, and was on the borders of Egypt, when a Roman envoy appeared.

They greeted from afar, the King using his voice and outstretching his hand, but the Roman did not take his hand. He held out a document to him; the King should read it before courtesies went further, that they might know how they stood. The King took the document, and read it; it was a resolution of the Senate at Rome, blunt enough. Not unreasonably he said he would discuss it with his friends before he answered. No! said the Roman; and then, says our historian, 'he did a thing which was looked on as offensive and thoroughly insolent (βαρὺ μὲν δοκοῦν εἶναι καὶ τελέως ὑπερήφανον). For he had in his hand a stick cut from a vine, and with it he drew a circle round Antiochus, and ordered him before he stepped out of it to give his decision about what was written. The King was surprised by this haughty act; but, after a few minutes' hesitation, he said he would do all that the Romans demanded. Then Popillius and his suite shook him by the hand one and all, and greeted him in friendly fashion. The letter told him to be done with the war against Ptolemy then and there. A fixed number of days was allowed him, and he withdrew his forces to Syria—angry and groaning, but yielding.'[1] Two things, no doubt, conspired to decide his action; he knew that Perseus, King of Macedon, had been defeated and finally ruined at the battle of Pydna earlier in the year; and he had been himself, earlier in life, a hostage in Rome for thirteen years and knew the Romans. His surrender was a notice to all the world, which all the world understood; the Romans were masters of all the world, and such kings as were still allowed their thrones had to obey. The King of Bithynia, Prusias II, had the odd inspiration to attire himself like a manumitted slave and to describe himself in so many words as 'the freedman of the Romans'.[2] Eumenes of Pergamum, proposing to visit the Senate, was forbidden to come. A quaestor met him at Brindisi as he landed; what did he want? he was to say at once, and, if he did not want anything, he was to leave Italy at once. He wanted nothing, he said, and went home, thoroughly understanding what was meant; and so did his enemies, the Gauls of Galatia, who were 'doubly encouraged to press on their war with him'.[3]

So much for kings; and the Greeks at large realized how well the Aetolian Agelaus had prophesied in 217 B.C. about the 'clouds in the West'.[4] The gesture of Flamininus in proclaiming at the games the 'freedom of all the Greeks'[5] was transitory; there was great acclaim

> Yet were the thoughtful grieved; and still that voice
> Haunts, with sad echoes, musing Fancy's ear:
> Ah! that a *Conqueror's* words should be so dear:
> Ah! that a *boon* could shed such rapturous joys!
> A gift of that which is not to be given
> By all the blended powers of Earth and Heaven.

Wordsworth was right, whether he had realized or not that it was the regular move among kings of the Macedonian dynasties to proclaim the liberty of Greeks. Polybius tells us of rival liberators, kings both, busy at once. Now another line was taken. A Roman envoy demanded of the Achaean League that all the men, named by a traitor Callicrates, as partisans or

[1] Polybius, xxix, 27.   [2] Polybius, xx, 18 (19).
[3] Polybius, xxx, 20.   [4] Polybius, v, 104.
[5] Polybius, xviii, 46.

friends of King Perseus should be sent for trial to Rome.
A thousand or more were named, and to Italy they were sent.
It is thought that the League Assembly voted this, in view of
a hypocritical rejoinder of the Senate to a plea for the liberation
of these men[1]—'the Senate was surprised tha they [the
Assembly] should apply to them for a decision on matters which
the Assembly had already themselves decided'. Hatred could
be keen enough among Greek politicians in ordinary times. But
here were a thousand leading Achaeans from all over the League
handed over to the Romans by a political opponent—surrendered
for trial on account of alleged services to the lost Perseus,
actually got rid of by a cunning opponent and never tried at
all—simply detained, distributed among Italian towns (largely
in Etruria) the boundaries of which they might not leave; and
there they were kept year in, year out—sixteen years unless they
chanced to die earlier. Their opponent, who had betrayed them,
did not retain his hold on the League, and again and again
embassies were sent to beg for their freedom or at least for their
trial. It was of no use. The Senate's reply was negative, doubly
negative—'We do not think it the interest either of Rome or of
your *dêmoi* that these men should return home'.[2] Your *dêmoi*—
the word meant parishes at Athens, here it was to mean
localities; in other words the Senate told them that Rome did
not recognize the League and would neither try nor liberate
the captives. Rome had to stand in with Callicrates and his
partisans. The result for the captives and their friends was 'utter
despair and paralysis of soul', all hope was lost. Polybius, on
another occasion,[3] speaks of the ravaging of land, the destruction
of trees and gear, leaving no place for repentance. A great
mistake, he says, to deprive men not only of present good but
of hope for the future; it makes men into beasts (ἀποθηριοῦντες)
and creates hatred that is ineradicable. The Italian captivity
was like Dante's hell—'All hope abandon, ye who enter here'.

'Utter despair and paralysis of soul'—ὁλοσχερὴς ἀθυμία καὶ
παράλυσις τῆς ψυχῆς. The injustice of the Romans, the hateful
treachery of fellow-citizens, the dragging years, the repeated
refusal to listen to embassies or to try the prisoners, and then

[1] Polybius, xxxi, 8.   [2] Polybius, xxx, 32 (Loeb edition).
[3] Polybius, xxiii, 15.

the death of one and another till after sixteen years two-thirds of their number were dead in exile. Exile is a word with painful suggestions in any community, but nowhere had it more misery than among Greeks. The centuries had revealed to what lengths of savagery Greeks would go to escape exile or to avenge it. These exiles had no such opportunity; there was nothing for them but ineffectual hate, utter despair and paralysis of soul. This was what the Roman domination of the world meant. To be sane, a man must reach some judgment upon life, some interpretation of life in Matthew Arnold's phrase. Perseus, Antiochus, the League—the strange concatenation of events round 168 B.C.—the raw injustice of the captives' fate—what could it all mean? Men in that age speculated on Fate and Fortune; they did for centuries; they do still. And Polybius quotes a writer of 'a hundred and fifty years ago'.[1]

'One is often reminded, and only too much, of the words of Demetrius of Phaleron. For in his treatise on Fortune, wishing to give men a perfectly distinct view of her mutability, he fixed on the period of Alexander when he overthrew the Persian Empire. This is what he says: "If you will consider not endless time nor many generations, but only these last fifty years before us, you will be able to understand in them the cruelty of Fortune. For, fifty years ago, do you think that the Persians or the King of the Persians, or the Macedonians or the King of the Macedonians, if some god had foretold them what would be, would ever have believed that at the time when we live the very name of the Persians, who once were masters of nearly the whole world, would be utterly lost, and that the Macedonians would conquer it all, a people whose very name was formerly unknown? But nevertheless Fortune, who makes no treaty with our life, who always defeats our calculation by some new stroke and displays her power by her surprises, is even now, I think, showing to all mankind by planting the Macedonians into the high prosperity of the Persians, that she has merely lent them these blessings until she changes her mind about them." This has come about in the case of Perseus. Demetrius, as if by the mouth of some god, uttered these prophetic words about the future. And I, as I wrote and reflected on the time when the

[1] Polybius, xxix, 21.

Macedonian kingdom was destroyed, I judged it to be right not
to pass over it without remark. I was an eye-witness of what
befel. It seemed to me my part to say the fitting word and
quote Demetrius. For he seems to me in this utterance to have
been more divine than a mere man; for nearly a hundred and
fifty years ago he made a true forecast of what was to happen
afterwards.'

Was there rhyme or reason in the course of human affairs, in
history, in the individual life? That was the question; and it is
clear that for long Polybius leaned to the suggestion of Demetrius;
a good many references can be gathered about *Tyche* doing this
or that; and, as one reads the history of the Hellenistic kingdoms,
there are certainly odd occurrences, unexpected events and so
forth, which dislocate the lives of individuals and sometimes
have some bearing on the history of peoples. The problems,
then, before Polybius or any other of his fellow-captives are
two—is it really Fortune, and she alone, that disposes events
for great nations; and, if the answer to that question is negative,
then the second becomes urgent, what is the explanation of
Rome's unexampled dominance in the whole world and of
the strangely short period of time in which she was able to
acquire it?

But before we attempt his answers to his problems, a little
should be said about the man who is trying to solve them. He
was an Arcadian of Megalopolis, the son of a prominent
statesman in the Achaean League, Lycortas; and somehow one
feels that from childhood he lived and moved in a political
atmosphere. He was about thirty-two years of age, when he was
deported. He had held office in the League as *hipparch*, which
may or may not have involved duties with cavalry. In any case
he was interested in army matters all along—a soldier as well
as a politician. He had been sent, no doubt in a minor capacity,
on some mission to Egypt and had seen Alexandria. He had
spent some part of 169 B.C. in the Roman headquarters in
Macedonia (xxix, 24). He had taken some part at the funeral
of Philopoemen, the patriot of the League, and had been in
some contact with him while he lived; and at some date not
determined Polybius wrote a life of Philopoemen. The fact that
he also was denounced by Callicrates may or may not be

evidence of some importance or promise. There cannot have been a thousand persons of exceptional significance; Callicrates cast his net widely, and was resolved not to have an opposition. It was like the new king in the Gospel story who made sure by having the opposition rounded up—'bring them hither and slay them before me'. Callicrates was saved that trouble; the Romans took them for him. As son of Lycortas and himself beginning to climb the political ladder, it was inevitable that Polybius must go.

But the point to be noticed is that he went already a man of some experience, bred in politics, and quick to recognize what was going on, and, noticeably, the relation between events. The year 168 had seen the collapse of Perseus, and the surrender of Antiochus, and in 167 had followed the triumph of the wretched Callicrates. This conjunction of events affected his thinking; he looks out on the whole world and takes a conjunct view (σωματοειδής is his word i, 3; iii, 32); history must be universal. And his experience gave him another principle, which he expresses in the long and clumsy word αὐτοπάθεια (xii, 25, 7)—a typical Hellenistic word, like too many in his pages. Long and ugly that polysyllable may be, but it represents a real idea. The historian must himself have done things (cf. xii, 25), seen things (cf. xii, 27), had personal contacts and taken part in some measure in great counsels and great actions. Otherwise he is exposed to the danger of what Polybius caustically calls the βιβλιακὴ ἕξις—the 'document habit' we might call it, or, worse still, the habit of mind that depends on other men's books (xii, 25, h, 3), the failing of Timaeus, who did his work on a sofa at Athens for fifty years (xii, 25, h). This does not mean that the historian is not to read; we shall see that a very significant library was in the house that Polybius frequented. Polybius had been a hunter in Arcadia and continued to hunt in Italy, and when he compares Timaeus to the painter who painted stuffed animals, his meaning is clear. The painter needs to know the living animal, and so, he suggests, does the historian. But perhaps we are looking ahead too quickly.

II

To Italy then in 167 Polybius went, and there he stayed for sixteen years. He was perhaps not so strictly limited in his movements as some of his friends. At all events he gives his readers a survey of Italy, and we recall that one part of αὐτοπάθεια was *autopsy*; the historian must have *seen* sites, cities and scenes of action for himself. But Rome was more than the centre of a geographical area, and he became acutely interested in her history. He deals with the first Punic War, for which (as for much else) he is among our chief authorities, if not far and away the chief; but it is more upon the half century before the year of great events that brought him to Italy, that he would concentrate the reader's attention—the 'less than fifty-three years' in which the Romans brought nearly the whole inhabited world under one rule (i, 1, 5). Again and again he emphasizes that it is not so much the fact that is important as the cause— the why and the how; and he asks, in that prelude, 'who is so worthless or so indolent as not to wish to know by what means and under what polity' the Romans did it all. To that we must return. Meanwhile the achievement of Rome. Of prime importance is Hannibal. The vast scope of operations involved and the spirit with which both sides pursued their purpose demand attention (viii, 1); Sicily, Spain, Italy itself are at stake, and the war is ended in Africa. The battle of Zama was one 'on which everything depended and which assigned universal dominion to the Romans' (ἡ μὲν οὖν ἐπι πᾶσι γενομένη μάχη καὶ τὰ ὅλα κρίνασα 'Ρωμαίοις, xv, 15).[1]

He tells us that Rome could muster against Hannibal 70,000 horse and 700,000 foot (ii, 24); that the Punic invaders brought against all this rather less than 20,000 men; but then they were led by Hannibal.

'Who could withhold admiration for Hannibal's generalship, courage and power in the field, who that considers the length of this period [218–204 B.C.] and reflects on the general engagements and minor battles, the sieges, the revolutions and counter-revolutions in states, the vicissitudes of fortune, and in

---

[1] Cf. xv, 9, 2, the Romans fighting περὶ τῆς τῶν ὅλων ἀρχῆς καὶ δυναστείας; cf. xv, 10, 2. Mr Paton in the Loeb translation in xv, 15 takes τὰ ὅλα as referring to the whole operations of the war—not quite without warrant.

fact the course of his design and its execution in its entirety? For fourteen continuous years Hannibal maintained the war with the Romans in Italy, without once releasing his forces from service in the field, but like a good pilot keeping those great numbers free from sedition against himself or among themselves, though his armies, so far from being of one nation, differed also in race. He had Libyans, Spaniards, Ligurians, Celts, Phoenicians, Italians and Greeks, who neither in law, custom, speech nor anything else had any natural affinity. Yet the skill of the commander was such that those differences, so manifold and so wide, did not disturb the obedience to one word of command and to a single will.'[1]

It is a noble portrait of a great soldier; and it will be noticed that nothing is said of his owing his great successes in all these years of war to Fortune. Similarly when Syracuse is besieged, its long resistance is due to the great Archimedes, and again not to Fortune. And Rome's victory over Hannibal—can it have been the reckless work of Chance, or Fortune—$\tau\acute{v}\chi\eta$—'displaying her power by her surprises'? We begin to divine the answer to one, or to both, of his main questions.

Whatever the translation of $\tau\grave{a}$ $\acute{o}\lambda a$ in the passage about the battle of Zama, there is no doubt that the victory was a decisive event in the world's history. The overthrow of Philip and of Perseus followed in turn, and the subjection and humiliation of Epiphanes and the Achaean League. Rome was supreme, and it begins to be felt, at least by the Romans and by their German apologist, that such a supremacy left weaker powers no right to consideration or to justice. *Hoc volo, sic jubeo, sit pro ratione voluntas*—the words that the Roman satirist puts into the mouth of the Roman woman, might have been used by the Senate. Indeed, their language to the Achaean League is little different; it was the kind of talk used by King Artaxerxes when he dictated the so-called King's Peace in 387 B.C.—unless his employment of the word 'just' makes a difference. Constant Martha makes a rapid survey of the actual deeds of a group of great Romans whom we are shortly to see from another angle. 'Is it for justice', he asks, 'that Scipio Aemilianus will blot out the cities that are the rivals of Rome, that Laelius, future president of

[1] Polybius, xi, 19.

the repressive commissions, will pursue with atrocious severity the friends and partisans of the Gracchi, that Furius Philus, as consul, will violate without shame the treaty made with the Numantines, that Galba will massacre 30,000 disarmed Lusitanians, that Cato will demand with so much persistence the entire destruction of Carthage?' He might have added a sentence from Polybius (xx, 16, (15) = Strabo, C 322)— 'Aemilius Paullus took seventy cities in Epirus, after the conquest of the Macedonians and Perseus, most of which were in the country of the Molossi; and enslaved one hundred and fifty thousand people'. And it must be remembered that 'enslaved' is not a metaphor; it embodies the bleak fact that 150,000 of the inhabitants were sold as slaves. So strong and so definite is the supremacy of Rome; what is its explanation?

But that is not all. A hundred years later Cicero speaks of all the wealth of all the world becoming massed in a few hands, while Rome looks on and nothing is said; it has been going on for many years.[1] It was true, and Polybius witnessed it—'after the destruction of the Macedonian kingdom the universal dominion [of the Romans] was undisputed, and after the riches of Macedonia had been transported to Rome, there was a great display of wealth in men's private lives and in public affairs'.[2] In particular, the art of conquered peoples was pillaged freely. Polybius discusses the removal of the art treasures of Syracuse in 212 B.C., quietly and sensibly;[3] it was in its way reasonable, for people aiming at world empire, to appropriate all the gold and silver of the conquered—such things were clearly factors in the enemy's strength and their confiscation would increase the strength of Rome. But paintings and reliefs did not add to military strength, and to take them was invidious. Cato had comments to make on the spoils of Syracuse. Again in 189 B.C. Marcus Fulvius Nobilior took Ambracia, by agreement; he allowed the Aetolian garrison to leave the town, but he took away the objects of art (τὰ ἀγάλματα), statues and pictures, of which there was a great number, as Ambracia had been the royal seat of Pyrrhus.[4] So it went on; and Mrs Eugénie Strong says that by about this time Rome was 'the greatest museum

[1] Cicero, II in Verrem, v, 48, 126.   [2] Polybius, xxxii, 11 (xxxi, 25, Loeb).
[3] Polybius, ix, 10.   [4] Polybius, xxi, 30 (=xxii, 13); cf. Livy, xxxviii, 9.

of the world'.[1] When in 146 B.C. Corinth fell, Polybius records
what he saw—pictures thrown on the ground and soldiers
playing draughts (πεττεύοντας) on them; and he names two
famous pictures so used.[2] But Polybius managed to save the
statues of Philopoemen, he adds, for which service even a modest
historian may be forgiven for saying that a marble statue was
set up of himself. The art acquisitions of Verres in Sicily a
century later hardly need to be recalled; and Pausanias tells
us that again a century later (or a little more) Nero removed
from Delphi five hundred statues of gods and men, robbing
Apollo.[3] Pliny however says—or the extant text says—that some
thousands of statues were left at Delphi.[4] When Byzantium
became Constantinople, it also was adorned with works of art
collected from such places as still had them; and when the
Goths entered Rome at last, the city had incredible numbers
of statues.

Side by side with this passion for annexed art flourished other
interests. Gladiator shows were in high favour, and Terence
sadly records how an audience forsook a play of his for the sight
of some boxers. But a story from Polybius dated 167 B.C.—the
year of his arrival—will suffice. Lucius Anicius in that year
included in the celebration of his triumph a great performance
of celebrated flute-players; but they did not please him, he
wanted more spirit (ἀγωνίζεσθαι μᾶλλον). Perhaps he had
misunderstood the meaning of the Greek ἀγών. At all events the
flute-players at last saw what he wanted and made a suitable
pandaemonium—a proper battle (ἐκ παρατάξεως ἀγωνιζομένων).[5]
As we read this story, it is of interest to remember what Polybius
says of his native Arcadia and the training in music given to the
boys, with the result that, while elsewhere men hire musicians,
in Arcadia they make their own music.[6] One can only suppose
that this was a part of the education of Polybius himself. No
wonder he found the flute-players' episode ludicrous, as he says.

So much for the general aspects of Rome, victorious, increased
with goods, turning to art and showing signs already of a
brutality, primitive or degenerate, which was in years to come

---

[1] Eugénie Strong, *Art in Ancient Rome*, vol. i, p. 73.
[2] Polybius, xxxix, 2 (13) (=xl, 7); quoted by Strabo, C 381.
[3] Pausanias, x, 7, 1.   [4] Pliny, *Nat. Hist.* xxxiv, 36.
[5] Polybius, xxx, 14 (22).   [6] Polybius, iv, 20.

to produce terrible results. The problem is still before us which Polybius had to solve, if he was to think and to remain sane; what was the explanation of Rome's greatness? We have yet to look at the intellectual life of Rome, into which Polybius found an entry.

III

One does not read far in Cicero before one discovers that it was to this period of Roman history above all others that he looked back with admiration and regret—the golden age, which is always apt to be one or two generations behind us. If we say that Cicero idealized the middle years of the second century B.C., we shall probably be right, but it does not follow that he was wrong because he idealized them. The Roman people, and notably the Roman Senate, had faced gigantic tasks and a supreme peril, and had come through victorious. It was not unlike the age of Elizabeth or of Chatham in our own history; no doubt there were dark patches in England and in Rome in the periods of which we think, 'nevertheless', as Pindar says, 'when a glory from God hath shined upon them, a clear light abideth upon men, and life serene'.[1] Cicero does not quote this passage of Pindar, but it represents more or less his feeling about the period of the younger Scipio, of Laelius and of the great Cato, 'citizen, senator, general, a man in a word eminent at once for prudence and diligence and indeed every virtue'.[2] Ennius had recently died; Lucilius and Terence were still writing—unless indeed we are to accept the odd Roman anticipation of the Baconian heresy, that Laelius was the real author of Terence's plays.

Plutarch picks two men of the period as subjects for biography, both of interest, Aemilius Paullus the conqueror of Perseus, and the old Cato himself. As one reads that life of Cato, one feels that Cicero has indeed idealized the old man. Granted that he was, as we read just now in the *Brutus*, 'citizen, senator, and general', adorned with every virtue and so forth, the Cato whom Plutarch pictures is not quite the benign old sage of the *de Senectute*, but the Cato that his own day knew, forceful, shrewd, pungent of speech, with a good many traces about him of the

---

[1] Pindar, *Pythian* viii, 95.   [2] Cicero, *Brutus*, 294.

promoted peasant, with the peasant's tastes in elemental pleasures, e.g. occasional festive intoxication, and the peasant's sense of the value of money. If we are to believe that he studied Greek in his old age, and like Solon grew old learning many new things, we might also apply Horace's *amore senescit habendi*. They tell us that his *de Re Rustica* betrays the presence of a revising hand; perhaps, but it still reminds one of Plutarch's *Life* in places. But great men have to be accepted as they are—to be 'painted with their warts'—and Cato stands out as a great man, if not in the annals of mankind at least in his own age, a characteristic and significant figure. We shall find at the end a contact between him and Polybius, which suggests earlier and very friendly relations. It is the Cato we know in Plutarch—rough-spoken, shrewd but kindly.

But beside these Romans, there were also Greeks of some historical importance in Rome. There was Panaetius of Rhodes, a Stoic and the intimate friend and fellow-traveller of Scipio. It was work of his which Cicero says he 'followed but did not translate' in the first two books of his *de Officiis*.[1] It was remarked by Sir John Mahaffy that Polybius is silent about Panaetius, and he wonders whether Polybius a little exaggerated his own influence with Scipio—in other words, may have been somewhat jealous of Panaetius.[2] Heitland inclines to agree with him, but aptly observes that we have Polybius' history only in a fragmentary state, so that any allusion made may have been lost.[3] Warde Fowler says that Polybius introduced Panaetius to Scipio;[4] the German, Wunderer, thinks that Polybius owed much to Panaetius,[5] though he does not name him. A comparison of their dates seems to reveal that Panaetius was some twenty years younger than Polybius.[6] Whatever the facts about their feeling for each other, there can be no doubt as to their acquaintance, quite apart from the picture that Cicero draws of the two of them in conversation with Scipio on the subject of the State.[7] We can well believe that such discussions took place among them; and, if they did, it cannot have been without real

---

[1] Cicero, *ad Atticum*, xvi, 11, 4 (Tyrrell and Purser, no. 799); *de Officiis*, ii, 60.
[2] Mahaffy, *Silver Age*, p. 93.　　[3] Heitland, *Roman History*, § 659.
[4] *Social Life in Rome*, p. 114.　　[5] Wunderer, *Sprichwörter bei P.*, p. 55.
[6] The dates are: Polybius, c. 200 to c. 120 B.C.; Panaetius, 180–111 B.C.
[7] Cicero, *de Republica*, i, 21, 34; cf. Velleius Paterculus, i, 13.

illumination to the exile, wrestling with the problems, which we have recognized to have occupied him.

Panaetius is credited with toning down the harsher aspects of the older Stoicism, and becoming one of the pioneers of the great influence which Stoicism had upon the lawyers of Rome and through them upon the law of the world. Roman law was already being modified in the direction of sense and humanity by the conception of *Jus Gentium*, the law common to the races of men, chiefly of the Italians to begin. The conception of principle pervading law had early been introduced, and the Twelve Tables had been a staple in the education of Roman boys. The Stoic brought in a new and greater principle; what was the origin, he might ask, of so many coincidences among the laws of all states—of those coincidences on which the *Jus Gentium* rested; what could it be but the Law of Nature? Nature lay at the base of the Stoic conception of the world and of all human life; Nature had made men thus and so, and had implanted certain things in the mind of man, which could not be rooted out. These were obvious physical laws which conditioned the life of men—laws of food, rest, growth and reproduction: and there were moral laws, laws of thought too, which were as valid. In so far then as man's legislation coincided with what Nature had already made inevitable foundations of all human life, man's laws would be right and valid. The consensus of mankind was a Stoic principle; where all men agreed, in spite of the differences of stock, state and age, they were probably right; all men believed in gods of some kind and in divination—consequently to disbelieve in these, to reject the unanimous movements of the human mind, was to incur danger of error, which Nature would punish with disaster. Apply this reasoning to law, and the *Jus Gentium* is reinforced; it represents assembled fragments of the Law of Nature. It was a grave doctrine, which appealed to men, possessed already of the conception of law based on principle; it explained much, and it suggested much; and as the generations passed the great Roman lawyers came more and more under the influence of this great Stoic teaching. Living in Rome and in the circle of the best minds, Polybius must have seen the beginning of this great and beneficent movement. Here were men, both of his own race and Romans, round him, able in all sorts of ways and deeply interested in the handling of ideas. The atmosphere in which he lived gradually made Demetrius of Phaleron look a trifler. The Romans, as he came to know them, had so much to suggest to an observant mind. They were victorious in war on a scale never yet known to mankind; they had a government, which had grown of itself and was not the clever invention of any Plato or Lycurgus, but combined the best features of all known government; law among them was something of a science and was becoming a philosophy. Let the personal influence of Panaetius, his junior, as we saw, have been great or little, the environment in which Panaetius and other Stoic thinkers counted so much, could not but affect a serious observer, a student of history past and present.

But Panaetius was not the only Stoic philosopher in Rome in those years. In 155 B.C. the Athenians had a controversy with the town of Oropus. The issue was not of any great importance to posterity; but, Rome being supreme, the Athenians took the ingenious step of sending as an embassy to the Senate the three outstanding philosophers of Athens. They came, they spoke, they were heard, and they made an immense impression. Aulus Gellius,[1] of the *Attic Nights*—a picturesque or even romantic title for a collection of note-books—tells us that 'these three philosophers were Carneades of the Academy, Diogenes the Stoic, and Critolaus the Peripatetic. When they were admitted to the Senate, they made use of Gaius Acilius, a senator himself, as their interpreter; but beforehand each of them separately for the sake of display had lectured to a large company. Rutilius and Polybius declare that all three aroused admiration for their oratory, each in his own style. Carneades, they say, spoke with vehemence and power, Critolaus with art and polish, Diogenes with restraint and sobriety.' And then the serious Gellius adds a word of his own, which we should be careful to remember, 'each of these styles, as I have said, is more brilliant (*illustrius*) when chastely and modestly adorned; but when rouged and bepowdered, it becomes mere jugglery (*cum fucatur et praelinitur, fit praestigiosum*)'. Plutarch, in his *Life* of Cato Major (22),[2] tells us how the most studious of Rome's youth

---

[1] *Attic Nights*, vi, 14.
[2] Cf. Pliny, *Nat. Hist.* vii, 112; Heitland, *Roman Republic*, § 657.

would gather to these Athenian philosophers, and listen with admiration. 'The charm of Carneades especially, which had boundless power, and fame not less than its power, won large and friendly audiences, and filled the city like a gale with the noise of his praises. Report spread that a Greek, amazingly clever, bewitching and enslaving everybody (πάντα κηλῶν καὶ χειρούμενος), inspired a strange passion in the young men, which turned them altogether from other pleasures and occupations and made them rapt for philosophy (ἐνθουσιῶσι).' A good many Romans were pleased to see the youngsters (τὰ μειράκια) take to Greek culture and consort with these brilliant men; but it did not please Cato, and he dealt with the situation effectively. These great men ought to be teaching in Athens; the Senate ought to decide the matter one way or the other and let the envoys go. It is not hard to see why he wanted them to go. Carneades had a sceptical tone; he maintained, they said, some principle one day and demolished it the next; how much better for the young Romans to give ear, as of old, to the laws and magistrates of Rome. So pled Cato. But Carneades left behind him a great reputation, and Constant Martha maintains that he was indeed the great pioneer of philosophy in Rome, that he effectually taught the Romans to think, and he asks what might not have been the result of the conquest of Greece and the Greek East by a race untrained to think.[1] Diogenes the Stoic may have made less noise, but perhaps had a more constructive influence. Cicero speaks of him from time to time.

There was another figure in Rome, who demands our attention. We saw that Antiochus Epiphanes had been a hostage in Rome for thirteen years. There was now another prince of the Seleucid house in the same position, twenty-three years old— most of which years he had spent in Rome. He felt that the crown of Syria belonged more justly to himself than to the children of Antiochus; but the Senate, Polybius tells us, thought that the incapacity of a child on the Syrian throne would suit Rome's interests better (συμφέρειν τοῖς σφετέροις πράγμασι) than the presence there of a man like Demetrius in the prime of life. That was explicit enough; but the Senate overlooked the

---

[1] Martha, Études Morales (Carnéade à Rome), p. 128.

fact that Polybius and the prince were friends. Perhaps they hunted together. At all events the intimacy meant for Polybius a practical knowledge of the affairs of the dynasty; and when a second application of the prince for release was refused by the Senate, Polybius hinted to him that it was well not to stumble on the same stone twice.[1] Prince and Achaean were alike victims of the same selfish policy, and, as we read elsewhere,

> Misery still delights to trace
> Its semblance in another's case.

So far we have looked at Rome in general, at what was patent to every man who would look at it—the records of statesmen and generals, the growing dominance of Rome in the world at large, the assemblage of spoils and especially of works of art, the advent of Greek philosophy, the presence or insolent exclusion of princes. All this meant education and enlightenment to a man susceptible of enlightenment and interested in observation. But Polybius had other advantages and opportunities to which we must turn.

IV

This brings us to what Warde Fowler, very intelligibly, called 'one of the most delightful passages in all ancient literature'.

At an earlier point reference was made to Aemilius Paullus, the conqueror of Perseus, and the dreadful devastation he made among the Molossians. It represented one phase of Roman character, and we have to realize that one phase does not exhaust the significance of a character. Paullus is one of Plutarch's heroes, a man with some generosity, as his pleading for the captive King Perseus shows,[2] and, unlike many Romans, he was superior to money. We read in Plutarch of the immense wealth annexed in Macedon after his victory, in Polybius a similar story of Spain;[3] and after all he died so poor that to pay his widow her jointure his sons had to sell real estate. Of all that had belonged to Perseus, Paullus would only take his library for the use of his sons, and a silver bowl (weighing five pounds) for his son-in-law—the first silver plate that ever came to that family.[4] To this library Polybius and Scipio owed their in-

---

[1] Polybius, xxxi, 2 (12); 12 (20).   [2] Plutarch, Paullus, 37.
[3] Polybius, xxxii, 9 (=xxxi, 22, Loeb).   [4] Plutarch, Paullus, 28.

timacy—'the acquaintance began with the loan of some books and conversation about them'. For it should be explained that the two sons of Aemilius Paullus were adopted into other famous families and became Fabius and Scipio.

The acquaintance began with books, and then we read that these two young men secured that Polybius should be allowed to remain in Rome, when the rest of the Achaean prisoners were being distributed among other towns. The intimacy thus grew more and more close, and one day Polybius was walking with Scipio when the young man, aged eighteen, his junior by some fifteen years,[1] surprised him. He suddenly spoke, in a quiet and subdued voice, and with the blood mounting to his cheeks; 'Why, Polybius,' he said, 'why is it that, though I and my brother eat together, you usually address to him all your questions and explanations, and pass me over? I suppose you have the same opinion of me which I hear the rest of my countrymen have. For everybody thinks me indolent and stupid, I hear, quite unlike a Roman in outlook and ways, because I don't choose to plead in the courts. And they say that the family I come of requires a different kind of representative, not the sort that I am. That is what troubles me most.'

'In the gods' name,' rejoined Polybius in some surprise, 'don't talk so, and don't have such a notion in your head. It is not for any want of appreciation of you, or to pass you over, but because your brother is the elder I begin and end my remarks with him, and address my explanations and advice to him in the belief that your opinions are the same as his. But now I am delighted to hear you say that you are pained to think yourself less spirited than a member of your family should be; for that shows that you have a high spirit. I would gladly devote myself to you and help you to speak and act as is worthy of your ancestors.'

While Polybius was still speaking, Scipio grasped his right hand in both his own; and, pressing it warmly, said, 'Would I might see the day on which you would count all else secondary and give your mind to me and live with me! For then I shall seem to myself worthy of my house and my ancestors.' Polybius

[1] If Polybius was born in 200 B.C. and Scipio, as we read, in 185, this episode will have happened very soon after the deportation.

was happy to see the enthusiasm and the affection of the boy, yet at the same time he was embarrassed when he thought of the high position of the family and the wealth of its members. Yet after this hour of mutual confidence the boy was never separated from Polybius and preferred his society to everything else.

So Polybius tells the tale of the beginning of a lifetime of friendship; and it might be hard to say which gained more from it. Each brought great gifts to their union; their traditions were different, but they were great traditions and the men were signally able to understand and to profit by the difference of outlook. It was sixteen years before Polybius was permitted to leave the environs of Rome, and it is an easy guess that long before that day came he had made a beginning with his history. There was the library of King Perseus, and it is clear that other books were available; for it seems unlikely that Perseus would have had a copy of Fabius Pictor. In spite of his caustic words about the βιβλιακὴ ἕξις, it is obvious—too obvious, now and then—that Polybius had read widely in previous historians, not all of whom he esteemed. It has been suggested that, at any rate in prose, he was much less familiar with the great writers before Alexander than with the lesser men of a later day. Not unnaturally; for Alexander had made a new world altogether, in which world Polybius had to live. But echoes are to be found of the phrase of Thucydides and Herodotus. At all events, that first year gave him a friend and a notable library.

Twenty-one years later Polybius stood at Scipio's side, when Carthage had fallen, and they watched the great city burning; and Scipio turned to him with the confession of a strange foreboding that another great city might yet find a similar end, and 'either deliberately or the verse escaping him', he quoted two lines of Homer:

ἔσσεται ἦμαρ ὅταν ποτ᾽ ὀλώλῃ Ἴλιος ἱρή.

A day shall be, when holy Troy shall fall.[1]

Prince Demetrius, as we saw, was held at Rome and was longing to get away; and in the nick of time there came from Syria his foster-father with strange news of happenings there, and it was suggested that, if he could once get away, and could

---

[1] Polybius, xxxviii, 21, 22 (Loeb) = xxxix, 5; *Iliad*, vi, 448.

each Syria, if it were only with a single slave, the kingdom was his. But how to get away? Demetrius turned to Polybius for guidance, who introduced to him a certain Menyllus of Alabanda, the very man for the job. Menyllus found a Carthaginian ship at the Tiber mouth, which was to carry sacred offerings from Carthage to Tyre; and he hired it as if for his own return to Egypt. This permitted its equipment and provisioning without any suspicion arising. The prince planned escape with three confederates, a dinner party, a hunting expedition near Circeii to hunt the wild boar, each of the group to reach Anagneia with one slave and some story of others to follow. Polybius was ill in bed, but knew all that was planned; and, feeling uneasy in case the dinner were prolonged and too much drunk, he sent an anonymous message to the prince to be ready at once—five lines of Greek verse, some of it Euripides and the νᾶφε καὶ μέμνασ' ἀπιστεῖν of Epicharmus. The prince received it, read it, guessed the sender and took the hint; he felt unwell, broke off the party and left the house. Before dawn the anchor was up and the ship had set sail; and it was four days before the escape was detected, by which time the prince was in the Straits of Messina. The Senate met on the fifth day and decided it was too late to catch him. So he reached Syria and became King; and one feels that the triumph belonged in a sense to Polybius and was another stage in his education. The story has had to be abridged here, but in the original it suggests that the historian was a better writer than some critics, ancient[1] and modern, have recognized.

So the years passed, in reading and writing and hunting, and in intercourse with significant men. And then at long last Scipio went to Cato; and the great rough red-headed[2] senator pled for the exiles in the Senate. There was a long debate; men spoke for and against the release of the Achaeans; some people can never get over the idea of peril. Cato rose and said—'as if we had nothing else to do! here we sit all day disputing about some old Greeks, as to whether they ought to be carried to their graves by bearers in Rome or in Achaia!' So release was voted;

---

[1] Dionysius of Halicarnassus, de Comp. Verborum, 4, groups Polybius with three others, and five et ceteras, as authors whom nobody finishes.

[2] Cf. couplet in Plutarch, Cato, 1.

and then came a small episode which is very revealing. For i
shows that Polybius might be unpractical and yet recognize a
situation and quote a jest at his own expense; and it shows a
side of Cato, which suggests that Cicero was not altogethe
astray in his picture of kindly old age. Polybius wanted the
Senate to pass a further vote, that the exiles on their return
should recover the honours they had had before their deporta
tion sixteen years ago. He asked Cato what he thought about it
Cato 'smiled and said that Polybius, like Odysseus, wanted to
go back into the cave of the Cyclops, as he had forgotten hi
cap and his belt'.[1]

So Polybius returned to Greece, but he did not stay there
We read of him at Carthage, at Numantia, at the fall o
Corinth, and conducting an exploring expedition along the
Atlantic coast of Africa. One's impression is that he never
quite finished his History; he says he did; but it looks as if he
still kept it by him for revision. Zeno of Rhodes, his contemporary, had published his work; and, when Polybius wrote to
him about his mistakes about the topography of Laconia, Zeno
was troubled, greatly troubled, but the work was out and beyond
recall; still he took Polybius' letter kindly.[2] So one judges that
Polybius kept his work by him to mend it as it might need—and,
as may well happen, never got the last corrections adjusted
though he lived to eighty and was then killed by a fall from his
horse. But a man may correct too long and yet fail of com-
pletion, and a book, like a child, can be watched over too long
by an anxious parent.

V

So the captivity of Polybius ended; and we may ask what it
did for him. It did a great deal. Other men know from
experience that a great cut in life's story, a big interruption
breaking off the even tenour and throwing the man into a new
environment, may be no bad thing. It may be painful; he may
find himself 'moving about in worlds not realized' and may
resent it; he may be angry with his fortune in life, with life
itself—and yet by and by realize what a blessing in disguise
the painful break in his life had been. It is at least worth

---

[1] Polybius, xxxv, 6 (Loeb) = Plutarch, *Cato Major*, 9.
[2] Polybius, xvi, 20.

recalling that the great predecessors of Polybius in History had all three been exiles. 'It was my lot to be in exile after my command at Amphipolis.' So runs the brief sentence of Thucydides; and Herodotus, after all he had done for Halicarnassus, had to leave it. He does not tell us that himself, but posterity knew it, and it is pretty plain from his narrative. And Xenophon had to live at Scillus, in exile, as he avows.

We have seen something of what Polybius gained. He came to know Rome at first hand and to understand the Roman people; and as he learnt to understand them, he admired them. A brave people, a people of spirit, whom disaster strengthens.[1] Bad streaks in that character he knew well enough, as our story has shown; and, though some readers have rashly put him down as servile in his attitude to the Romans, he is very explicit in criticism of them. And a man is apt to judge a people by the men he knows and likes best.

We have seen how the fall of Perseus moves him to quote the words of Demetrius of Phaleron about Fortune. We do not know, and cannot know, the dates at which he wrote his various books; still less can we plot out for ourselves a chart of his corrections; and, as we have seen, it looks as if he had never achieved his final revision. His life seems to have been a full one; the Romans set him to draft constitutions for the conquered Greek states, which he did; for Pausanias tells us that, wherever the Romans accepted his suggestions, things turned out well. But the History suffered. Forty long books written out in rolls, how could he check and correct all he said? But from time to time the correction is made and the reader must accept it, and apply it where necessary. Thus he says, in so many words, 'the progress of the Romans was not due to Fortune ($\tau\acute{\nu}\chi\eta$) as some Greeks suppose, nor was it automatic, but it was entirely reasonable that after they had schooled themselves in affairs of such character and such greatness, they not only struck boldly for universal supremacy of dominion, but achieved their project' (i, 63, 9). In fact, as he says elsewhere—and it looks like a criticism of Demetrius (and perhaps of those who quote him?)— 'to talk of *Tyche* is not proper; it is vulgar' (ii, 38, 5). The sixth

---

[1] See the following passages: i, 64, 6; xxvi, 29, 1; i, 20, 11; and with reference to disaster, iii, 75, 8; 85; 86; 94; 112, 9; xxvii, 8, 8; and (after Cannae) iii, 118, 7.

book of Polybius[1] is devoted to an analysis of Rome's constitution and her military methods, of Roman character and honesty. The account given of the Senate is peculiarly valuable. The upshot is that Rome fairly won her position in the world by sheer merit—a great people indeed, with cruel defects and some bad omens, but none the less a great people. The exile may have come to Italy bitter as any other exile; he lost his bitterness, and he solved his problems; he wrote his history and achieved his purpose, showing his readers—Greek, Roman, modern—not only the significant facts, given with a passion for truth, but the how and the why, which he tells us once and again are more important.

Let us sum the thing up, and it will best be given in a paragraph from Gibbon.[2] 'The Greeks, after their country had been reduced into a province, imputed the triumphs of Rome, not to the merit, but to the FORTUNE of the republic. The inconstant goddess, who so blindly distributes and resumes her favours, had *now* consented (such was the language of envious flattery) to resign her wings, to descend from her globe, and to fix her firm and immutable throne on the banks of the Tiber. A wiser Greek, who has composed, with a philosophic spirit, the memorable history of his own times, deprived his countrymen of this vain and delusive comfort by opening to their view the deep foundations of the greatness of Rome. The fidelity of the citizens to each other, and to the state, was confirmed by the habits of education and the prejudices of religion. Honour, as well as virtue, was the principle of the republic. The sage historian, who excited the virtue of the younger Scipio and beheld the ruin of Carthage, has accurately described their military system, and the invincible legion superior in active strength to the Macedonian phalanx of Philip and Alexander. From these institutions of peace and war, Polybius has deduced the spirit and success of a people incapable of fear and impatient of repose.'

---

[1] Cf. in particular, Polybius, vi, 56.
[2] Gibbon, *Decline and Fall*, chap. xxxviii.

Chapter VII

CICERO AMONG HIS BOOKS

I

Holbrook Jackson's *Anatomy of Bibliomania* is clearly modelled
on a more famous book. Title and arrangement are designed
to recall it, and it is a high compliment to the author to say
that they do. The modern work is all about book-lovers—eight
hundred pages filled with stories of them, quotations from them,
aspects of their enthusiasm, their quaint weaknesses, their
lovableness. One may doubt at times whether anybody, not
engaged in correcting the press, ever does—or perhaps ever did
—read *through* either *Anatomy*, but either of them is good to read
in, a book to come back to and to be idle with, so full of 'fine
miscellaneous feeding'. One of Mr Jackson's book-lovers is
Cicero, who of course deserves his place in that genial company,
a book-lover from boyhood to death. One sentence, quoted
from him by Mr Jackson, stayed long in my mind, and at last
I turned it up—*si hortum cum bibliotheca habes, deerit nihil*; 'if you
have a library and a garden, nothing will be wanting'. What
a charming sentence, a summary of earthly felicity! It is in a
letter to Varro[1] and it is dated 46 B.C., when Cicero was sixty.
But a shadow falls across the sentence. Tyrrell and Purser read
in bibliotheca, and comment: 'We frankly give up this passage
as it stands, and yet it looks as if it was sound. Cicero may have
been fond of flowers, as some commentators say, but why should
the garden be in the library? besides *hortus* is generally used for
a vegetable garden.... If we might read *hortum cum bibliotheca*—
cū having fallen out after *tū*...we should get some kind of
sense.' We often get some kind of sense in Cicero's letters; and if
we may turn to the opening of *de Finibus* v, a very characteristic
piece of Cicero's writing, we find enthusiasm for gardens at
Athens, the *hortuli* of Plato and the *horti* of Epicurus—gardens
which one cannot readily suppose to have been devoted entirely
to pot-herbs.[2] Perhaps some difference may exist in usage

---

[1] *ad Fam.* ix, 4; no. 466 in Tyrrell's great edition.
[2] Cf. also *ad Q.F.* 118, *hortus domi est*.

between singular and plural; and it is a sad tradition of scholarship to choose the duller reading or interpretation, to assume
that the great author would be matter-of-fact and unwilling to
sparkle or even to twinkle. But Cicero, as a hundred letters
show, did not cultivate dullness; he was willing to sparkle and
to twinkle, and frequently does both. Yes! when he writes to
Atticus or to Trebatius Testa; but Varro? He comes near it in
the previous sentence; *tu si minus ad nos, nos accurremus ad te.*
Still even if he limits his desires to a vegetarian supper served in
the library, there we have the two great book-lovers of the age
meeting among books, and that is where we want to see them.

Varro was one of St Augustine's authors, who more than once
emphasizes that he was the most learned of Romans, a man
'who read so many things that we wonder he had leisure to
write anything, and wrote so many that we scarcely believe
any man could have read so many—a man great in genius and
great in learning'[1]—a magazine inexhaustible whence Augustine
drew endless ammunition for the destruction of paganism. So,
too, says Servius, the great commentator on Virgil—'Varro
everywhere the enemy of religion'. So Cicero meets Varro in
his library, whether with a garden outside or a frugal supper
within—perhaps both.

Cicero clearly loved a library. Every man, wrote Oliver
Wendell Holmes, is afraid of books who has not grown up among
them; he himself was at home with them, like a stable boy
among horses, he says. So with Cicero. He reminds his brother
of their father's passion (*studium*) for educating his boys,[2]
admirable and wise man as he was, who, as Cicero says in
another passage, when his health gave way, occupied himself
with letters[3] (*qui cum esset infirma valetudine hic fere aetatem egit in
litteris*). He speaks of the 'manifold pleasure he had found in
the studies in which he had lived from boyhood';[4] and there
was some range in these studies. Like a Roman boy of his
period, he learnt the Twelve Tables by heart *ut carmen necessarium*,
which in half a century had dropped out of the schoolboy's
curriculum;[5] and, at the age of an English undergraduate, he
made a Latin translation of Xenophon's book *Oeconomicus*, which

---

[1] Augustine, *de Civitate Dei*, vi, 2.   [2] *de Oratore*, ii, 1, 1.
[3] *de Legibus*, iii, 1, 3.   [4] *de Republica*, 1, 4, 7.   [5] *de Legibus*, ii, 33, 59.

Ruskin planned to have as the first volume of his 'library for shepherds'.[1] While still quite young (*admodum adolescentulus*)[2] he translated Aratus into Latin verse. He was not himself a poet, in spite of Plutarch's statement that, for a while, he had high repute as best poet of the Romans; the fame of his oratory abides, but many gifted poets sprang up and his poetry has fallen into neglect.[3] We recall Juvenal's mockery and the quip of Tacitus about the other writers of verse, Caesar and Brutus, who were no better than Cicero but luckier, for fewer people knew of their doing it.[4] Yet modern students of the Latin hexameter recognize that Cicero's treatment of it marks a stage in its development; no one would compare him with Virgil, but Cicero also had an ear that told him plainly that a Latin must not use the licenses of his Greek models—the language would not stand it. We see the same thing in Horace a generation later; he wrote Alcaics and Sapphics, but not as Alcaeus and Sappho had written them, nor as Catullus did in his pioneering days. Plutarch further tells us that Cicero in his young days was nicknamed 'the Greek' and 'the scholar' (Γραικὸς καὶ σχολαστικὸς ἀκούων), 'names which the vulgarest Romans are apt to throw about'.[5] Long years afterwards in the book on Human Duties (*de Officiis*) which he wrote for his son, he took occasion to speak of the great contribution made to mankind by scholars 'whose interests and whose whole life has been devoted to the pursuit of knowledge'; they have trained many to be better citizens and of more practical use to their country, and he speaks of what he owes, and perhaps his country through him, to his own teachers.[6] And he goes on to speak of the writers of books, particularly about laws, customs or political science (*disciplinam rei publicae*) and what they have done for men in active political life.

This brings us back again to the library. Here is a letter of the year of Caesar's consulship (59 B.C.) written to Atticus; Cicero has gone away, and he is going to be idle—he won't write a book—no, not the Geography he had thought of: 'I have so taken idleness to my bosom (*sic enim sum complexus otium*) that

---

[1] *de Officiis*, ii, 87.
[2] *de Nat. Deor.* ii, xli, 104. Cf. *pro Archia*, 14.
[3] Plutarch, *Cicero*, 2.
[4] Tacitus, *de Oratoribus*, 21.
[5] Plutarch, *Cicero*, 5.
[6] *de Officiis*, i, 44, 155.

we cannot be separated. So I either delight myself with books
of which I have at Antium *festivam copiam* [it sounds very like
schoolboy slang], or I count the waves; the weather does not
lend itself to catching lizards.'[1] A holiday, suggesting that *dolce
far niente* which the younger Pliny describes—*illud iners quidem
jucundum tamen nihil agere nihil esse.*[2] But Cicero was a man of
more active mind than Pliny, and he must have books. He
had, we learn, some eight country houses beside his house in
Rome, and there is every indication that Antium was not his
only country place furnished with books; how could his *Tusculan
Discussions* have been written without books at his hand? And
it was not only books that a library needed. The elder Pliny[3]
speaks of the Roman's passion for setting up in his library
statues or busts of 'those divine and heavenly men, whose
immortal spirits do speak still, and ever shall, in those places,
where their books are'; 'even if exact portraits of them are not
to be had, we want something of the sort; the lack of it kindles
in us a great desire and longing to know what the man was
like'; and he instances Homer. No one can imagine a contemporary bust of Homer, but a later age produced one of
singular beauty, and nobility. Homer *ought* to have been like
the traditional bust. It is notorious what a passion Cicero had
for works of art;[4] Atticus had to buy them for him;[5] and so did
Fadius Gallus;[6] and there were dealings with Damasippus; and
first and last the impression is given that Cicero leaned to
extravagance in this direction, for a man of his resources. But
he did not, we learn, buy without intelligent appreciation. The
speeches against Verres tell much of Roman acquisitiveness
where Greek art was concerned. No one suggests that Cicero
used the methods of Verres in acquiring works of art. No doubt
originals appealed to him; but one surmises that, like other men,
he might at times be limited to those 'Roman copies', which
are counted so inferior, but to the makers (and purchasers) of
which we of more modern times have every reason to be

---

[1] *ad Atticum*, ii, 6.   [2] Pliny, *Letters*, viii, 9.
[3] Pliny, *Nat. Hist.* xxxv, 9; cf. H. N. Wethered, *The Mind of the Ancient World*,
p. 208; quotes Philemon Holland's translation.
[4] See Torsten Petersen, *Cicero, a Biography*, p. 210f.
[5] Cf. *ad Atticum*, i, 4 (no. 9 Tyrrell); references to busts and books; *ib.* i, 10, 11.
[6] *ad Fam.* vii, 23; no. 126 in Tyrrell and Purser.

grateful. A 'Roman copy' is better than none. Cicero would rather sit on a garden chair of Atticus, under the bust of Aristotle, he says, than in the curule seat of the Roman magistrate.[1]

But, after all, books were the main thing. A man, Paetus, offered him a collection, and he playfully tells Atticus that as the Cincian law (now nearly 150 years old, and rather like a dead letter), which limited gifts to advocates, did not hinder it, he meant to accept the books. So 'if you love me, if you know that I love you, make every endeavour—through friends, clients, guests, yes, and freed men and your own slaves, that not a leaf is lost. For I have tremendous need of those Greek books, which I suspect he has left, and the Latin ones which I know he has. There is not a day but I feel an increased sense of rest in literature, whatever time is allowed me from the labour of the forum'; so with a final appeal for Atticus' usual kindness under-lined (as it were) the letter ends.[2] 'Take care', he writes in another letter, 'not to part with your books to any one; keep them for me, as you promise. My enthusiasm for them holds me, just as my disgust does for everything else; you would not believe how much worse, and in how short a time, you will find everything than when you left.'[3] At another time, he writes of enjoying (*pascor*) the library of Faustus Sulla—perhaps the very volumes that his despotic father, the dictator Sulla, had brought back from Greece, as we read that Aemilius Paullus had done a century before with the library of King Perseus.[4] The library that Sulla thus acquired was very rich, we read, in works of Aristotle and Theophrastus, at that time not very familiar to the reading public. Plutarch and Strabo[5] explain the mis-adventures of this library at Scepsis in Asia Minor before it came into the hands of Apellicon and of Sulla. It would add to the interest if we could be sure that Cicero was reading the books in Theophrastus' own copies. At any rate Atticus must not suppose he is amusing himself at Puteoli and the Lucrine lake—perhaps, we are told, an allusion to oysters and not to scenery.[6] Yet again, he tells Atticus he has received from Vibius

---

[1] J. S. Reid, Intr. to *Academics*, p. 7; *ad Atticum*, iv, 10.
[2] Tyrrell, *Letters*, vol. i, Intr. p. 35. *ad Atticum*, i, 20 (Tyrrell no. 26).
[3] *ad Atticum*, i, 11.   [4] Plutarch, *Sulla*, 26; *Aemilius Paullus*, 28.
[5] Strabo, C 608–609.
[6] Cf. Tyrrell on the letter, no. 121, in his second volume.

a copy of Alexander of Ephesus, an 'inept poet' and careless, but not quite useless; so he copies him out and sends him back.[1] It was the only, or the most obvious, way to be sure of a copy of a book you wanted. Caerellia, an elderly and wealthy lady, who lent Cicero money on one occasion, 'aflame, to wit, with the passion for philosophy', gets ahold of his books *de Finibus* and copies them out—gets the books, he says, from the copyists of Atticus, not from his own staff; his own copy had never been out of his sight, and his staff were hardly equal to making even a single copy; but he would not have Atticus find fault with his servants—'Ah! me! how I do harp on trifles! (*Hui, quam diu de nugis*).'[2]

This last story reveals what is known from other sources. One must not quite speak of Atticus as Cicero's publisher, conditions were so different before the age of the printing press. But Atticus kept a large number of literary slaves, *librarii*, who acted as copyists,[3] and by their means copies of Cicero's works reached his friends—Varro, for instance[4]—and no doubt others; it is conjectured it would not be without some profit to the very businesslike Atticus. 'I sent you my speech', he writes (xv, 13, 1) 'and leave it to your discretion to keep it or to publish it' (*Ejus custodiendae et proferendae arbitrium tuum*). He sends Atticus a revised version of his *de Senectute*, with a lot of additions between the lines; 'have it copied on large paper (*in macrocollum*) and read it privately to your guests, but, as you love me! when they are in a good temper and well-fed, that they may not vent their rage on me, when it is really you they are angry with' (xvi, 3).

The reproduction of books, each individual copy made by hand and very generally by slave labour, had its bearing on all branches of study. Pronunciation was the source of spelling mistakes; fatigue and carelessness counted; and where lines ended with the same letters, not infrequently a line or a passage would be lost, as the eye swept onward and the mind was inattentive to the sense. That is not peculiar to antiquity; an American printer, reprinting a book of my own, dropped a line;

---

[1] *ad Atticum*, ii, 20; 22.
[2] *ad Atticum*, xiii, 21a: see Tyrrell and Purser, vol. iv, p. lxxi.
[3] See Tyrrell and Purser, vol. i, Intr. p. 45; J. S. Reid, *Academics*, Intr. p. 36 note. See also Boissier, *Cicero and his Friends* (tr.), p. 128.
[4] *ad Atticum*, xiii, 25.

whoever may have been reading the proof failed to notice the omission; and the paragraph was wrecked so far as sense went. The amusing Synesius, about A.D. 410, writing to his son, playfully defends his use of bad copies; the gap that breaks the thread (τὸ ἐνδεὲς εἰς τὴν ἀκολουθίαν τῆς ἀναγνώσεως) exercises the mind, which has there and then to weave something in (προσυφαίνειν) and should gain in confidence from not depending too much on the eyes.[1] Plutarch tells us of a law at Athens that standard texts of the three great tragic dramatists were to be kept, and the actors forbidden to alter them. Here and there, as we pursue Cicero among the libraries, his own and others, we come on a Greek from Amisus called Tyrannion, who taught Cicero's nephew, the young Quintus, meddled somehow with that library of Theophrastus, was invoked to rearrange and restore Cicero's own library (or one of his libraries) 'the remains of which [he writes in 56 B.C.] are much better than I had expected', thought badly of Eratosthenes, and incurred some grumbles from Cicero for being dilatory (cessator). Still he did very well, all considered, with Cicero's books and their arrangement; and Cicero goes on to request Atticus to send him two of his library slaves to help Tyrannion in pasting leaves together and procuring the parchment tags 'which I think you Greeks call σίλλυβοι'.[2]

Here we have to recall that the books were rolls of papyrus, perhaps 35 feet long, made by glueing or pasting the plant's leaves together, very liable to get out of order. They were kept rolled up and lying flat perhaps on a shelf or vertical in a receptacle like a bandbox; and in either case the tag on the end of the roll was necessary for its identification. All this is familiar, but one forgets sometimes to reflect on the consequences of what is familiar; how few of us realize what English life was like before the devising of matches and electric torches! It was not the vogue yet in Cicero's day to use the paged book; and the roll was infinitely less convenient. One of the things that strikes the modern reader of Polybius notably is his apparent change of mind as to the parts played by Chance and Providence in human affairs (τύχη and πρόνοια), and his failure to adjust his work to his later view. His books are long; and to hunt up

[1] Synesius, Dio, 15.   [2] ad Atticum, iv, 4.

every reference to Chance or Providence in a series of many rolls would have cost immense expenditure of work and time; and till the fall from his horse killed him at the age of eighty, Polybius had a busy life; so the tangle remains to this day.

When we come to consider the many philosophical and political writings of Cicero, it will be relevant to bear in mind the practical obstacles that a library of papyrus rolls put in the way of research, quite apart from the difficulty of access to old or out-of-the-way books. The use of the cyclopaedia is common enough to-day in spite of reference libraries, so that some excuse should be made in advance for a busy man writing in Latin, with a Greek summary at his elbow. I have long wondered how Herodotus contrived to carry all his information, acquired here, there and everywhere by word of mouth and from books; and what possible conveniences he had for making, keeping and adjusting notes. A century after Cicero, Pliny the naturalist must obviously have had some system of note keeping; but he was (so to say) a professional polymath, which Cicero was not. It is in fact asserted, for Professor Reid is emphatic in denying it, that Cicero was a 'dabbler'.[1]

II

Not a dabbler, on the contrary 'his appetite for every kind of literature was insatiable, and his attainment in each department considerable. He was certainly the most learned Roman of his age, with the single exception of Varro.' So Dr Reid. Only we have not to expect miracles; there are limits which the human mind knows—time is short, life is crowded, fatigue attends the most active; and what people who live near any of the three great libraries of England forget—very pardonably—is that books are not always accessible. *Habent sua fata libelli.* 'Time and chance happeneth to them all', as the history of scholarship tells us. To go no further, we can recall the strange discovery by Cardinal Mai of Cicero's own *Republic* in a palimpsest, and the emergence of Aristotle's *Constitution of Athens* from a mummy case; and how many famous books have depended on single copies! Probably, as Joseph Mayor suggests, Cicero had not read all the authors and books referred to in §§ 25–43 of the

[1] Cf. Intr. to *Academics*, p. 6.

first book *de Natura Deorum*, nor all the Epicurean books mentioned in the following sections. It is only Professor Saintsbury of Edinburgh who read every printed book in English. Cicero used, as we all do, the work of predecessors, who were not in every case infallible. Velleius, the Epicurean, in the *de Natura Deorum*, summarizes the views of earlier thinkers, and it is indicated by modern scholars that he makes mistakes. To this the reply is suggested that Epicureans did; but no! that will not do, for the man who replies to him compliments him on his summary, which must prove—that Cicero did not notice the mistakes? Very likely; but we must not quite exclude the fact that a polite controversialist will often begin with a dexterous compliment. We must not exclude this possibility; but there looms up from the ruins of Herculaneum another possibility. A charred manuscript, cleverly saved from crumbling and adroitly transcribed, seems to supply a 'source', or to suggest one. Scholars are not at one about the name—was it Phaedrus? was it Philodemus? or somebody behind one or other or both of them? It is not of first importance to us—or perhaps to anybody—to decide. 'The Germans', wrote Andrew Lang (dealing with Appian in *The Daily News* in 1899), 'are most industrious and ingenious in these researches [as to the "sources" of extant authors], but the books to which they refer are usually lost, like those of Tanusius Geminus.' This author, says Smith's *Dictionary*, 'seems to have lived about the time of Cicero. The exact nature of his work is uncertain'—all of which, to one type of mind, makes him more fascinating. Lost authors, like insoluble problems, are always best; hundreds of writers of books have married wives; but *did* Swift marry Stella? How dull it would be, if we knew! It is interesting to find that scholars are again and again perplexed as to Cicero's sources; sometimes he names them, which may go some way towards settling the question; sometimes he leaves posterity guessing.[1] Here we will not add to the number of the guesses.

He was really a man of the widest range of interests, as his allusions, his quotations and his requests for information prove. 'He purposed, as we are told, to write a comprehensive history

[1] See the remarks of Dr Keyes in the introduction to his Loeb translation of *de Legibus*, p. 292.

of his country, and to combine with it much about Greece, and in general to work into it the tales and myths he had gathered'—but public affairs and private troubles stopped him. So Plutarch in his *Life of Cicero*;[1] and in one of his own letters, already quoted, he was thinking of a Geography, but that Tyrannion and others had doubts about Eratosthenes the Greek geographer whom he must have been meaning to use—and Cicero was tired of writing and had that 'jolly lot' of books to fall back upon at Antium.[2] Of course, to project a book does not necessarily imply ability to write it, or even a very strong purpose; we recall the forty thousand treatises which Coleridge, according to Lamb, failed to complete—or perhaps ever to begin. Cicero, at all events, made a sketch of early Roman history in the beginning of his *Republic*, with an attempt to correlate Roman and Greek Chronology. Criticisms of the great Greek historians occur from time to time in his pages—Thucydides *prudens severus gravis* but not a model for the Roman law courts; Xenophon charming, but neither is he the model for those courts;[3] Herodotus—*quid Herodoto dulcius*?[4] And he speaks also of Pherecydes, Hellanicus and Acusilaus; but one would not so categorically say he had read them. But turn to *de Finibus*, book v and the second chapter; the scene is Athens, and the appeal of the city, to which the speakers confess, is surely a bit of autobiography. He had six months in Athens as a young man—or rather young; and Atticus lived there. '"All over Athens", said I, "I know there are many reminders of eminent men in the actual places where they lived"'; but for the moment he thinks of Carneades and the hall where he lectured. Yes, says Piso, every one of us has something that appeals to him; what says our friend Lucius? Lucius, it appears, had sought out the beach at Phalerum where they say Demosthenes used to practise declamation; he has visited the tomb of Pericles; but there is no end to it in this city (*id quidem infinitum est in hac urbe*); wherever we go, we tread historic ground (*in aliqua historia vestigium ponimus*). And Quintus has already spoken of Oedipus and the beautiful lines with which the *Coloneus* of Sophocles begins; and Atticus could not forget Epicurus. And Marcus is haunted by Plato—*deus ille*

---

[1] Plutarch, *Cicero*, 41; cf. *de Legibus*, i, 2, 5.   [2] *ad Atticum*, ii, 6.
[3] *Orator*, 30, 32. Cf. Quintilian, x, i, 33.   [4] Fragment, 239, 49 (Nobbe).

noster Plato[1] and *Platonem illum tuum*;[2] and Socrates, as he knows
him in Xenophon, appeals to him with his refusal to meddle
with problems of Nature that seem irrelevant to human life.[3]
We read of Cicero undertaking translations of the *Timaeus* and
the *Protagoras*,[4] which would hardly be dabbler-work, and
Demosthenes' *Crown* and the reply of Aeschines. We may also
recall his pride that he, a man of Arpinum, discovered the grave
of Archimedes at Syracuse and pointed it out to the Syracusans
who had forgotten where it was.[5]

In one place and another he discusses the authors who deal
with Roman history, and whom we only know in fragments
and references and hardly esteem—Fabius Pictor, Caelius
Antipater, and some who are weaker still[6]—feeble, clumsy,
long-winded: but then there is the great Cato, *qui tibi semper in
ore est*, author of the *Origines* and of a hundred and fifty speeches
which, we are told, were still available for Cicero's reading—
Cato, the genial old sage of *de Senectute*. And three times in his
Republic he refers to Polybius, 'unsurpassed in chronological
accuracy', and a profound student of Roman institutions, with
whose views readers find him in much accord. Polybius of
course was a Greek and wrote in Greek and 'our national
literature is deficient in history' (*deest historia litteris nostris*).[7]

III

At the end of a letter of May 45 B.C. there come words lightly
written, which have become famous. The letter is a short one,
about this and that, touched on and left—a small financial
affair between two men not very well known to history, a letter
to Caesar, a purchase of gardens (two in question), a rumour of
a divorce; and then: 'As to the Latin language, be easy in your
mind. But you will say: "What? when you write on such
subjects?" Ἀπόγραφα *sunt*—they are transcripts; and they don't
give me too much trouble. I only supply the words; and I have
plenty of them—*verba tantum affero, quibus abundo*.'[8]

---

[1] *ad Atticum*, iv, 16.   [2] *de Legibus*, i, 5, 15.
[3] *de Republica*, i, 10, 15.   [4] See Teuffel, *Latin literature*, p. 308.
[5] *Tusculans*, v, 23, 64. Elsewhere he calls Cato's character a 'problem for
Archimedes', *ad Atticum*, xii, 4.
[6] *de Legibus*, i, 26.   [7] *de Legibus*, i, 2, 6.   [8] *ad Atticum*, xii, 52.

Lightly written phrases; and much has been made to turn on them. Cicero's philosophical and political writings, then, would be mere translations—easy work for a man whose words come so readily—*quibus abundo*; he simply overflows with words, and he says so. And the inference seems plain. The value of the books must depend on the authors whom he is transcribing into Latin—Philodemus or whoever it was—Panaetius—Posidonius —the authors he borrows, writes to Atticus about, and names in one treatise or another. But it is clear, long before one reaches book xii of the correspondence with Atticus, that Cicero knew very well to whom he was writing and wrote with an assurance, which the years justified, that his friend understood his speech, and understood *him*. Not every reader of the correspondence has understood either the man who wrote the letters, or what happens when two such friends correspond. When one reads a public speech of Cicero's, his mastery of the art of public speech quickly becomes apparent—at least, if the reader knows any-thing about audiences. To sway a popular audience you must watch them as you speak; it will not do to read from a manu-script—unless it is to be a state paper, or is already a sermon, for divines hardly realize that theirs is a specialized constituency, tolerant of tedium and instructed already. It is very quickly clear that Cicero meant to be listened to, meant to be heard and to be followed; and when you address such an audience you have to be lucid, far more lucid and far more emphatic than some of his commentators would ever suppose. The idea has to be repeated, if it is to be taken in, but the audience is not to realize that it is repeated; it must be in other words and look different; and if the orator can say it three times without the audience suspecting his sense of their dullness, so much the better. Further, if he can (it is a real art) give the listeners the feeling that they are actually mastering propositions which require some real power of mind to apprehend—better still! He is making them value themselves, and the second or third time the idea comes, it is recognized as something one can definitely assimilate.

So much for public speech. When it is a common audience, say the thing three times; when you are writing to Atticus, that will not be necessary; it will hardly be necessary to say it once.

'A nod's as good as a wink to a blind horse', the Scots used to say. It was not needful to underline things in a red ink in a letter to Atticus—or to complete the sentence; half a hint was enough between them. Furthermore, it is to be remembered that undiluted vanity was not one of Cicero's traits. Vanity, if you like. 'Periautology' Plutarch calls it—talking about himself.[1] Boissier says indeed that Cicero had no passion for the glory of being 'original'—'C'est à peu près la seule vanité qui lui manque'—which is worth remembering. But when he writes to Atticus, his humour plays about his vanity; writing to his intimate friend, he laughs gently at his own foibles, which he recognizes well enough.[2] *Quibus abundo!* 'Oh! I have lots of words'; and Atticus twinkles as he reads, and decides he can indeed be 'easy in his mind', *securi animi*, about the Latin language.

But when a correspondence is published, it may get into wrong hands. Who ever had such *jucunditas*? asks Quintilian. One who reads those letters, says Cornelius Nepos in his short eulogy of Atticus (16), does not much crave for a connected history of those times. No, indeed, for you are living in intimate daily intercourse with two of the most gifted men of the day; and even if we have not the letters that Atticus wrote, with men like Cicero and William Cowper and Charles Lamb you know the man to whom they are writing from the texture of the letter. There is no doubt, as you open the Cowper volume, whether the letter you stumble on is to William Unwin or to John Newton. This leads one to say that Cicero had no notion of writing to Theodore Mommsen, who read him with contempt and called him a 'journalist'. It is eighty years since Mommsen's *Roman History* was translated into English, nearly ninety since it appeared in German; and E. A. Freeman's words about the author still stand—Mommsen, he wrote, 'cannot understand that a weak state can have any rights against a strong one'; 'almost every page is disfigured by the writer's unblushing idolatry of mere force'.[3] One would think he was describing

---

[1] Plutarch, *Comp. Cic. et Dem.* 2.

[2] Cf. Horace, *Satires*, i, 10, 13, the urbane, *parcentis viribus atque Extenuantis eas consulto.*

[3] Freeman, *History of Federal Government*, p. 534; and *Essays*, II, p. 270.

the spiritual ancestry of Adolf Hitler rather than the work of an historian. Even the calmer spirit of J. S. Reid is stirred to say: 'had Cicero by any chance been author of a proscription, he would probably have been one of Mommsen's heroes'.[1] Cicero was not *echt deutsch*, as one can see even in Teuffel's matter-of-fact pages. The French really understand the Latin type, the 'urbane' type, better; the Gauls, says Sainte-Beuve, early found their way to the Capitol. Boissier is a far better interpreter of Cicero than Mommsen, as any human reader of *Cicero and his Friends* knows, whether he has read that most delightful book in French or in English.

And now to return to the ἀπόγραφα, and the words with which Cicero 'overflows'. The question is not, what does Cicero say, but what does Atticus understand? Words, said the great English man of science (he must have been more!), 'were given us to conceal our thoughts'. It is not enough to ask what the heavy-footed literalist—the χαλκέντερος of the Greeks—would make of Cicero's words; Cicero was not writing for him, but for Atticus, a spirit as little likely to misconstrue him as Charles Lamb's correspondents, such as Wordsworth, Coleridge or Thomas Manning were to mistake him. We can believe that Atticus was not deceived by the word ἀπόγραφα, nor by the modesty of Cicero's rôle as a mere translator. Men of his type are never mere translators; and whatever German scholars make of him, there are American scholars—or were, for Tenney Frank and Sihler are gone—who tell us better. The books, says Frank, 'often, even when they are to some extent mosaics, give us very precisely the Ciceronian pattern'; they illustrate his own convictions reached through his own experience.[2] A parallel; Coleridge dwelt on the shrewd reading of the soul shown by Shakespeare when he gave us Romeo in love with Rosaline before Juliet dawned on him. Nonsense! said some of Coleridge's critics; Rosaline was in the book from which Shakespeare took the tale—'à qui gloire soit rendue', as Voltaire said. As if Shakespeare did not show his genius in his borrowing as well as in his omissions. Stapfer brings out how faithfully he would reproduce North's Plutarch, which is surely a great tribute to

---

[1] J. S. Reid, Intr. to *Academics*, p. 26 note.
[2] Tenney Frank, *Life and Literature in the Roman Republic*, pp. 216, 217.

the Greek biographer. And Cicero, we may assure ourselves, could be trusted to borrow or discard, as genius prompted— always allowing a little for haste, a weakness with great men of affairs. When someone, reading Theodore Roosevelt's vigorous *Winning of the West*, remarked that he was in a great hurry when he wrote volume iii, 'he always was' rejoined a friend of the president. Teuffel is far from satisfied with Cicero's work; he complains of errors, haste, no settled results. But, after all, it was not exactly settled results that interested Cicero or that he wanted to give us; it was not the conclusion, but the question that interested him; he would look at it this way and that way, and a third way if there was one. 'Then a question is education?' we read in Xenophon's *Oeconomicus*. 'It is just this inconclusive-ness of Plato's thought', wrote Gilbert Murray,[1] 'that has made it immortal. We get in him not a system, but a spirit.' Some-thing of the same sort might be said of Cicero. This is not to equate him with Plato, 'his god'; but, after all, dogma, 'settled results', may not be philosophy—certainly not of the Academic school to which Cicero leaned. The point is made that we have to distinguish between Cicero handling speculative or analytical problems and Cicero dealing with problems of conduct, and to recognize that he is surer and more definite on the latter. As to the gods, Warde Fowler advanced the view that Cicero's interest in the 'nature of the gods' is pre-eminently intellectual; he misses in it the note we find so often in the Psalter—not unnaturally; Cicero is not—could hardly have been—the 'Gott-betrunkener' man that Spinoza was. Cicero avows his plan of giving opposing arguments; it was the tradition of Aristotle, and there seemed no other way so likely to produce a probable result.[2] He will not copy the Stoic who will not move the breadth of a foot from Chrysippus—*a Chrysippo pedem nusquam*.[3] Legend used to say that R. L. Nettleship was once challenged after a Balliol lecture—was he or was he not, 'paid by the college to have a definite opinion on these subjects?' It is an old rule, and a safe one, that we have to take genius on its own terms. Cicero's career had not been one to make him a dog-matist, even if Nature had given him that temperament.

[1] Gilbert Murray, *Greek Literature*, p. 312.
[2] *Tusculan Disputations*, ii, 3, 9.　　　　[3] *Academica*, ii, 143.

Nature had not given him that temperament; and the omission vexes the Mommsen type. Here is a man whose mind moves; it even swings; he is swayed by his feelings; he writes in many moods. To-day he writes to Atticus in hope and gaiety; to-morrow's letter is all depression; what can be made of such a man? Some critics cannot understand that a man may reveal wavering moods to an intimate, who yet shows a firmer front to the world. Scripture gives a double portrait of Jeremiah, most sensitive of men in his self-revelation, and 'a brazen wall' to the Jewish community. The sensitive nature, that can overcome its sensitiveness and act with decision, is surely not a contemptible one, even if at times an acute observer can recognize a moment of weakness. Courage has been defined by a well-known Scottish novelist as 'being afraid and not "letting on".' No one will wisely deny that there were weaknesses in Cicero's character; there are in most characters; but a man of letters, with a gift for expression, for self-revelation, will be peculiarly apt to let such weaknesses escape concealment. It must be much simpler to be 'stodgy', to be incapable of responding to impression, incapable of feeling emotion or betraying it; but it will be duller. Such people do not write books or letters that any one *wants* to read; and the Roman world wanted to keep, and did keep, masses of Cicero's writing; and the Renaissance world read them with joy, and even the modern world, in spite of certain heavy critics, recognizes that this was one of the masters of literature.

Ἀπόγραφα sunt! Well! Suppose they were? Where are the books of Panaetius and Posidonius? How much of their name and fame do they not owe to Cicero—'amateurish', as the kindly Warde Fowler says[1]—hurried, eloquent, liable to make slips and worse errors than slips, but readable? 'Let us not forget', wrote Andrew Lang about St Augustine's story, 'that the guide on the way to the city was kind clever wordy vain old Marcus Tullius Cicero.'[2] Torsten Petersen[3] quotes the suggestion that Cicero's philosophical treatises have had a more profound influence than any other works belonging to ancient

---

[1] W. Warde Fowler, *Roman Ideas of Deity*, pp. 3, 4, 10.

[2] Andrew Lang, *Adventures among Books*, p. 167. He refers to Augustine, *Confessions*, iii, 4, 7, *Hortensia*.

[3] T. Petersen, *Cicero, a Biography*, p. 589.

Greece and Rome, with perhaps the single exception of Plutarch's *Lives*. He will not quite commit himself to this claim, but he emphasizes the fascination the books have exercised for generations. It is at least significant that in one and another treatise we get the reaction of a man of genius to Greek thought—the first man of genius who was not Greek himself whose reaction we can measure, and a man who, as no less a critic than Martin Luther points out, lived 'in so many great dealings and businesses?', 'in great care, and had upon him great burthens, labour and pains'. 'No man', he adds, 'rightly understandeth *Cicero's* Epistles, except he hath been exercised in chief Government twentie years.'[1] Luther is clearly right in his judgment; the philosophical books were written by a man of affairs.

But they were written by a man of letters, who never, except in his exile, when his house in Rome was destroyed, and no doubt his library with it, when his spirit for the time was broken, wrote a clumsy sentence. This cannot be said of all the philosophers. Affinity is traced between the sixth book of Polybius and Cicero's *Republic*; they are 'the real results of the early Stoic teaching at Rome', and it is observed, alas! by every reader how little Stoicism had done to develop style in Polybius, a great historian, a thinker, but of all great historians hampered by the most lumbering pen. The journal of Marcus Aurelius can be read, and should be read; but it is not read for the charm of its style. Cicero was read for that reason, and so was Plato; and in each case the thinking of mankind gained. Men were charmed into reading, and bore away more than they realized.

Panaetius—Posidonius 'the philosophical wizard'[2] who modified Stoicism 'to make men at home in the universe'[3]— Philodemus (if it was he)—these men supplied the Greek summaries on which Cicero worked, which he modified, rewrote, humanized and made readable. Other names are mentioned—Dicaearchus, and 'heavens! what a huge heap of him I had piled at my feet! Oh, a great man'[4]—Demetrius of

---

[1] Henry Bell, translation of Luther's Table Talk, published 1652, pp. 508–509.
[2] W. Warde Fowler, *Roman Ideas of Deity*, p. 142. Cf. Augustine, *de Civitate Dei*, v, 5, *Posidonius magnus astrologus idemque philosophus*.
[3] Edwyn Bevan, *Stoics and Sceptics*, p. 98.   [4] *ad Atticum*, ii, 2.

Magnesia; Caesar has crossed the Rubicon and Pompey ha
fled from Rome, and Cicero writes to Atticus:[1] 'I remember a
book being given you by Demetrius of Magnesia, dedicated to
you, entitled "*On Concord*"; I wish you would send it to me'
—and by and by he sends it back[2]—and Serapion the geographer
(should he be mentioned?), 'you have done a most agreeable
thing in sending me Serapion's book, though—between you
and me!—I hardly understand the thousandth part of it', but
Cicero will pay Atticus for it.[3] But there is little use in trying
to compile a catalogue of lost authors, whom he read in whole
or in part, used and very likely discarded. A Californian
bookseller once explained to me that he 'did not sell books
but text-books'—a great distinction, and a real gulf between
the two classes. Two more groups of Cicero's writings have to
be looked at, and then we can pass to the books that were books
indeed—the books that he really liked, that influenced him, that
stir in his mind and suggest themselves to him.

When Cicero writes of the State, different strains are recognized. Of course a man who writes a treatise *On the Republic*
and follows it up by another *On Laws*, has Plato before his mind—
the mere titles prove that, but a hundred other things speak of
Plato's influence. Yet there were later thinkers who were laid
under contribution—Panaetius again and Polybius, the friend
of Scipio the younger, who used to discuss the question of the
State with him, and whom Cicero brackets as 'best versed of
all the Greeks in what bears on the State', whether he means
by *rerum civilium* things Roman or more generally Politics.[4] But
once again, we are warned by Tenney Frank—and we surely
ought to have thought of it—that a Roman of Cicero's own
political experience writing of the State will not draw all his
material or all his ideas from the books of other men, and these
not Roman but Greek. How could he have? And when it is
plain all along that his ideal commonwealth was not an
impossible pattern laid up in the skies (if there), but the actual
Rome of history in its great period, conqueror of Hannibal and
Carthage, of Philip and Antiochus, home, nurse and inspiration
of Cato and all the great Romans, it becomes easier to believe

[1] *ad Atticum*, viii, 11.   [2] *ad Atticum*, ix, 9, 2.
[3] *ad Atticum*, ii, 4.   [4] *de Republica*, i, 21, 34.

that autobiography as well as the library has its part in these books. They at least are not ἀπόγραφα, and Cicero brought more than words to them. In passing, one may recall how the 'Dream of Scipio', with which he concluded his *Republic*, had a separate existence and history, and survived in the Commentary of Macrobius, quite apart from Cardinal Mai's palimpsest. And perhaps one may suggest that it is not so very far behind (if at all behind) the more general revelation of Er the son of Armenius. It is remarked that here again, in his writings on politics, he shows changes of mind, or at least inclination to change, and the explanation is obvious. He lived in a changing world, a world of furious changes—foe became friend, and friend foe, in fresh alliances and conflicts, the whole political scene kept changing and little wonder if different aspects of longstanding questions received new emphasis. All the shifting was not done by Cicero; nor, on the other hand, was he of the younger Cato's type, the poseur who would never change, the self-conscious archaist who discarded a shirt out of compliment to his great-grandfather (whatever the greater Cato's attitude to shirts; he at least was no Gandhi), and who fancied himself (so Cicero put it) to be living in Plato's Republic and not in the dregs of Romulus.[1] Yet perhaps Cicero did share something of Cato's weakness, if weakness it was; in the old phrase of Roman history he 'did not despair of the Republic'; and there are those who would say that he ought to have despaired of it— people who would prefer Isocrates to Demosthenes, and the school of Mommsen and Hitler. To cherish an impossible ideal is at least as much to the credit of a man's intellect as to give way at once to the squalid realism of surrender to the master of the moment; yes, even if a new order is to supervene and prove permanent, which it does not always.

The third group of Cicero's speculative writings is again a large one and concerns Oratory. Here again there were Greeks who had written before him and were writing alongside of him, Aristotle long ago, Dionysius of Halicarnassus a little after his day. Cicero's *de Oratore* has charm, his *Orator* less. But, while a master stylist has a right to be heard respectfully when he speaks of his art, he is far more significant when he exercises

[1] *ad Atticum*, ii, 1 (dated June 60 B.C.).

it—when he *does* the thing instead of talking about it. Horace's
Art of Poetry we read, as Augustine Birrell said, because we like
reading Horace; his *Odes* stand on another footing, and are a
thousand times as well worth reading. The critics note two or
three things about Cicero's reflexions on Oratory. First of all,
as we have seen already, Cicero realized that Latin was not
Greek. So much would seem obvious, but the history of one
literature and another reveals that men of real education and
even of genius fail at times to recognize that one language will
not stand what is possible in another. The story of Edmund
Spenser and Gabriel Harvey illustrates it. Modern analysis, we
are told,[1] has proved that despite Greek theory about the use
in prose of iambus, dactyl, paean and so on for clause endings,
and Cicero's loyalty to such suggestions, 'his ear had shaped a
truer Latin rhythm than his scholarship or his logic'. The fact
is that Art is not very amenable to Science. The literary artist,
we are told, is self-educated;[2] Homer's minstrel says so, and
explains that it is God who teaches him.[3] There are rules
enough which the great artist knows, which he may have
formulated himself, and he will keep to them—till he thinks it
better not to, and then he will break the rules, he will transcend
them, and their violation may be glorious, more triumphant
than even their observance could ever have been. Cicero coined
words that mankind has adopted; even the grocers, as R. Y.
Tyrrell pointed out, have laid hold of his 'quality' and 'quantity', which was not the fate of their Greek archetypes; and in
another order of words we are told that he gave us 'Providence'.
Finally, Dr J. W. Mackail has put it all in a sentence: 'Ciceronian
prose is practically the prose of the human race.' Erasmus may
have said that of all men he hated most the 'apes of Cicero',[4]
which is very intelligible. But Cicero was not one of his apes;
he originated; he showed men at large how to write and how to
speak; no style could be clearer, or more natural; Torsten
Petersen cannot be far astray in comparing his style to
Thackeray's. 'If it is not lucid, it is not French', is a saying of
Frenchmen; and that lucidity is Latin and Ciceronian.

---

[1] Tenney Frank, *Life and Literature in the Roman Republic*, p. 155.
[2] T. Petersen, *Cicero, a Biography*, p. 424.
[3] Phemios in *Odyssey*, xxii, 347.
[4] Erasmus, *Ep.* 351, to Budaeus, 15 February 1516–17.

And the great artist who taught all Europe to think and to
write is taken literally, when he tells his friend ἀπόγραφα sunt,
verba tantum affero! And this is supposed to be criticism.

IV

But it is time to turn from Dicaearchus and Serapion and their
kind, from the men who wrote text-books and summaries to the
real literature in which Cicero lived.

In the year 59, the year of Caesar's consulship, Cicero is
weary of things and wants to get away and stay away—to go
(say) to Egypt and not return to Rome till people miss him
(cum aliquo desiderio reverti). But—and he quotes Homer (Iliad,
vi, 442)

αἰδέομαι Τρῶας καὶ Τρῳάδας ἑλκεσιπέπλους (ad Atticum, ii, 5).

The words are Hector's; he says them to Andromache when she
would have him stay out of the battle. 'Surely', he says (in
Walter Leaf's translation), 'surely I take thought for all these
things, my wife; but I have very sore shame of the Trojans and
Trojan dames with trailing robes, if like a coward I shrink away
from battle. Moreover mine own soul forbiddeth me.' No one
can read it without feeling it to be one of the noblest passages
in Homer himself, in all literature, that is; and it haunts Cicero.
The words, says Tyrrell, are often quoted by him in his letters;
we may find them, at least the first two of them, in the letters
to Atticus vii, 1, 12; xiii, 13; xiii, 24; and these last two letters
belong to the year 45—to the period when his daughter was
dead and all his political ideals shattered by the despotism of
Caesar. This means that, life through, the conception of duty
shaped itself to him in one line of Homer and that it abides.
Men are possessed by a line of Shakespeare, a verse of Scripture,
which is always with them, decus et tutamen, so to speak; conscience
uses the quotation. What can it imply but that this comes from
a book which has stirred the man, when a single sentence from
it can shape conduct on all occasions, can shape life itself?

Now turn to one or two more letters, and here is some more
Homer—

εἷς οἰωνὸς ἄριστος ἀμύνεσθαι περὶ πάτρης (ad Atticum, ii, 3).

That is Hector again (*Iliad*, xii, 243):

> ἀλλὰ τὰ μὲν προτετύχθαι ἐάσομεν ἀχνύμενοί περ
> (*ad Atticum*, vii, 1; *Iliad*, xviii, 112; xix, 65),

that is, 'we will let bygones be bygones';

> οὐχ ὁσίη φθιμένοισιν—
> (*ad Atticum*, iv, 7, 2; *Odyssey*, xxii, 412),

three words from a famous passage and one of them wrong; he thinks of Odysseus—

> οὐχ ὁσίη κταμένοισιν ἐπ' ἀνδράσιν εὐχετάασθαι;

or again, once more a slight misquotation of a famous line,[1]

> πολλὸν ἀριστεύειν καὶ ὑπείροχος ἔμμεναι ἄλλων
> (*ad Q.F.* iii, 5 and 6; *Iliad*, vi, 208; and xi, 784).

The misquotations, if our common experience is to be trusted, mean surely that the quotation haunts the heart and that it has not been turned up in a concordance (even if there was one). There we may cease to quote for the moment, unless a reference or two in lighter vein are worth recall to fortify a strong position. Turn again then to the letter with which we began (*ad Atticum*, ii, 5), and Homer comes again three lines down—

> Πουλυδάμας μοι πρῶτος ἐλεγχείην ἀναθήσει
> (*Iliad*, xxii, 100)

and Cicero explains that Polydamas with his ready blame in this case is *Cato ille noster*, 'who alone outweighs a hundred thousand in my eyes'. In a later letter (*ad Atticum*, vii, 1) Polydamas comes again, and this time he is Atticus himself. And then there is Varro touched off in another letter (*ad Atticum*, xiii, 25, 3) and a line much less likely to be remembered than one or two already given:

> δεινὸς ἀνήρ· τάχα κεν καὶ ἀναίτιον αἰτιόῳτο
> (*Iliad*, xi, 654).[2]

---

[1] It is suggested to me that Cicero's texts may not have been ours; perhaps, but one would rather have expected the recension of Aristarchus to be in his hands.

[2] Another out-of-the-way line (*Iliad*, vii, 93) near the end of the long letter to Atticus from Laodicea (*ad Atticum*, vi, 1, 23) with Tyrrell's note, no. 152.

It is worth while to remember Dio Chrysostom's remark about Homer.[1] Homer gives every man, he says, as much of himself as the man can take. It stands that Cicero was able to draw a good deal from him.

At previous points references have been made to his intimacy with Plato and Xenophon, to the appeal exercised upon him by the *Oedipus Coloneus* of Sophocles on the actual ground of the scene. To these may be added a sentence or two of Plutarch, based on passages of his books and echoes of his talk: 'he said of Aristotle that he was a river of liquid gold, of Plato's dialogues that Zeus, if it were his nature to use human speech, would speak like that. Theophrastus, too, he used to call his own especial delight; and when he was asked which of the speeches of Demosthenes he thought the best, he answered "the longest".' The index shows many references to Isocrates, only two to Pindar. He even praises Nicander of Colophon—not indeed his snake-bite poem but his *Georgics*, 'written by a man, who had no connexion with the country, by sheer poetic faculty of no rustic order'.[3] Tyrrell is warm in praise of his 'splendid translations' from the Greek poets—from Homer in *de Divinatione* (ii, 63, 64) and in *de Finibus* (v, 49), and from Aeschylus and Sophocles in the *Tusculans* (ii, 19–35), which were so good that they were long assigned to Accius, and 'which no judicious critic can read without recognizing a dignity and even splendour of diction not surpassed in Latin literature'.[4] An amusing and quite short letter to Atticus tells of a meeting with Pompey, and all but accidentally reveals excursions in out-of-the-way corners of Greek literature. Pompey talked much with Cicero that day, we read—'very dissatisfied with himself, as he said (you must not omit that in speaking of Pompey). He scorned Syria, he ran down Spain—once more, as he said. Yes, I think that all along, where he is mentioned, we must repeat the refrain "as he said"—just like καὶ τόδε Φωκυλίδου'—the catchwords with which Phocylides used to begin his two-line aphorisms.

Taking all these passages together—and many more references might be gathered—the reader must feel that here is a long and

---

[1] Dio Chrysostom, xviii, 8: ἀφ' αὑτοῦ διδοὺς ὅσον ἕκαστος δύναται λαβεῖν.
[2] Plutarch, *Cicero*, 24.   [3] *de Oratore*, i, 16, 69.
[4] R. Y. Tyrrell, *Latin Poetry*, p. 18.

intimate knowledge of Greek masterpieces, which must mean more than any assemblage of useful summaries from which ἀπόγραφα should be taken. The speech for Archias, the Greek poet whose citizenship had been questioned, makes quite explicit Cicero's avowal of his debt to Greek literature and his delight in it from youth to age.

When we turn to Latin literature,[1] we find the same enthusiasm in Cicero for study, the same devotion to the poets—none of them the peers of Homer and Euripides, but the pioneers of national culture. It was notorious how fond he was of reading them. Quintilian remarks how Cicero avowed that he had been helped by those most ancient writers, men of genius even if deficient in art.[2] Indeed, of the fragments of the old-time literature—how many preserved by Cicero himself, it would be hard to conjecture—perhaps the most impressive survivals are due to his sympathy.

Moribus antiquis stat res Romana virisque.

'This verse Ennius seems to have uttered as it were from an oracle, so brief and so true is it.' Thus he begins the fifth book of his *Republic*. The line is famous—beautiful in structure, profoundly true in sentiment, almost, one might say, a prophecy of the *Aeneid* itself. No 'lack of art' about it; but Ennius is not always on that level. And yet in rougher verse of the old primitive style, we have often enough the same quality of Roman thought. Thus in the *de Officiis* (i, 12, 38) Cicero quotes 'that noble passage of Pyrrhus on the restoration of the captives: "I ask not gold for myself, nor shall you give me a price. Not huckstering the war but fighting—*non cauponantes bellum sed belligerantes*—with iron, not with gold, let us each decide on life or death, whether Fortune wills it that you reign or I; whatever she bring, by valour let us discover. And take this word therewith: whose valour so ever the fortune of war has spared, their freedom I am resolved to spare. I give them to you; take them; I give them with the blessing of the great Gods." A royal thought indeed and worthy of the Aeacid stock.' It is clear that

---

[1] He counted no Roman properly *eruditus* who did not know the national literature; *de Finibus*, i, 2, 5.

[2] Quintilian, x, i, 40. There is a caustic chapter in Gellius, *Attic Nights*, xii, 2, slashing Seneca for fatuous criticism of Cicero's pleasure in Ennius.

a great reader has found a great poet. No wonder Ennius is a favourite with him.

There would be little gained for the moment in making a transcript of all the fragments of Ennius to be found in Cicero's work. I prefer to take a page from his *Tusculans*,[1] where he quotes from the *Captive Andromache*. Cicero at heart disliked Epicureanism; his *de Senectute* has a Stoic tinge, which is perceptible in other works; the issue between the two systems seems never very far away. There is criticism of Epicureanism at large in his book on the Nature of the Gods. But in this Tusculan passage there is another approach. He takes the picture of supreme suffering as drawn by the greatest poet his country yet knew, and asks in effect what Epicurus has to offer the broken heart. But let him speak for himself.

'Epicurus must admit all this—or else what I have quoted word for word must be struck from his book—or, better still, the whole book abolished; for it is stuffed with pleasures. Let us ask, then, how one is to be freed from pain who speaks thus: "O heaven! it is fortune not race that fails me; for a kingdom was mine—that thou mayst know from what a station, from what wealth, from what sphere, my fortune has fallen in ruin." What then? Are we to press on her a cup of mead that she may cease to lament—or something or other of that sort? Look you! here is another passage from the same poet:

"The great glory is gone; I need thy help, oh Hector." We ought to come to her aid; she wants help.

"What succour am I to seek or to find? On what hope in exile or in flight dare I rely? Of citadel and city am I bereft. Whither shall I fall, whither turn? No altar stands for me in the house of my fathers; broken and scattered they lie, temples burnt with fire, the high walls scorched, defaced, and the pinewood...."

'You know what follows, and these words above all:

"Oh my father, oh my country, oh house of Priam, temple guarded by the portal that creaked on high! I have seen thee, while the wealth of the barbarian was all about thee, the ceilings

---

[1] *Tusculans*, iii, 19, 44–46; the passage is also cited in *de Oratore*, iii, 58, 217, as an illustration of fitting word and movement to the idea of sorrow; evidence of Cicero's interest in the play.

embossed and panelled, thyself adorned with gold and ivory, in royal mode!"

'Oh splendid poet! although he is despised by these singers of Euphorion. He realizes that the sudden and unforeseen falls with a heavier blow. So he piles up royal magnificence, which looked as if it would last for ever—and then he adds—what does he add?

"All this have I seen in flames, Priam's life reft from him by violence, the altar of Jove defiled with blood." Splendid poem! In fact and word and movement alike sadness! Let us take her sorrow from her! How? Oh, put her on a down cushion, bring in a flute girl, set a light to a pan of incense, look out a nice little drink and something to eat. For these, forsooth, are the "goods" by which the heaviest sorrows are done away. You, Epicurus, were saying just now that you conceived of no others. I would agree with Epicurus that she should be called back from sorrow to the contemplation of "goods" or blessings, if I could agree with him as to what is good.'

That is to say—when you penetrate into the spiritual, Epicureanism is futile; and Ennius has opened the door into the spiritual, and in that realm Cicero moves with the great poet; the deepest things lie open to him in the pages of Ennius; and Epicurus will not serve. It is the real refutation of hedonism; the broken heart is too serious a thing for that foolish talk;[1] and again, when Epicureans talk of the universe framed by the fortuitous concourse of atoms, do you think, Cicero says, that by jumbling alphabets together, you could one day toss out Ennius all ready for the reader?[2]

Ennius is not by any means his only love among the old poets, though (one guesses) chief among them. He cites Pacuvius, Caecilius, Terence and Plautus, Accius and others; but for the moment a line from Naevius will suffice, a line to which he has given a currency which it might not otherwise have had. Hector, he says, in Naevius, rejoices:

Laetus sum, laudari me abs te, pater, a laudato viro.[3]

The fact is that Cicero was steeped in his country's literature,

---

[1] Not to swell my text, another favourite quotation of Cicero's from Ennius is from his *Medea in Exile, utinam ne in nemore Pelio.*

[2] *de Nat. Deor.* ii, 37, 93.   [3] *Tusculans,* iv, 31, 67.

and, as with every well-read man, it came spontaneously to his mind, uncalled but relevant.

We must turn, however, for a moment, to another possible section of his library—possible but not more than possible. 'The singers of Euphorion', we saw, despise Ennius—very needlessly, Cicero thinks. 'Are we to pass over Euphorion?' asks Quintilian; 'if Virgil had not thought well of him, he would never have mentioned in the *Bucolics* "songs written in Chalcidian strain".'[1] Perhaps not; but Virgil's friend Gallus had been translating them, and in his early days at least Virgil responded a good deal to the modes of Alexandria. Cicero clearly did not; but here and elsewhere he shows that he was aware of new fashions in verse. Thus, returning in 50 B.C. from Cilicia, he writes to Atticus from Brindisi, after a crossing as lucky as Atticus could have had himself with his genius for good luck; 'so fair for me

flavit ab Epiro lenissimus Onchesmites';

Onchesmus was an Epirot town not otherwise very famous. Somehow Cicero strikes out this line of verse; laughs and says: 'This spondaic line, palm off as your own on any of the neoterics'[2]—the fin-de-siècle people, he might have said at the end of Victoria's reign. He makes it clear that he knew their fancies in verse but without much admiration. Incidentally we are told that Cicero quotes Catullus once or twice; Catullus speaks of the lobe of the ear being soft, and so does Cicero![3] 'The rain, it raineth every day'—so any allusion to rain must prove that an English poet had read *Twelfth Night*. It is odd that Cicero should have needed Catullus (nearly twenty years his junior) to tell him that the lobe of his ear was soft. A remark of Dr J. W. Mackail, in writing of Palgrave of the *Golden Treasury* and his attempt at a second selection, is worth recalling: 'And indeed the judgments in poetry of a man of seventy are likely to have lost much and gained little in the years of declining life.'[4] This can befall a man earlier; and a man of Cicero's traditions was little likely to turn to a juvenile 'singer of Euphorion'; the 'marriage of Peleus and Thetis' was

---

[1] Quintilian, x, i, 56; Virgil, *Eclogues*, x, 50.
[2] *ad Atticum*, vii, 2.
[3] R. Y. Tyrrell, *Latin Poetry*, p. 93 note; *ad Q.F.* ii, 13, 4, and Catullus, 25, 2.
[4] See Palgrave, F. T. in *Dictionary of National Biography*.

of another type from what he favoured in poetry—clever and
pretty enough, Alexandrine and trivial, not the real source of
Catullus' fame with posterity.

To one contemporary he refers quite definitely, and, if he is
to be allowed to say what the manuscripts give us, with real
judgment. He writes to his brother Quintus: *Lucretii poemata,
ut scribis, ita sunt, multis luminibus ingenii, multae tamen artis*—and
that is all.[1] Editors, one and another, have a passion for
inserting a negative before one or other of the clauses; but it is
difficult to see why Cicero should insist on their antithesis
between genius and art. One feels that they have taken too
much to heart the famous antithesis Ovid made about Ennius.
St Jerome tells us that 'Cicero' edited Lucretius, and the guess
has been hazarded that he meant Quintus Cicero, in which
case he might better have said so. Munro and Tyrrell both
believe that, though Cicero never quotes a passage from
Lucretius, 'his philosophical works undoubtedly show acquaintance' with the poem.

In conclusion, we have seen Cicero from youth to age responsive to literature, Greek and Latin, a lover of books, an
addict of *lectiunculae*[2] as well as of intensive study. It cannot be
too strongly emphasized how he enjoyed reading, as he seems
to have enjoyed everything he did. 'You Greeks are always
boys', we read of the Egyptian priest saying to Solon; and it
could have been said of Cicero. Put a book in his hand or a
pen, and he will fall to it with the freshness and zest of a boy.
Playfulness, good humour, happy quotations, gay or serious,
haunt his writing. 'Metellus', he writes, 'no, he isn't a human
being really but [and a quotation slips out] "sea-shore and airy
void and sheer solitude".'[3] No wonder that his letters were
kept and published, whether Tiro or Atticus gave them to the
world, and that the world decided to go on reading them and
does still. Literature is a thing men play at and labour at—
trifle with it and kill it with erudition; not so Cicero; he knew
how to handle it; he enjoyed it, and it passed into his constitution, quickened his mind, and formed his style, won him

---

[1] *ad Q.F.* ii, 9 (11); Tyrrell and Purser, vol. ii, no. 132. And cf. Munro on
Lucretius, ii, 1092.

[2] *ad Fam.* vii, i, 1.

[3] *ad Atticum,* i, 18.

readers. Yes, says Quintilian, 'and he can be loved'.[1] The heavy-minded miss this and that in one or another of his books; they would not have written them as he did. No, they would not; we can believe it. But let us turn once more to Luther's Table Talk and reach an end. 'Cicero', he said, 'handled the best and finest Questions in Philosophie; as *Whether there bee a God? What God is? Whether hee dealeth with humane affairs? And that there must bee an everlasting minde etc.*....Cicero was a very wise man; hee wrote more than all the Philosophers and read all the Grecian books through....Cicero, a wise and diligent man, suffered and performed much; I hope (said *Luther*) God will be merciful to him.' And every human reader will say 'Amen!'

[1] Quintilian, ii, 5, 20, *etiam amari potest.*

Chapter VIII

PRINCE OF DIGRESSORS

No one who has followed Coleridge's reading will doubt, I think, his acquaintance with Pausanias.

J. L. Lowes, *The Road to Xanadu*, p. 393.

I

Of all men who ever wrote guide-books, Pausanias must be nearly, if not quite, the most conscientious; and he writes for the actual traveller. He followed the road both ways, we are told, out and back, with the clear intention of making plain to those who might come after him the relative position of places and things. The wayfarer should not be lost in any tangle of cross-roads; everything should be exact and explicit; and after sixteen centuries modern travellers and explorers find ruins and sites precisely where he said they were. Always interested in what he is doing, Pausanias writes without raptures—more usually of the works of men than of the works of Nature. A man, of course, cannot well write a guide-book and avoid mentioning rivers and mountains, even if he is writing for people who will be travelling by train. Pausanias thought of men who would be on foot or on mule-back; rivers and mountains would be their guideposts, as it were, and both would sooner or later have to be crossed; and for a traveller on foot in any land, particularly in a Southern land, it is important to know where drinkable water is to be found. So Pausanias constantly speaks of springs and tells the reader where he will find them. He even says of one forlorn place, that water has to be carried there from half a mile away (x, 35, 9). He does not as a rule spend many words on country scenes;[2] Greeks rarely did; and, though in his period it was the way of rhetoricians to write up a prospect, perhaps most people to-day

---

[1] The passages cited by Professor Lowes deal with the Alpheus going under sea to join Arethusa. Coleridge used the translation of Thomas Taylor (1794), a book which was also in Wordsworth's library.

[2] Cf. W. G. Clark, *Peloponnesus*, p. 34, 'I do not remember, in all his book, a single phrase implying any sense of landscape beauty'.

who love the country would prefer not to read their efforts; and the more brilliant, the less one would wish to read them. A man needs remarkable powers of intellect, at any rate to-day, if he is to hold the reader with his rhetoric. It was not always so, as the later Greek world makes only too clear.

Pausanias was no rhetorician; when he lets himself go over scene or sculpture, he will tell us that it is 'worth seeing' (θέας ἄξια), which is not the language of hyperbole. Sir James Frazer, author of the elaborate commentary on Pausanias, was indeed something of a rhetorician; with all his learning, he had a naïve fancy for getting an artificial glitter on his narrative, and at times his facts suffer—as the reader of his selection of Cowper's Letters will find in the introduction, where a craving for brilliance—unless indeed it is pure *odium theologicum*—gives a twist to the plainest facts about John Newton and his successor Thomas Scott. So when Sir James Frazer expatiates on the defects of style, which he and, indeed, others note in Pausanias, perhaps his own gifts and instincts betray him. He finds the style loose, clumsy, ill-jointed, ill-compacted, rickety, ramshackle, and so forth. No one would guess it at all from his rendering of the text; perhaps like King James' translators of the Bible he felt himself more limited in translation than in original composition; in any case, his translation is a most readable piece of work, which at least one reader will gratefully own he has long used as a bedside book, reading in it or through it as might be, with great satisfaction, and glad to come back to it.

Pausanias is an eminently conscientious writer. 'It would be difficult to find a guide more accurate', wrote Henry Holland, a century or so ago, in his *Travels in Albania*. H. F. Tozer, in his *Geography of Greece*, says the same; and Frazer ends his long and critical introduction with a warm tribute to him. His book 'will be read and studied so long as ancient Greece shall continue to engage the attention and awaken the interest of mankind'; and Frazer anticipates that nothing can come to light to shake the confidence of reasonable and fair-minded men in his honour and good faith.

It is from one of the most charming of modern books on contemporary Greece that I borrow the title of this essay[1]; and

[1] Mrs R. C. Bosanquet's *Days in Attica*, p. 173.

perhaps a little explanation is needed. Pausanias is careful of his roads, is careful of everything; a widely-read man (e.g. with Herodotus at his finger-ends, as W. G. Clark put it— cf. ii, 30, 4), a man with a very wide knowledge of Greek literature, Greek history and Greek legend—and much more passion for genealogies than he suspected[1]—he never comes to any place of any consequence at all but he thinks of its history at large and its literary associations in particular. And then emerges what, in spite of all criticism of his handling of language, is surely a triumph of style. In the shortest compass he somehow gives immense masses of fact from book or memory or both. Much of the history of the Hellenistic period depends on him. Sometimes he gives us the rather Herodotean hint that it is his function to tell and not to criticize; sometimes he adds comment, which may be shrewd enough, or may look inconceivably naïve. It comes to this, wherever he goes you are to be made at home— not that he would use so emotional a phrase!—but, after this, it will not be a strange place; you will know too many of the people by name to be strange there; and you will know their stories. Like himself, you may not quite believe all the stories; that is no matter, you will be glad to know them. The squire of the village may not be descended from William the Conqueror, as he says—nor the noble of Corinth from Herakles— but they think so, or would like you to think so; and that is more important than a certificated pedigree with all the generations— except one or two, perhaps, unfortunately obscured, as is so unfortunately liable to happen. Take the opening of the book on Laconia (book iii); it is a little difficult to believe that Lacedaemon was a historical person, son of a lady Taygete, husband of a daughter of Eurotas called Sparta, and father of a son called Amyclas; and that they all gave their names to the local scenery, mountain, river and town. And there are plenty more figures of old legend in that first chapter— Herakleids, Dorians, twin princes, and so on. When we reach Messenia, we have many pages of history, ancient and less ancient, some of it likely enough to be true, not to be doubted

---

[1] Still he offers a caution on one occasion: 'the old legends, being unencumbered with genealogies, left free scope for fiction, especially in the pedigrees of heroes' (i, 38, 7). So, probably, most of his modern readers will have surmised.

at all, and some of it better than true perhaps—of the William Tell and King Arthur kind, not true perhaps but dynamic, and therefore significant. 'Up, guards, and at 'em'—if the Duke of Wellington never said those words, many things he did say were of less consequence.

Are we to count these expatiations into legend and history as digressions? Hardly, for how else is a guide-book to be written? Pausanias is not compiling a book for motorists, an affair of road-maps and recommended hotels. If memory serves, he does not mention an hotel. His book is for historians and antiquaries, and eminently for people interested in ancient art—in statues, pediments, pictures—and perhaps even more for those who care for shrines and gods and heroes, and strange traditions about them from the remote past—strange usages that survive, peculiar to one place or another, with the still stranger explanations that local priests and guides offer to your inquiries. 'The world is so full of a number of things', as the Scottish poet told us, you would hardly believe half of them. But there they are. As Herodotus said six hundred years before, given long enough time anything may prove true.

Posterity may be grateful that Pausanias lived when he did, in the reign of Marcus Aurelius, dating himself by the two hundred and seventeen years since the refounding of Corinth by Julius Caesar (v, 1, 2), who, by the way, also refounded Carthage (ii, 1, 2). The barbarian had not yet swamped historic Greece. The Gauls had long since raided it, and had been swept off into Galatia (i, 4, 5; and book x, 19–23); the Costobocs, whoever they were, had more recently attempted it (x, 34, 5); but Slav and Turk were names that the Greek world had not yet heard; and the new religion from Palestine, preached indeed in Athens and Corinth a century before by St Paul, had either not reached Pausanias or did not interest him. The Panagia and St Elias had not begun to usurp the shrines and functions of the old gods. Nor was Pausanias very much interested in the speculations of Greek philosophy—perhaps not at all. He was a man 'of common clay' says Frazer—'what Antony à Wood was to Oxford', says Tozer. Yet not so very common clay; for common clay rarely produces a book you can read and read again; and, at least to my mind, Pausanias is not nearly as irritable as Antony à Wood. Still, he can say a shrewd thing on occasion; 'as to the age of Hesiod and Homer, I have made the most precise investigation, but I do not care to write about it, knowing as I do how apt to find fault people are, and not least those who in my day preside over epic poetry' (ix, 30, 3). They might be à Wood's Oxford contemporaries, so sure of themselves and their scholarship, and so disagreeable. (All the same, when he digresses from Achaia to the climate, the cities and sanctuaries of Ionia, he cannot help just mentioning the river Meles near Smyrna, and the grotto near its springs, 'where they say that Homer composed his poems', vii, 5, 12.) Or again, one recalls his caustic Greek proverb about 'worshipping God with other people's incense' (ix, 30, 1). Yet again, the Ionians, changing sides back and forth in war, 'to use an Ionian expression, painted both walls' (vi, 3, 15). But Pausanias does not often let go in such criticism; perhaps he would be commoner clay, if he did. Still, allowing the author of a historical guide-book a wide margin in historical allusion, it would not be quite unkind to him to suggest that this reflexion upon contemporary students of literature might be called a digression. Let us call it so; and as we read him, we shall find many more—digressions all of them, and glimpses that leave us less forlorn. It is very often a man's digressions that reveal his character and interests, and that may reveal even more—the outlooks of his day, for instance, the traditions of his caste, and so forth; and if he is that happy combination of common clay and the genius for interesting people—if it is not absurd to suppose such genius to be of common clay—so much the better.

In what follows the endeavour will be to confine myself to Pausanias as 'prince of digressors'. Nothing will be written here that will enable a reader to find his way down a street of Corinth or Lebadea (though we shall visit the latter town); nothing will be said to enable him to identify a single sculpture; dates will be withheld; nothing will be found here but what is at least gently irrelevant to a *Periegesis of Greece* strictly conceived. Only our author's digressions will be considered. The aim is to see the man and linger about with him when he forgets the main aim of his work—unless indeed, as sometimes happens in literature, the digressions are the real business. Here at least they will be—the digressions, that is, of Pausanias; if the reader finds further consideration of the guide-book, that will be a digression. Just so much should be said; Pausanias, not unlike Herodotus, gives us a *caveat*. 'I am obliged', he says (vi, 3, 8), 'to say what is said by the Greeks, but I am not at all (οὐκέτι) obliged to believe it all.' No, one is not obliged to believe it all; for indeed 'most things in Greece are subjects of dispute' (iv, 2, 3).

II

We begin with myth, and with a champion myth (x, 4, 4). At Panopeus on the frontier of Phocis and Boeotia there stands by the roadside a small building of sun-dried brick (πλίνθου ὠμῆς), in which is an image of Pentelic marble; some say it is Asclepios, some that it is Prometheus, and the latter offer evidence. For by the river gulley lie two stones, each big enough to fill a cart. They have the colour of clay, yet not earthy clay, but such as would be found in a gulley or sandy torrent, and they smell very like the skin of a man. They say these are remains of the clay, out of which the whole race of mankind was fashioned by Prometheus. Here at the gulley is the tomb of Tityos. The circumference of the mound is just about one-third of a furlong and we are told that the verse in the *Odyssey*, 'lying on the ground; and he lay over nine roods', refers not to the size of Tityos, but to the place where he lay, the name of which was Nine Roods. Cleon, a man from Magnesia on the Hermos, used to say that men are incredulous of wonders, who in the course of their lives had not met yet greater marvels. He himself, Cleon said, believed that Tityos and other men had been as tradition said they were. For he had been at Cadiz; and he with the rest of the crowd had sailed out from the island, so bidden by Herakles, and when they came back to Cadiz they found a man of the sea cast ashore; and *he* covered five roods; he had been hit by God with a thunderbolt and was burning. So said Cleon (x, 4, 4–6). And so says Pausanias, without any expression of doubt or dissent. The lumps of clay or stone smelt of human flesh, and that made the story probable; and Cleon's general canon is only too true. Men who have seen nothing but what is to be seen in the streets of their own town do not realize that Nature does stranger things than they suppose. Herodotus at least held this belief. 'I do not know if this is true', he says about a story of gold-mining: 'I write what is said. Yet all things are possible', and he offers an illustration from his own experience (iv, 195); though what he saw is much more probable than Cleon's story. Still elsewhere we read of mermaids washed ashore dead on the coast of Gaul,[1] though no hint is given that they are as enormous as this man of the sea. Cleon's story falls rather short of making the Prometheus relics convincing.

Sometimes Pausanias is rather more critical. He briefly refers to a story of a musician called Cycnus becoming King of the Ligurians on the other side of the Eridanus river beyond the land of the Celts (he is not thinking of Caesar's Gaul); and then they say that after his death he was transformed by the will of Apollo into a swan. 'I am ready to believe', he continues, 'that a musician became King of the Ligurians, but that a man turned into a bird, is to me incredible' (i, 30, 3). The only relevance of the swan is that Socrates was alleged to have dreamt of one on the night before Plato became his pupil. But at a later point, when he writes of Arcadia, he speaks of lycanthropy and how Lycaon became a wolf (viii, 2, 3). Polybius mentions an Arcadian tale, cited by Plato, of a man turning into a wolf, but he seems to imply that it was a myth or an allegory (vii, 13, 7); he was an Arcadian himself, and we may be sure that it never happened among his acquaintance. When Polybius says that Philip V of Macedon lived 'the life of a wolf' (xvi, 24, 5), he means something else. But Pausanias is convinced by the story; the Arcadians have told it from of old, and it has the additional merit of probability. For the men of that period, because of their righteousness and piety, were guests of the gods, welcomed at their tables; the good were openly honoured by the gods, whose wrath as conspicuously fell on the wicked. Why, men in those days—some men—became gods, and to this day they keep their privileges ($\gamma\acute{\epsilon}\rho a$); and he cites Herakles and the Dioscuri and others. So that one might well believe that Lycaon became a wild beast, and Niobe the daughter of Tantalus a stone. But in my day, he says, to such an extent has wickedness increased and spread over every land

[1] Pliny, *Nat. Hist.* ix, 5, 9.

and all the cities that—apart from flattering talk addressed to rulers—no one is changed from a man to a god; and the wrath of the gods is reserved for a distant future, when the wicked have departed from this life. Truth comes into discredit too often, of old and nowadays, because of lies built up on a foundation of fact. Thus they say that ever since Lycaon's day a man is changed into a wolf at the sacrifice of Zeus Lycaeus, but, if he abstains from human flesh for nine years, he becomes a man again; otherwise, he remains a wolf. Thence he digresses still further; they say that Niobe on Mt Sipylus weeps in summer; and—further still—he has heard that griffins have spots like leopards and Tritons speak with a human voice, though some say (and Wordsworth seems to support them, we notice) that Tritons blow through a shell with a hole in it. In fact, those who enjoy the marvellous are rather apt by nature to make it more marvellous still, and so they ruin truth by mixing it with falsehood (viii, 2, 5–7). In the next chapter he gets back to history of a sort—Lycaon's son and the foundation of cities in Greece and Italy; and then Lycaon's daughter is transformed into a she-bear by Hera, and is shot by Artemis, but Zeus made her into a constellation—unless indeed the constellation is so called out of compliment to her, for the Arcadians point out her grave.

The reader must make of all this the best he can; and he may agree with H. F. Tozer that Pausanias is 'a very quaint figure— the thorough archaeologist—completely destitute of humour'— that he is in short a sort of Herodotus with all his wit (in the widest sense of the word) eliminated.[1] It is perhaps unfair both to Mr Tozer and to Pausanias to string these phrases so abruptly together. It may be common clay, as Frazer says, but it surely takes unusual forms. One might be tempted to make a very abrupt judgment upon the man who wrote the chapters just summarized, but old acquaintance forbids it. The man has evidently a genial gift of digression; and perhaps he is as credulous as these passages suggest; but think of his other gifts— his close observation (for which you must read him at large), the range of his interests, and his constant appeal to the reader. Much that he writes is frankly absurd from our point of view—

---

[1] These phrases are gathered from Tozer's *Geography of Greece*, pp. 25–29.

his etymologies as improbable as his myths, or more so—and yet absurdity seems no complete account of him. The greatest of English biographers had certainly a genius for being absurd; no doubt of that, if you try to imagine yourself reading his Johnson on publication, before it became a hallowed work. Pausanias' book is quite different, in every way you can think of it, from Boswell's; but you *can* read it, and you want to read it; it has some sort of charm, not so readily recognized as Boswell's but a real charm, which it may take us more time and more quotation to analyse. 'Dear garrulous Pausanias!' cries Mrs Bosanquet, and one can understand her.

We need not linger over oracles and omens at this stage, but two suggestions may be made. Some thought may be given to the evolution (if that is the right word) of Cyamites, a sort of bean-hero of Attica (i, 37, 4); Pausanias will not be sure of his origin; perhaps a hero was needed to discover beans, because the discovery was not to be attributed to Demeter—'whoever has been initiated at Eleusis or has read the so-called Orphic writings, knows what I mean'. So does Sir James Frazer, it would seem; beans, he says, were prohibited to Eleusinians and Orphics, as, we learn elsewhere, they were to Pythagoreans. Without further remark Pausanias proceeds to register some big and beautiful tombs. But we may turn to quite another passage (ix, 16, 7), where he tells us that 'Greek legends have generally discrepant forms'. Thus the Megarians (and it is very silly of them) falsify the story of Theseus (i, 41, 5) for purposes of their own, clean against the true tradition.

III

Reference has been made already to the lavish use of History by Pausanias, for which posterity is indebted to him. It is, for instance, of interest to learn that the Macedonian custom was not to erect trophies; Philip set up none for his victory at Chaeronea, nor Alexander for his triumph over Darius (ix, 40, 7–9). Pausanias explains at an early stage in his book on Attica that 'the age of Attalus and Ptolemy is so remote that the tradition no longer remains, and those who associated with the kings for the purpose of chronicling their deeds fell into neglect still earlier' (i, 6, 1). A man, he says, who is the intimate of a king must inevitably write to please him; if Philistus was justified in concealing the most impious deeds of Dionysius because he was hoping to be allowed to return to Syracuse, there is surely plenty of excuse for Hieronymus writing to please King Antigonus (i, 13, 9). No wonder that Greek stories are discrepant. Nor need we look back at his genealogies; he seems, as I have said, unconscious of their great appeal to him—'those who want to find pedigrees for everything', he says, make Pythes the son of Delphos and derive the name Pytho from him (x, 6, 5); but Pausanias recalls and quotes the story of the dragon killed by the arrows of Apollo and of its body rotting, whence the name from *pythesthai*; and so he digresses to the various attacks made through the ages on Delphi (x, 7, 1)—by the Euboean pirate, by the Phlegyan nation, by Pyrrhus the son of Achilles, by Xerxes, by the Phocians, down to the Gauls and to Nero (who stole five hundred bronze statues of gods and men).

No history is too ancient for him. He speaks of the Bacchiads of Corinth, of the Herakleidai, of Spartan wars with Argos, in all of which Herodotus was at least one of his sources. Helen's suitors we may pass by, merely noting with him that Achilles cannot have been one of them (iii, 24, 10). He surveys the 'benefactors of Hellas'—Miltiades, Leonidas, Themistocles (one is glad to see that name), but *not* Aristides, who imposed tribute on the islander Greeks. 'But those who took part in the Peloponnesian war against Athens, and especially those distinguished in it, one might call the murderers of Hellas, yes, and all but its wreckers (καταποντιστάς)'. Cimon and Epameinondas, founder of such famous cities as Messene and the Arcadian Megalopolis, and Aratus one would count among the benefactors, and last of all Philopoemen, after whom Greece ceased to produce valiant men (viii, 52). Evander, familiar to us in the *Aeneid*, an Arcadian and son of a nymph, receives honourable mention (viii, 43, 2). Even Mummius, sacker of Corinth, is gently handled, the first Roman to dedicate an offering in a Greek sanctuary (v, 24, 4). After which it seems odd to find Augustus explained, 'emperor of the Romans after Caesar the founder of the modern Corinth' (ii, 3, 1). The Roman forum is 'a marvel (θαῦμα) for size and style' (x, 5, 11). And he has references to wars in Britain (viii, 43, 3) and Germany (viii, 43, 6), practically contemporary. Finally (not that there is an end to it anywhere but here) 'my reason for introducing this account of Sardinia into my account of Phocis is that the island is little known to Greeks' (x, 17, 13)—a sentence which almost justifies (if it needs justifying) the title I have borrowed for this essay.

History covers more than politics—inventions, for instance, are significant. King Pelasgus, who must be very ancient, invented huts, as a protection against rain and heat, and also the sheepskin coats, still worn by the poor in Euboea and Phocis, and not quite unknown in modern Greece (viii, 1, 5). On another plane the Samians Rhoecus and Theodore were the first to melt bronze and cast statues, and Theodore made the famous signet ring of Polycrates (viii, 14, 8); and we read of the inventor of the perfect flute, who greatly delighted audiences by the expression of his face and the movement of his whole body (ix, 12, 5).

But a last word or two on politics. 'We have yet to hear of democracy bringing prosperity to any people except the Athenians, who attained greatness by its means'—Herodotus, you will remember, said something like that (v, 78); for the Athenians excelled the Greek world in native wit, and least of all men disregarded the established laws—and there Pericles in Thucydides' pages seems to have given him a clue (Thucydides, ii, 37; Pausanias, iv, 35, 5). The Argives always loved freedom (ἰσηγορίαν, the Herodotean word) and self-government from the most ancient times, and limited to the utmost the authority of their kings (ii, 19, 2). But the curse of Greece has always been treachery, 'never absent from Greece since time began'—every state in Greece, except Sparta, suffered more from it than from plague (vii, 10, 1; 3). Yes, and it was well said, he thinks as he contemplates the fate that overtook Demosthenes for all his love of his country, that a man who throws himself heart and soul into politics and puts his trust in the people, never comes to a good end (i, 8, 3). Isocrates won a reputation for prudence by keeping out of politics and public life (i, 18, 8). Elsewhere he concedes that even a democracy may be capable of a just resolution; for the Athenians conceded the honour of a public

burial and a commemorative inscription to slaves who fought
for Athens against the Persians, and fell (i, 29, 7).

IV

We have seen how reluctant Pausanias was to venture an opinion
as to the dates of Hesiod and Homer (ix, 30, 3). He tells us that
the Cypriots claimed Homer for their island, and that the people
of Ios show a tomb alleged to be his; but once more, in spite
of his reading books and oracles, he will not express a view of
his own as to the poet's age or native land (x, 24, 2–3). But he
is clear that, like Demosthenes, fortune used Homer badly, that
he knew poverty, beggary, and blindness on foreign soils
(ii, 33, 3), but went on making poetry none the less, though
Thamyris, also blind, 'sang no more' (iv, 33, 7; cf. x, 30, 8).
The god at Delphi called Homer at once ill-starred and blest
(viii, 24, 14; the actual oracle quoted x, 24, 2). Pausanias is
not as orthodox a Homerist as Strabo, for he accepts the
Homeric hymns as genuine, and tells us that Callinus and many
respectable critics (ἄξιοι λόγου) count the *Thebaid* Homer's; he
does not say that he goes so far himself, but he puts the poem
next after the *Iliad* and the *Odyssey* (ix, 9, 5). He tells us of
people who say that Pisistratus collected the poems of Homer
which were scattered and preserved only in broken memories
(ἄλλα ἀλλαχοῦ μνημονευόμενα), but by someone's slip at least
one name, an obscure one, was changed (vii, 26, 13). Of course
Homer is incessantly quoted by Pausanias as by all the Greeks.
Homer wandered far and wide, and 'esteemed the largest of
princes less than the applause of the people' (i, 2, 3).

As to Hesiod, he was perhaps of manners too rustic to
associate with princes, or did not care to roam (i, 2, 3). An
ancient tripod still stands on Helicon, which they say Hesiod
won in a contest at Chalcis (ix, 31, 3). Other authorities say
he beat Homer himself in that contest. The Boeotians round
Helicon, Pausanias says, hold that Hesiod wrote nothing but
the *Works and Days*, and not all of it; for they delete the address
to the Muses; they have a leaden tablet, very time-worn (which
he saw), on which the poem is engraved. Other people, however, say Hesiod wrote a lot of other poems—e.g. the *Great Eoeae*

(the poem on famous women, where each paragraph begins ἢ οἵη), the *Theogony*, etc. He recurs to the possibility that the *Theogony* is Hesiod's, but he does not definitely accept it (viii, 18, 1). Hesiod, however, he says, was murdered at last, and his bones were brought to Orchomenos, as the Pythian priestess bade; a crow had helped to find them (ix, 38, 3–4). Pindar's house was still to be seen, but in ruins (ix, 25, 3); it was a long time since the great Emathian conqueror bade spare the house of Pindarus, and time was less kind. The poet's iron chair was still shown at Delphi, and stories told of him. On other poets we need hardly linger—Alcman, Alcaeus, Corinna, Telesilla, Rhianus, or Orpheus, the subject of many discrepant legends (ix, 30, 4–6). It is interesting to read in his pages that Aeschylus said that a dream of Dionysus bidding him write tragedy was what started him (i, 21, 2); a story that reminds us of Caedmon. Incidentally we may note that in Pausanias' judgment there is not in all mankind a people so indifferent to poetry and the praise of poets as the Spartans (iii, 8, 2). This is hardly a digression, and it shows how little the centuries had changed that unpleasing race. Why, even the Laconian dialect is 'the least musical of languages' (iii, 15, 2).

V

Pausanias, as we have seen, has been compared, distantly, with Herodotus. Of course the theme of Herodotus was a world war—the first of world wars, and the theme of Pausanias was the antiquities of Greece, a very different matter; but he also has the wider interests, and, relevant or irrelevant (we will not be more precise about it than he), he looks abroad from time to time, as well he might, if, as is deduced from his book, he came from Lydia. In particular, he is interested in natural history—not, of course, so exclusively as Aelian or the elder Pliny.

'It appears,' he says, 'to be a characteristic of the Greeks to admire what they see abroad more than what they see at home. For while distinguished historians have given us the minutest descriptions of the Egyptian pyramids, they have not even mentioned the treasury of Minyas and the walls of Tiryns, which are not a whit less wonderful' (ix, 36, 5). Pausanias does not say he has seen the Pyramids; he does say he has *not* seen the walls of Babylon and Susa (iv, 31, 5).

To begin then with what seems strangest, he had travelled, he tells us, in 'the land of the Hebrews'. It is *à propos* of the fancy that the river Alpheus passed under the sea from Elis to Syracuse, to mingle his waters with those of Arethusa. Similar tales of the undersea passage of rivers he quotes elsewhere (ii, 5, 3); the people of Phlius and Sicyon claim that the Maeander from Phrygia traverses the sea somehow and becomes the Asopus in Greece; and the Delians make a similar claim upon the Nile—if indeed the Nile was not actually the Euphrates! Thus, he says, the Nile runs successfully through a certain lake as if dry land, to emerge into Egypt and reach the sea opposite Pharos. 'And in the land of the Hebrews, as I know myself, the river Jordan passes through the lake called Tiberias, and then enters another lake called the Dead Sea and is lost in it. The Dead Sea has qualities quite unlike those of other waters; living creatures float in it naturally, without swimming; dying creatures sink to the bottom. Hence the lake is barren of fish; danger stares them in the face (ἀπὸ τοῦ φανερωτάτου) and they flee back to their native water' (v, 7, 4–5). As in other cases, his analogy fails somewhat of being analogous. In another place he tells us of a Sibyl at Cumae, named Demo, whose bones are preserved in an urn in a temple there; and she suggests to his mind another prophetic woman, Sabbe by name, who lived 'among the Hebrews who dwell above Palestine'. Her father, it was said, was Berosus; but some say she was a Babylonian, others an Egyptian. And then he swings back to Dodona and the 'Doves' (x, 12, 9–10). He records the tomb of a Silenus in the land of the Hebrews, which proves, as other such tombs prove, that the Silenuses are a mortal race (vi, 24, 8). It is not very clear that there is much difference between Silenuses and Satyrs; elderly Satyrs bear the other name; and he tells of a western voyage on the Atlantic, on which Euphemus, a Carian, said he and his ship were driven on to certain islands; and, reluctant as the sailors, who had been there before, were to put in, they had to; these islands were inhabited by satyrs, red-haired creatures with tails little less than the tails of horses, who attempted to carry off the women from the ship (i, 23, 5).

From other statements, e.g. Strabo's, who however seems doubtful, perhaps these islands (plural as they are) were Ireland. At all events in the Orphic *Argonautica* (1170 ff.) we read

νῦν γὰρ δὴ λυγρῇ τε και ἀλγεινῇ κακότητι
ἔξομαι ἢν νήσοισιν 'Ιερνίσιν ἆσσον ἵκωμαι.

We might ourselves be digressing if we attempted a precise date for that strange poem; suffice that it belongs probably to a later century than Pausanias. Nor must we let the Silenus tempt us to wander too far afield. We return to the land of the Hebrews to a very strange object. For 'in the city of Jerusalem, which the Roman Emperor razed to the ground, there is the tomb of a native woman called Helena. The door of the tomb, like the rest of it, is of stone; and there is a contrivance by which it does not open until the year brings back the same day and the same hour. Then the door opens by its own mechanism, unaided, and shortly afterwards shuts of itself. This happens at that time, and at any others you could not open it if you tried; force will not open it but only break it down' (viii, 16, 4–5). The digression follows the account of the tomb of Aepytus to which Homer alludes (*Iliad*, ii, 604). For any one who remembers another Helena, mother of Constantine, reputed discoverer of the True Cross at Jerusalem, the digression raises curious questions; the coincidence is so odd as to tempt one to wonder whether it is more.

As Pausanias surveys the world, he finds a strange variety of unexpected creatures. Some are familiar to us already—the Arimaspi, for instance, of whom we read long ago in Herodotus —those one-eyed men described by Aristeas of Proconnesus who fight the griffins for gold. The men are all one-eyed from birth, and the griffins are like lions but with the wings and beak of an eagle (i, 24, 6). Again in Libya are wild men and women among other incredible monsters (ii, 21, 6); Procles, a Carthaginian, said he saw one of these wild men who had been brought to Rome, and conjectured that the famous Gorgon, slain by Perseus, had been one of the tribe. Her head, Pausanias says, lies buried under a mound near the market-place of Argos. On giants he is particularly well-informed; the bones of one are preserved with much veneration in the gymnasium at Asopus (iii, 22, 9), while the grave of another was disclosed near

Antioch as the result of the diversion of the river (viii, 29, 3).
The oracle of Clarus revealed the name of this last giant; it
was Orontes, an Indian, and he was about eleven ells high
and—this is important—he had not, as a silly popular story
asserts, serpents instead of feet. India has the necessary conditions for producing creatures of great size and strange
appearance; so why not a human giant?[1] After all, the human
race was produced by the sun warming the earth. Climate
works marvels, as we shall see.

For beside giants he discusses Tritons, starting with a story
of Tanagra (ix, 20, 4). The Triton concerned used to attack
the women purifying themselves in the sea. So they prayed to
Dionysus, and he came and conquered the Triton. But there
is a variant to the story, less dignified but more probable; it
was cattle the creature attacked, till at last a bowl of wine was
put out for him, and he drank and slept; and a man of Tanagra
chopped off his head as he slept. The image there is headless,
and the story about Dionysus is rationalized. But Pausanias
saw another Triton at Rome, a smaller one, a scaly creature
with gills and a big mouth, with the teeth of a beast; 'the eyes
blue, I think', hands, fingers and nails like the shell of the
murex, and a tail like a dolphin. That was not all he saw at
Rome; for there was a rhinoceros with two horns on its nose,
a shaggy Paeonian bull, Indian camels the colour of leopards,[2]
and an elk (something between a stag and a camel). From
these actual beasts, he strays to the *Martichoras* described by
Ctesias, the man-eater with three rows of teeth in each jaw and
a tail that shoots spikes at its enemies—which he thinks in the
main false, the product of terror; probably just a tiger, he thinks.
Probably the wild animals of Greece, if found at all in Libya
or India, would be different. The rivers of Greece, at all events,
breed no dangerous brutes, like the crocodiles of the Nile and
Indus, to say nothing of the hippopotamus which is as bad
(iv, 34, 2–3). Man is not the only animal differentiated by
climate. Look at the asps of Libya and of Ethiopia; in the latter
country they are as black as the men. So careful ought we to

---

[1] One might add the big Celts (Cabarenses) 'who dwell on the borders of the
frozen desert' (i, 35, 5)—this a digression from the knee-bones of Ajax, as big as
quoits.

[2] Were they giraffes? *Diversum confusa genus panthera camelo,* Horace, *Ep.* ii, 1, 195.

be to avoid hasty judgment and reckless incredulity. He has
never seen a winged serpent, but believes them possible; a man
of Phrygia had produced a scorpion winged like a locust.
Herodotus also believed in winged serpents, we remember
(ix, 21). Pausanias has seen swarms of locusts, in Asia, and seen
them destroyed, one swarm by a storm, one by heat, one by
sudden cold (i, 24, 8).

Pleasanter than such creatures, surely, is the silkworm (*ser*) of
the Sêres, a good deal bigger than those kept by English school-
boys, longer lived too, living four years, at which age the Sêres
give it food that makes it burst, and the bulk of its silk thread is
found inside it. Seria is an island in the Red Sea, as Herodotus
called it, though English people call it the Indian Ocean; but
another story says it is a deltaic island formed by the river Ser.
It may be remembered that in the *Odyssey* and Sir John
Mandeville most strange places are islands. The Sêres, some
said, are a kind of mixture of Scythians and Indians—not too
bad an attempt to represent the Chinese, when one recalls that
all the land East of the Indus was 'Indian'.

The mention of India leads us naturally on to digressions;
India, a land of barter with no coined money (iii, 12, 4), first
launched the doctrine of immortality, which Plato adopted
(iv, 32, 4); and then, of course, there are elephants (vi, 26, 6);
and Pausanias remarks how odd it was that Homer knew ivory
but not the elephant (i, 12, 4). He discusses whether we should
speak of the tusks or the horns of the creature, and decides for
horns, for he sheds them every year; and Pausanias claims to
know, for he saw an elephant's skull in a temple in Campania
(v, 12, 2–3). So it goes on. Cochineal—mosquitoes—famous
trees—white blackbirds and other albino creatures (viii, 17, 3)—
all tempt him to digress—and notably the singing fish of the
river Aroanios, which however would not sing for Pausanias,
and did not for Edward Dodwell.[1] He gives a strange account
of ebony, derived from a Cypriot, who told him it has neither
leaf nor fruit, and is not a plant of the sunlight, but a growth
underground (i, 41, 5). The cork oaks of Arcadia are more
probable altogether (viii, 12, 1), and the white poplar that
Herakles brought to Elis (v, 14, 2). The unguent of roses from

---

[1] *Tour*, vol. ii, p. 445; trout, he says; Pausanias, viii, 21, 2.

Chaeronea will keep wooden images from rotting (ix, 41, 7). But it is needless to try to catalogue his references to Natural History, which afford him endless temptation to digress; Nature's creatures and ways are so strange.

Elsewhere in this volume something is said about the springs of Hellas, a constant matter of reference with him. Here we may be content with a reference to the signs of coming earthquake vouchsafed by the god (vii, 24, 7); the prelude is unseasonable weather, heavy rains or drought, a hazy sky, the drying up of springs, storms of wind, unfamiliar stars, and 'a violent rumbling of winds blowing underground'. Earthquakes are of different types, the deadliest leaving no trace of human habitation; Helice was swamped in the sea, and a town on Mt Sipylus was swallowed in a chasm, from which water streamed out and the lake called Saloe was formed (vii, 24, 7–13). It may be relevant to recall what our own contemporaries tell us, that, the more familiar men become with earthquakes and their effects, the more they dread them. Finally, and we may leave Nature and her ways for the time being, the Ocean is not a river, but the utmost sea that men can sail; it washes the shores of Iberians and Celts, and the island of the Britons lies in it (i, 33, 4).

VI

When we turn to consider the gods, we touch what is clearly from start to finish one of the main interests of Pausanias; and here perhaps it may seem that we leave our proper theme, for what he says of the gods is hardly digression. His whole book is an assemblage of information about temples and images, special local legends and peculiar rites, ceremonies and offerings, the various surnames or by-names given to the gods in various places—many indeed—and the strange images or objects in which the divine is embodied. Thus 'in the olden time Greeks worshipped unwrought stones instead of images' (vii, 22, 4), and the people of Pharae in Achaia still adore thirty square stones, giving each stone the name of a god. Near Mantineia, he finds a sanctuary of the Black Aphrodite (viii, 6, 5), for which name he gives an explanation: her function is chiefly exercised at night. A 'black Demeter' is recorded near Phigalia, in

Arcadia (viii, 42, 1). Xenophanes, the reader will remember,
found black gods somewhere in the Mediterranean; but his
caustic lines about the horses making a god suggest a
simpler and more straightforward explanation. Again, at
Chaeronea the god most honoured is the sceptre which Homer
says Hephaestus made for Zeus, and which was passed on till
we find Agamemnon wielding it. There was a story as to how it
came there, but Pausanias believed it was brought by Agamemnon's daughter Electra. It had not indeed a temple, but a man
kept it in his house for a year at a time, and day by day flesh
and cakes were set out on a table beside it (ix, 40, 11–12). It
was, he believed, the only genuine and authentic work extant
of Hephaestus, though others were alleged (ix, 41).

But while 'many a wondrous sight may be seen, and not a few
tales of wonder heard in Greece, there is nothing on which the
blessing of God rests in so full a measure as the rites of Eleusis
and the Olympic games' (v, 10, 1). As we shall see, a dream
warned him to be silent about the Eleusinian mysteries, but
he has many pages, full of interest, about Olympia. Not
all Olympic victors however have had statues erected to
commemorate them (vi, 1, 1), nor all great men in other
spheres.

Occasionally a strain of rationalism shows itself in his remarks.
They say, he tells us, that Tyndareus put the fetters on Aphrodite
Morpho in Sparta—a symbol, some said, of the fidelity of wives
to husbands, or, said others, it was to punish the goddess for
bringing his daughters to shame. But that Pausanias cannot
accept for a moment; it would be too silly to suppose he could
punish the goddess by making a cedar-wood doll and giving it
her name (iii, 15, 11). On Taenarum Greeks say Herakles
dragged up the dog from hell, but 'no road leads underground
through the cave, and it is not easy to believe that the gods
have an underground dwelling in which the souls of the dead
gather'; and he quotes the explanation of Hecataeus of Miletus
that the said hound of hell was a mere snake; Homer was not
responsible for the name Cerberus and its three heads (iii, 25, 5).
But on the whole Pausanias is no rationalist—'when I began
this work, I used to look on these Greek stories as little better
than foolishness; but, now that I have got as far as Arcadia, my

opinion about them is this: I believe that the Greeks who were accounted wise spoke of old in riddles and not straight out; and accordingly I conjecture that these stories about Cronos [swallowing a foal instead of his son and afterwards a stone instead of Zeus] are a bit of Greek philosophy. In matters of religion I will follow tradition' (viii, 8, 3). Possibly it is 'a bit of Greek philosophy'—or is it a line of verse readjusted?—that he gives us when he tells us that 'Sleep is to the Muses the dearest god' (ii, 31, 3).

Naturally he stands by the stories of divine vengeance. The gods of Greece took vengeance on the Arcadians at Chaeronea by the hands of Metellus, for there they had abandoned the other Greeks to Philip (vii, 15, 6). The god routed the Gauls from Delphi (i, 4, 4; viii, 10, 9). The Cabiri took terrible vengeance on those who profaned their sanctuary (ix, 25, 5–10). Mithridates and his impious admiral Menophanes (who razed Delos to the ground) alike met punishment (iii, 23, 5).

In the temple of Asclepios at Aegium in Achaia, Pausanias tells us he fell into religious discussion with a man of Sidon. The stranger maintained that the Phoenicians had juster ideas of the divine nature than the Greeks; in the Phoenician story Asclepios was the son of Apollo, but no mortal woman was his mother. 'Asclepios', said the Phoenician, 'is the air, and as such is favourable to the health of man and of every living thing; Apollo is the sun...and gives the air its healthfulness.' 'Certainly', said Pausanias, 'that is just what the Greeks say; for at Titane near Sicyon the same image is called both Health and Asclepios, clearly because the sun's course over the earth is the source of health to mankind' (vii, 23, 7–8). Here he at least approached the school, largely Stoic, that identified the gods with natural objects, though he would never have been so reckless as some of them. Gods who could and would take vengeance could not really be identified with air and grain and drink. He resolutely held by their guidance and their personality. They guided him in dreams, he says. He had meant to give a full description of the Athenian sanctuary at Eleusis, but a vision in a dream forbade it, and he turned to 'what may lawfully be told to everybody' (i, 14, 3). Other dreams forbade him to tell of the sanctuary of Triptolemus (i, 38, 7) and of the rites of the Great Goddesses in the Carnasian grove in Messenia (iv, 33, 5).

But on one occasion he is more explicit. At Lebadea in Boeotia is the oracle of Trophonius, and he tells how a man must prepare for consultation. He must lodge for a specified time in a certain building dedicated to the Good Daemon and Good Fortune. He must observe rules of purity and abstain from warm baths; the river must suffice. There must be due sacrifices and a soothsayer—particularly the sacrifice of a ram on the crucial night, and its entrails must be favourable. Duly led to the place, he is given first the Water of Forgetfulness (*Lethe*), to clear his mind, and then the Water of Memory to help him to remember what he shall see below. Worship follows; and then clad in linen with ribbons, and wearing country boots, he comes to the oracle itself and its chasm. A ladder takes him part way, and then he lies on his back, and goes feet first into a cavity; something of a struggle to get his knees through, and then down he shoots, as if swept down by a river. He comes back feet first, and the priests set him on the chair of Memory not far from the shrine, and question him as to what he has seen and heard. He is then handed over to his friends, still over-powered by fear and unconscious of himself, and brought to his previous lodging, the Good Daemon's house. 'Afterwards he will have his wits as before, and the power of laughter will come back to him. I write not from mere hearsay; I have myself consulted Trophonius' (ix, 39, 5–14).

It has not been my lot to tramp afoot through Greece as some of my friends have done; but I find that the travellers, one and all, speak of Pausanias as the most accurate and reliable of guides. When he says a certain thing is in a certain place, it is there that they find it; and they find what he described. Nor is it topography alone; he has contributed materially to the history of Greek art, and here again I must refer the reader to the work of experts. But I write of him as I have found him, and as I have enjoyed him. It may be that he is, as Tozer said, wholly without humour, or else that such humour as visits him is of the dryest; but his gravity, the seriousness with which he describes and digresses, has its own appeal. 'Common clay' he may have been—or that may be just Sir James Frazer's fun,

his description of all who believe anything in religion, John
Newton, Thomas Scott and, no doubt, others. But it is no
common gift to be interesting through ten books of close detail,
with definite distances indicated, historical memories and minute
descriptions of sculpture. No! he has real gifts, and one can
read him and wish to read him again—'dear garrulous
Pausanias!'

Chapter IX

THE MIND OF ST PAUL

I

Our object to-day is the study of a great mind—that was the wish of the founder of this lectureship—the study of the mind of a man who has shaped the thinking of mankind, who has (in Thomas Carlyle's phrase) 'operated changes in our ways of thought'. There are in every such study antecedent conditions to be reckoned with; but there are times when we have to set our faces against archaeological detail and antiquarian interests, fascinating as they are. Nor at the moment will it be our task to analyse the philosophical conclusions of the man we study, still less to trace the sources from which he draws the modes of thought which give their shape and direction to those conclusions. An outline of this theology, if one could frame it, would appeal to some types of mind, but it would not represent St Paul. Like Plato and other formative men he is not reducible to what the French critic Taine called a formula. A despairing amateur with a camera said of a well-known figure in his college that nothing short of a cinematograph could photograph him. So it is with some great thinkers; they move too much to be reducible to any formula that would reveal any personality. But such minds repay study more than some which might be called more orderly.

In any case, if you want to study a man's mind (always assuming that you are yourself fit for such a task) there is a perspective to be considered; central things have to be central; the interplay of faculties and ideas has to be understood, and the main factors in the man's thinking have to be recognized and given their proper place and influence. What I think Epictetus meant by τὸ ἡγεμονικόν, the master-thing in the man—impulse, habit, factor of whatever sort—has to be at least identified, I do not say, explained, for the chances are that we shall not explain it even if he could himself. His arguments about it will commonly be after-thoughts—perhaps valid, very possibly irrelevant. Intuition is often ahead of explanation, and it is very generally the source of what means most to a man. Furthermore, we must be prepared for uneven development, particularly in so quick-minded a man as St Paul; for a certain want of symmetry, perhaps a very great want of it; for kinks in the skein; for survivals of his past which we may think ought not to survive logically or any way at all. It is a human instinct to hold on to something from the past, however much we renounce it—a human habit to love incompatibles and to keep them linked. Whatever another man's logic may demand, one cleaves to one's own story, one's own identity—and human nature is not simple.

No, it is not simple; and the question rises, *Can* personality be analysed and explained, and its elements ticketed? The deeper one goes, the less satisfied one will be with results in such an attempt. But, as Carlyle wrote in recommending Novalis, 'the most profitable employment any book can give us, is to study honestly some earnest deep-minded truth-loving Man, to work our way into his manner of thought, till we see the world with his eyes, feel as he felt and judge as he judged, neither believing nor denying till we can in some measure so feel and judge'.

With this conception of our task, we have to concentrate, as far as we can, on the man *himself*, as distinct from all the factors that shape, pull, push, or distract him—the influences of parents, pedigree, school, heredity, and environment. We tend to over-estimate such things. The poet Shelley is hardly to be deduced from his parents and his school. The great man will indeed react to all these things, and his reactions will be highly personal; and his rejections will be as significant as his acceptances. He is to be known in those reactions and rejections, and perhaps still more in the new emphasis on this or that which pervades his speech and his mind. He may very well be using old phrase, but it will be in a new way, a way of his own. The canon that Humpty Dumpty laid down to Alice holds with every man of genius; words have to mean what he intends them to mean, whatever the dictionary makers say. He will have, if not a new vocabulary, a new series of emphases—sometimes to be made out from what he himself says or writes, sometimes to be seen more clearly from what his disciples catch up from him and underline. A great man might often be advised to pray to be delivered from his disciples with their gift for wrong perspective, for parody; yet, as men like Plato and Alexander the Great show us, it may take generations to bring out the value of the great man.

II

Yet however emphatically we urge that the great man is himself, a new phenomenon, a creator, we have to remember that he is also heir. 'A good head and a good inheritance', Goethe postulated for a great man. But here we have to distinguish. Men—some men—tend to over-estimate their inheritance; it is a lovable trait. But at the heart even of this habit, it is not so much the accumulated heirlooms that count, nor the baronial hall, nor the ancestral acres, however many and whatever the soil, as the spiritual sense of a lineage, a consciousness of race and family. Alexander the Great believed himself descended from Achilles: the *Iliad* was all about his family and he carried it with him through Asia. Such a belief may make a man a hero or it may make him ridiculous—or both—as you or any other irrelevant person may judge. You can be too matter-of-fact in historical judgments, and you will not understand Alexander till you understand what it is to be descended from Achilles.

St Paul then was a Jew in the pagan world. The Roman poet spoke of a second language giving him an extra 'heart'. St Paul at Tarsus lived where two great languages met, Greek and Aramaic, and he thought in both. One or two plays upon words, not possible in Greek, show that he thought at times in Aramaic; and it is emphasized that, Hebrew of the Hebrews as he was, he read and quoted the Greek translation of the Bible; it was his Authorized Version, and, like ourselves, he would use it without referring to the original text. 'What advantage hath the Jew? Much every way!' So he said and so he thought. It is fairly clear that his education was not the academic education of the Greek, readily obtainable in Tarsus. Compare him with Clement of Alexandria, and you will not count him deeply read in Greek literature. No, but you cannot live among Greeks, even if you do not attend their professors, without learning something of their ways of thought. Witness Paul's appeal to 'Nature'—a central conception of the Stoics, but an idea that like evolution and relativity drifted outside the classroom. Anyone who will have the patience to read Jewish apocalyptic books will realize that, muddled as they were, their writers were touched by a consciousness of the Greek, perplexed indeed. The book of Wisdom shows, much more genially, the influence of Greek thought and word—God 'the first artificer of beauty', 'the universe the champion of the righteous'; if the older Hebrews had ideas of this type, they did not phrase them so.

It is to be noted that there were in Judaism and in Paganism parallel movements of thought—if we are not too Euclidean when we say parallel. The Tarsiot Jew of Paul's youth was not quite at the standpoint of his ancestor in Jehoshaphat's reign. The prophets had lived and written, the psalms had been gathered into familiar books, the Bible had been translated into Greek, and the Synagogue had grown up. The Temple and its sacrifices and services were already—little as Jews would have allowed so blasphemous a thought—obsolete, as appeared when, a few years after Paul's death, Titus destroyed the Temple in order to destroy Judaism, and its destruction made no difference, unless it was even a blessing. Judaism had become spiritual and did not need the blood of beasts for communion with God. Paganism had seen great changes too, a movement from practical atheism to pietism. Augustus 'restored' religion in Rome, and Horace wrote odes about it—neither of them quite a pietist, yet with a sort of conception of a real value in religion. Plutarch, a junior contemporary of St Paul, wrote interminably, but very readably, on the truth of old Greek religion, fortified by the sacraments of Isis.

To sum it up briefly, four movements in religion are very visible both in Judaism and Paganism—growing convictions, of course not uniformly held: there is no real standardization in religious ideas, even if you have a creed reinforced by an episcopate, which neither half of that ancient world had. Men were, however, moving to convictions, variously couched and variously reconciled with their opposites, of the unity of God, and of God's essential righteousness. They were coming to believe more and more in the reality and significance of the individual human soul, till its immortality became an urgent need. And, fourthly, they were convinced that, in spite of all that abstract philosophy taught, there was a possibility of some relation, some mutual understanding, between God and man—or at least between some gods and men. This is not archaeology. These convictions are indeed vital to religion; without them it is nothing. The movements are recognizable in Jew and pagan; but there is a contrast, a very deep one: Paul looked back to a spiritual inheritance very different from that which Plutarch cherished.

But here a *caveat* must be allowed; one based, if you will let me say so, on personal experience. Most people who study Plutarch, or who quote Greek 'mysteries', seem not to have themselves known a world that makes and worships idols. The late Mr Claud Montefiore pictured Paul looking over the fence, with some longing, at pagan mysteries. Waiving the question whether he could have seen mysteries or their adepts if he had looked over the fence, the suggestion implies unfamiliarity with actual idolatry. The Moslem in India does not feel this longing; Chaitanya does not appeal to him. He has his own religion, a passion for monotheism, his own mystics. So had the Jew, and to anyone with that passion for monotheism the very sight of the heathen gods is revolting—even nauseating. A street in Benares I can never forget, and I find the same reaction in St Paul's writing: how could a Christian have anything to do with devil-worship? How indeed? But it is worth noting that the Christian apologists of the second and later centuries know indeed that there are 'mysteries', but do not much care about them; their attack suggests that they found the centre elsewhere. And it is significant that the Christian vocabulary which has come down from those days shows little or no influence from the 'mystery religions'; *deacons* are not *daduchs*.

Yet the existence of those mystery cults, and the writings of Plutarch and Apuleius, highly unlike as these two exponents of religion are, supply evidence that the heathen world knew cravings for God not altogether unlike those of the Jewish psalmist, for contact with God and for immortal life. So much is true; but the Jewish conviction of sin, as an obstacle to communion with God, is hardly to be found in the pagan world. There was something of the sort—a sense of failure in life (familiar to the reader of Seneca's letters), technical impurity—but nothing that approaches the intensity of the 51st Psalm—'Against thee, thee only, have I sinned'. There was a movement to monotheism, a real movement, but compromised terribly by tradition as we see in Plutarch, while Celsus tries to effect a blend of monotheism and polytheism by a parallel drawn with Roman Emperor and civil service. A movement toward monotheism—but not the Hebrew's passion for One God. The Old Testament made a difference—'chiefly because to them were given the oracles of God' is a telling and a true sentence. Pagan religion never got clear of Isis and Cybele; Plutarch can give nothing up; the obscene image is a parable, and shall be kept. Put shortly, the pagan sought God—or goddess—in sacraments; the Jew sought Him in a purer mysticism, which has given us religious books, books not yet obsolete, but in daily use wherever religion is real to-day.

Parallel movements there were, then, and there was more. One of the great effects of the life and reign of Alexander the Great was a new sense that the world was one. His part in the movement toward monotheism is very real—one world, then One God. But one race of men? No, there remained division of races, above all an irremediable dichotomy between Jew and Gentile, final and fundamental. And yet could it be so? Jewish nationalists said Yes; Jewish apocalyptic writers, thinkers themselves in their queer way, said No. How could you decide? What was the mind of God about it?

And here Paul, with the Jews, held firmly that God's mind is not beyond some grasp of ours.

III

But, as Wordsworth says, 'here pause'. For we are coming now to our central theme, the mind of Paul. And once more a *caveat* seems necessary. The commentator Bengel suggested two centuries ago that a man proposing to interpret the New Testament should first ask himself what right he had to do it—*quo jure*. We may ask ourselves what right we have to try to interpret Paul. We know only too well the havoc made in life, for themselves and alas! for us, by people who interpret without intimate knowledge, who can knock you off an explanation,

simplified by omission of some vital factor. What is our qualification to understand Paul? It may be that in the discovery and
assessment of Truth pure reason is all that is required. But in
judging a man's mind and character something else is also
needed. As clear a perception of Truth as we can grasp—yes,
but also some capacity to share the emotions, the imaginative
life, of the man we are studying, some quick response to what
moves him, to what attracts or repels him, some sensitiveness,
if I may put it so, to his accent. For the accent is a part of the
man, and he knows it; it tells of home and country; 'may my
right hand forget her cunning', when he cares for it no longer.
But an accent is not fundamental? Is it not? Can you love
the man, if you dislike his accent? You cannot measure men
by *plus* and *minus*. In arithmetic, I believe, one deducts from
the other; in human character you have to add the *minus* to the
plus. And it is true of more men than poets that

> You must love him ere to you
> He will seem worthy of your love.

A further point—more *caveat*! A. C. Bradley once wrote that
we get more from the genius of a man of genius than from
anything else in him. There is always something inexplicable
in genius; how does it manage

> Out of three sounds, to frame,
> Not a fourth sound, but a star?

The effect of genius, its touch, its magic, its harmonies, reveal
it; but do we understand them? 'To feel and respect a great
personality', said Goethe to Eckermann,[1] 'one must be something oneself.' Yes, indeed, one must be something oneself, and
that is why the great interpreters of Paul have been Augustine
and Luther and (if you like) John Wesley. If you are not *quite*
'something yourself', you must at least have had some experience
along the same lines as the man you interpret, or you will be
outside him altogether. You may have the most accurate
knowledge of everything about him—about him and about—but
unless you have been inside him, it profiteth nothing. History,
said Benedetto Croce, is 'written by professors and other innocent
people'. J. B. Bury wrote about St Patrick, in the fullest posses-

---

[1] *Conversations of Goethe*, Eng. tr. ii, 337.

sion (far fuller than Patrick himself by any stretch of fancy) of everything round and about and outside St Patrick, and never inside him. Enough of *caveats*! or you will quote Bengel at me, *quo jure*.

IV

With so much prelude, we come to St Paul, and the first outstanding feature of his mind that we note is the quickness, the sensitiveness, with which he responds to what he sees, what he hears, and what he divines. The frequent references to Greek athletics in his writings suggest that as a boy at Tarsus he would watch and enjoy (whether sanctioned by his parents or not) the contests in running and boxing. 'Run to win', he says, and owns that he does not himself fight 'as one who punches the air'. He certainly did not at Antioch. These sports evidently appealed to him—spectacles of human skill, endeavour, and quickness; they come back into his mind when he wants a telling picture to stimulate his friends. In his early Jerusalem days we see the same alertness and energy. He recognizes quickly in the synagogue of the Cilicians that the Christian preaching of Stephen is a danger to Judaism; and he acts with decision and energy. When the revelation comes to him on the road to Damascus, there is the same quick realization of the situation, and the same quick thought of action—'What wilt thou have me to do?'

Again, wherever he goes, there is the same quick response to human contacts, the acquisition of friendships, and the uncomfortable recognition of unspoken criticism. Attempts have been made to count the men whom he actually names as friends, but precise tally above sixty fails us; Gaius was a common name, and we do not know how many of his friends bore it. It will be noted that his friends have predominantly Greek or Latin names, the latter apparently implying Roman citizenship, but it is clear that a good many of them must have been Jews. 'Jesus which is called Justus' is an illustrative case. But as clearly he made friends of Gentiles. It further illustrates his mind in this matter, as I think, that, while, perhaps oddly, he never uses the word 'friend', his feelings are shown by a long and pleasant series of alternative terms—'beloved', 'fellow-soldier', 'fellow-worker', 'fellow-prisoner', and so forth. Words

which tell of common experience, of adventure together in the
supreme work of serving Christ and preaching Him—words
which must have stirred deeply the men so described. Imagine
the feelings of (say) Aristarchus, a youth of spirit, when he finds
himself so heartily recognized by Paul as one of his team.

But a nature, quickly conscious of friendship and quickly
responsive to its unspoken indications (often the deepest and
tenderest), cannot fail to feel hostility and criticism however
veiled. Language, it has been said, was given to us to conceal
our thoughts. Paul's references to shame are significant. The
position when he spoke on Mars Hill is typical. There in the
centre of Greek culture, with the Acropolis and the Parthenon
towering above him, he speaks to the intelligentsia of Athens;
and how many of them could fail to recognize in the first few
sentences that he came from Cilicia? 'Solecism' is still in our
vocabulary, a word coined by the satirical to describe the speech
of the people of Soloi, a Cilician town not far from Tarsus. And
can we doubt that Paul was uneasily conscious there and then
that his listeners recognized the Eastern Mediterranean accent
and expected the worst? When he tells the people of Corinth,
the next town that he visited, that he has no rhetoric and no
philosophy, no Greek culture, that his language is just what it is,
what were his feelings in this avowal? Attentive reading brings
out that in the Corinthian epistles he alludes to a good many
criticisms made upon him at that place; and Greek criticism,
even when made by the less delicate minds, could be pungent
and revealing. These men read him, and he was sensitive to their
recognition of his limitations. 'The hidden things of shame'[1] is
not in English a very lucid expression; I think it means a secret
sensitiveness to criticism of his defects, a consciousness that,
preaching to Greeks, he too conspicuously lacks the fine elements
of their culture, that his speech bewrayeth him. And when he
tells the Romans that he is not ashamed of the Gospel, the
negative sentence implies, as it normally does, some awareness
that the opposite feeling would have been more natural; and
no doubt it was. No doubt he saw—it was only too plain on
Mars Hill—that intelligent people thought him a fool; no one
else could have talked of a resurrection; the Gospel 'can be held

[1] 2 Cor. iv. 2.

by no sane man' as Kharshish tells us in Browning's poem; and Paul knew perfectly well, before the blunter listeners burst out laughing, what they would think of his message. He knew it; he was sensitive within to their contempt; and he delivered his message. Elsewhere it is the same sort of story—'fightings without, and fears within', 'the sentence of death in ourselves', and so forth; and, curiously, never in all his extant writings the word 'courage' nor an explicit reference to that eminently Stoic virtue. (His references to timidity in the epistle to Timothy are worth notice, and may be taken as authenticating that epistle, or some part of it; the attitude to be read in them is too subtly personal for an imitator; timidity he understands, and he reads it in Timothy, but his criticism is delicate, associating himself with the instinctive shrinking that might prove the undoing of his friend.)

Another aspect of this quickness of mind appears in his tangents of thought. Corinthians, and perhaps others, were critical of swift and unexpected changes of plan that he made—critical, too, of the suggestion that such changes were in some way the outcome of guidance from above, an easy explanation of levity of purpose, of flightiness; what a man plans, he should stick to and carry it through. I suppose military history could tell of many battles lost through failure in quick recognition of a changed situation. 'The spirit' suffered not Paul to preach in the province of Asia or in Bithynia; a dream fetched him over to Macedonia. But, as Thoreau said in his *Plea for Captain John Brown*: 'any man knows when he is justified, and all the wits in the world cannot enlighten him on that point'. History has vindicated Paul on these occasions.

The tangent pervades his writing. A sudden idea strikes him, and he swings off at a right angle. To take an illustration from a questioned document—some people think godliness is gain; yes! it is gain, he adds in a flash. Quick transitions, digressions, insets, havoc with construction and grammar—the Authorized Version, any group of translators, will be liable to smooth down and obscure such things. But take the Epistle to the Galatians; Paul tells his readers what he said to Peter at Antioch (he was not beating the air), but how far down the page he is quoting what he said to Peter and where his words to the Galatian friends start again—who knows? At four points in this Epistle I have felt that the amanuensis broke down—small blame to him; and I suppose (this is a guess, of course, but I think it likely enough) that when Paul had written his own great conclusion in the large clumsy letters quite unlike the rest of the document, the amanuensis may have asked him what about those places where the author had outrun the scribe and the gaps stood; and that Paul laughed and told him to let it alone. A guess. . . . It is sound criticism when Luther, in the old English version of his commentary on that Epistle, says Paul has 'a strange and monstrous' way of writing; and when Erasmus tells us that 'Paul thunders and lightens and talks sheer flame'. Like all quick and sensitive natures Paul could be irritable; he wishes the people 'cut off who trouble' the Galatians. 'Written in gall, not ink', is Jerome's description of the first epistle to the Corinthians.

V

A man of many and quick thoughts, who reads a situation in a flash and as instantly can see the implications and suggestions that leap to sight when he or another speaks—we shall find further revelation of his mind and its make-up in the problems that persistently occupy him. A man can be estimated fairly accurately by the size and scope of the problems which he finds himself bound to solve—not less so when all his thinking centres in the endeavour to

> assert Eternal Providence,
> And justify the ways of God to men.

For this clearly is the master-task of Paul as thinker. All his problems involve God. Briefly, for we shall not at once be done with them, they may be grouped under five heads. What is the meaning of the Gentile world and the cleavage that separates Jew from Gentile; is it fundamental, a final decree of God, or was it a temporary ordinance to be abolished in due course? This, as we have seen, was a major perplexity to many pious Jews: could God have created Gentiles in order to eternally damn them? There follows the problem of God's righteousness, a concern of deepest gravity to the Jew, and involved in this question of the destiny of the Gentiles, and in much else. It may seem to some readers that one is overstepping the mark in suggesting that Paul is face to face with the old Greek antithesis of Nature and Law, φύσις and νόμος—august beyond Greek traditions as is the νόμος of which he constantly thinks—but Nature is one of Paul's concepts, if not herself a force at least a creation of God. Linked with this is his conception of the creation subject to vanity—perhaps futility would more closely represent his Greek in modern language—creation groaning and travailing, it would seem, in birth pangs—creation stretching out an anxious head (ἀποκαραδοκία) to see what sign there is of the sons of God, but still in bondage and doomed to decay. It is a problem, indeed, which the optimists hardly realize—a problem beyond solving by any easy confidence in Nature, whose preachers, the Stoics, looked forward only to a general conflagration. All these problems are upon the mind of Paul, and a yet greater difficulty besets him—his own unceasing struggle with sin, clearly a struggle that had begun before his conversion and, if the seventh chapter of Romans is biography and not rhetoric, continuing after conversion, as many a man has since found. A new allegiance to God does not end Satan's campaigns.

For we have to understand a besetting sense of failure that haunts Paul, as that chapter and other passages show. No more than any other Christian does he live in easy assurance of constant victory; if he is 'more than conqueror', it is victory plucked by Christ out of Paul's defeat. He does not carry all before him; he has the sentence of death in himself; there are many adversaries; but it is Christ who delivers him. Such experience is not peculiar to Paul; but one feels that with him conviction of sin is a deeper and more terrible thing than with the Rabbinic Jew, with whom Montefiore so unfavourably compared him. No dedication of a Day of Atonement to repentance, when 'the Jew does a lot of repenting and God does a lot of forgiving', avails for Paul: the hurt of his soul is not to be so lightly healed. As a result we find him reaching a depth of insight unguessed by the Rabbinic Jew—of insight from failure. There are no easy successes in the Christian life as he sees it. He will never be understood by critics who (if a phrase may be borrowed from common life, or from Plato) find it easy

to be good. Here, as we ought to know, other thinkers confirm
him, Christian or not.

> Wer nie sein Brod mit Thränen ass,
>   Wer nie die kummervollen Nächte
> Auf seinem Bette weinend sass,
>   Der kennt euch nicht, ihr himmlischen Mächte.

So Goethe, and Clough:

> 'Tis not the calm and peaceful breast
>   That sees or reads the problem true;
> They only know on whom 't has prest,
>   Too hard to hope to solve it too.

'It is from a tried and a varied and a troubled moral life', wrote
Walter Bagehot, 'that the deepest and truest idea of God arises.
The ascetic character wants these; therefore in its religion there
will be a harshness of outline, a bareness, so to say, as well as
grandeur.' Harshness of outline and bareness are not de-
scriptive of Paul's religion; it has a tenderness in its grandeur,
a sense of the forgiveness of God which alters every relation
with God and with man.

VI

Once more, if I am not deviating to too many *caveats*, I would
interpolate a question. Is it reason or passionate feeling that
reveals? Euripides, in a passage of his *Hippolytus*, shows how
the human heart craves a future life beyond the grave, and in
the next few lines laments that it is 'not demonstrated'; feeling
craves, and reason hesitates. Yes, but it is feeling that puts the
great question, that puts all the great questions, for after all
feeling is one mode of experience. Reason tries to answer these
questions; and if, as Euripides sadly says, it fails, the question
does not lapse, if the feeling that raised it was deep and true.
Something is gained when a question is put even if it is not
answered. 'Man was not born to solve the problem of the
universe', Goethe said one day to Eckermann, 'but to find out
wherein it consists.' Or, if a more Christian witness is wished,
St Bernard tells us that God is not sought in vain even when he
is not found. 'I grew more miserable,' writes St Augustine, 'and
Thou wast nearer to me.'

It is want of this gift of feeling that ruins some men where leadership is concerned. The Garibaldis enlist followers, because they offer them a passion which they recognize at once to be right, and Paul is a leader of men. 'A dynamic personality attracts men, and repels', it has been said; and Paul did both; and there was intensity alike in those attracted and in those repelled; indifference was impossible—except of course in such purely negative atmospheres as Mars Hill and its modern analogues. The appeal of Paul has never died; it is seen in the movements of the world's thought, in the response of deep and sentient natures to his great conceptions and to the great phrase in which they are embodied. Luther's words, said Jean Paul Friedrich Richter, were half battles. What of Paul's? Even other men's phrases become new when he uses them. 'The just shall live by faith', so Paul read Habakkuk, whatever the prophet meant by it in his Hebrew; and

> in his hands
> The Thing became a trumpet; whence he blew
> Soul-animating strains.

A mind for which nothing remains cut-and-dried, when it once gets round to it, nothing finished—a mind for ever moving, and grasping fresh aspects of the real—a mind instinct with the joy of discovery and (most of all) of such discoveries as came to Paul—has an appeal which a living nature finds it hard to resist. Compromise is not in his character; 'I intend to get to God', as Browning's man says; Paul is all for God and for ever alive. Yet, as we saw before, he is at times inconsistent, but from a certain charity; else could he have fallen in with the suggestion of the Jerusalem leaders and involved himself in the misadventure which ended in his long captivity at Caesarea and in Rome? Yet the motive for the moment was an honourable one. But the insight of the enemy was right; and the criticism and propaganda of the enemy were powerful factors in clearing his thought—once more an indication of his type of mind, its force and candour.

Finally, at this stage of our progress, his mind can be read and felt and judged by its effect on the universal thinking of the Christian church. His story revealed certain things; his reflection upon them made them clearer; his writing gave them permanent form and force, as we have seen. He reveals gaps and needs in human nature, and does it so powerfully that the complacent type of semi-Christian, terribly familiar in every age and every branch of the church, has never been able to conceal them again. Sin is, for every serious thinker, what Paul made it; he recognized it for what it is and gave it its classic expression. And the same is true of redemption. What he wrote of Christ's work in regenerating the human soul is one of the greatest contributions to sane thinking—to human life at large—that an individual man ever made. He had, as we sum him up, such a gift for experience and such a power of expression that his life and his interpretation of it are part of man's dearest inheritance for ever. Fresh epochs in religion have been made by men who took his contribution seriously and examined it. Once again a man's mind is to be read in its creative force, in the men and the types which he inspires and creates. For such work always depends on a penetrative grasp on the real factors in God's world.

VII

At an earlier point I spoke of the problems that exercised the mind of Paul; we have to return to them to see how he dealt with them. One fundamental feature of them all is the obvious division where there should be unity. Jew and Gentile was the first cleavage we noted. More significant is the problem of evil in its many aspects; why is the world haunted with evil, with pain, and with death? Why is there still with men in every age a question whether God or the devil is to have the last word, the final victory? It is *no* question, many will rejoin—men of high character. But will the victory of God be complete, without subtraction, with nothing lost—or will there be, as the Jews of Paul's day expected, Gentiles by the million in hell? Will it be a victory in which masses of men are to perish unredeemed? Central in all this is the problem of the Cross. Was the Cross a signal defeat inflicted on God by 'the rulers of this world', who are not Pontius Pilate and Caiaphas and the rest, but 'the rulers of this world's darkness', the legions of 'the prince of the power of the air'—the daemon lords of nature, as pagans represented them? For generations there were men in the Church perplexed in the extreme by the fact that Jesus suffered, when philosophers were so certain that God and a godlike man could *not* suffer. The universe took a lot of explaining. But there was worse. 'I became to myself a great question', wrote Augustine; and that question Paul knew, and he expounded it in the seventh chapter of Romans. When all is said, most candid men will own that, if the universe is a sad and perplexing problem, the most urgent problem is (each of them will say) 'me'. Paul knew this. What is the solution that is to explain all these difficulties and to reconcile man to man, man to himself, and man to God?

The Jew, as we saw, stuck to it, against the Neo-Platonist, that God is intelligible, that He is not to be defined in the philosopher's way as 'the deification of the word NOT'. Paul found his solutions in a fresh conception of God, which he found in three ways. He had been brought up to believe with every Jew that to his race had been given 'the oracles of God'; and, if it grew clear to him, as he lived in Christ, that the law of Moses was not God's last word to mankind, the oracles of God were yet not given in vain. Like the Stoics of his native Tarsus, he found in Nature a real guide to Truth—more certain for him than for the Stoics, as he was clearer about a God in Nature and had the Jewish 'oracles of God'. Consensus was the Stoic's test of truth; and here he had it in a stronger degree. But, above all, so significant that the rest might seem negligible, he was sure of 'God in Christ'; there was his great ground of certainty.

VIII

Once again, at this point, we had better cry 'Halt!' lest others do it for us, to cross-question us about Paul's solution of his problems. How did he reach it? they will ask. To which the first answer must be that *how* it was reached is less important than *that* it was reached. Still less important, I would suggest, is your explanation, or mine, as to how it was reached. Even his own explanation may not necessarily be final. For, as someone has said, 'life moves on ahead and analysis limps behind—a long way behind'. Call it intuition, if you like; he said revelation. In any case it has to be remembered that the terms coined by psychologists have not hard edges, nor indeed the phrases used by Paul. Ecstasy, the third heaven, unspeakable—none of these are amenable to what the scientist calls 'quantitative thinking'. There is no machine yet that will exactly measure love, patriotism, or disinterestedness. Suffice it, for the present, that Paul, in a life of thinking and suffering, of endeavour and failure, based himself on experience; and, as an outstanding American thinker put it, 'the universe backs the experience'. But the interpretation of the experience? There is only one other available, that offered by the Stoics; and the history of philosophy has nothing so significant to show as the world's respectful contempt for Stoicism, lock, stock, and barrel: the system left too much experience entirely out to be of interest to the human heart.

To come then to Paul's solution of his problems, his conception of the universe and the reconciliation of its clashing elements. The eternal cleavage of Jew and Gentile, and that of Greek and barbarian, he swept aside for ever. All round him were Stoics saying something of the sort; even the Roman dramatist would 'count nothing human alien'; but the distinctions of race and culture were not obliterated that way. Neither by argument from physiology nor culture, nor by Hellenism in spite of its being based on Alexander's one world and one human kind, were the old divisions to be healed. Nothing was strong enough to 'break down the middle wall of partition', as Paul saw; but in Christ there was no longer Jew, Gentile, Greek, barbarian, bond or free. As a modern has phrased Paul's thought, 'at the foot of the cross' none of those distinctions exist. God's gift of Christ to all alike, and Christ's death for all alike, were decisive. So it was then, and nothing else yet avails to sink race prejudice and colour prejudice.

'At the foot of the cross', the great problem of pain, if not solved, at least took on a new aspect. To Celsus, as to the Jew, the cross was the final proof that Jesus was an impostor. But the Christian world saw more—saw at last an antithesis, that the cross was either the final negation of God or a new revelation of God. Where was God when the tragedy (as men call it) of the crucifixion was taking place? Had He washed His hands of the whole thing like Pilate? Where was He then? 'God was in Christ', said Paul, 'reconciling the world to Himself.' The problem of pain is not solved in the abstract, but Christ had chosen pain; and if God was in Christ as He suffered, then, whatever you guess about the abstract, the practical problem is solved for some serious people—for Paul, in fact, who chooses that any element of pain which Christ did not endure, he, Paul, may experience, that between them they may share the whole gamut of pain. *Cadit quaestio.* Suffering and death are not to be final; because He lives, we shall live also; death has no more dominion over Christ, nor over Christ's people; nothing else was thinkable to a man with Paul's experience of the living Christ. And sin was not to have dominion, nor the rulers of this world's darkness; but all things were to be reconciled and united; Christ was to be all and in all. Read, for example, the first chapter of Ephesians or the eighth of Romans—but if possible without the haze that long familiarity with the beautiful words casts over them. Recall, if you will, what Augustine says of the hymns in the church: much as the beauty of the singing moved men's hearts and his own, the matter sung was more than the singing—*ipsum quod moveor non cantu sed rebus quae cantantur.*[1] Little wonder that Paul speaks in a new way of 'the God of peace', of 'joy and peace in believing', and affirms that 'we have peace with God', that we rejoice or exult ($\kappa\alpha\upsilon\chi\hat{\alpha}\sigma\theta\alpha\iota$) in Him. And, lest it be urged that this may be the language of mere emotionalism, let us recall what Paul wrote for no such purpose—that amazing story he tells us of his life of peril, shipwreck, beating with rods, bonds and afflictions in every city, and open-eyed adventure into fresh centres where the same awaits him. There is surely something valid in such an experience; he has reached something real, whatever *your* theory of it may be. 'I know whom I have believed', he says.

'We have peace with God', he says, adding 'through our Lord Jesus Christ.' So the solution of the last problem is in sight—the personal one, which after all presses harder on a man than any problem of the universe. Sin may still trouble, but it is not to rule; and a man who has peace with God may have peace with himself; God is the God of hope, and Christ, the

[1] *Confessions*, x, 33, 50.

living Christ, is to subdue all things to Himself; His 'working'
will be effective. And all comes from the amazing experience
of God revealing His Son in Paul, from which follows the glad
avowal: 'I am crucified with Christ; nevertheless I live; yet not
I but Christ liveth in me; and the life which I now live in the
flesh, I live in the faith of the Son of God who loved me and
gave himself for me.' Yes, says Luther, 'read with great
vehemencie these words *me* and *for me*'. No wonder that, with
all his fightings without and fears within, the note of joy is heard
so often in Paul. The universe backs the experience, and the
living Christ 'must reign'.

INDEX

CAMBRIDGE: PRINTED BY W. LEWIS, M.A., AT THE UNIVERSITY PRESS